THE QUEERING OF
CORPORATE AMERICA

ALSO BY CARLOS A. BALL

The First Amendment and LGBT Equality: A Contentious History

After Marriage Equality: The Future of LGBT Rights (editor)

Same-Sex Marriage and Children: A Tale of History, Social Science, and Law

The Right to Be Parents: LGBT Families and the Transformation of Parenthood

From the Closet to the Courtroom: Five LGBT Rights Lawsuits That Have Changed Our Nation

The Morality of Gay Rights: An Exploration in Political Philosophy

Cases and Materials on Sexuality, Gender Identity, and the Law (coeditor)

QUEER ACTION/QUEER IDEAS
a unique series addressing pivotal issues within the LGBTQ movement

BOOKS IN THE QUEER ACTION SERIES

Family Pride: What LGBT Families Should Know about Navigating Home, School, and Safety in Their Neighborhoods, by Michael Shelton

Out Law: What LGBT Youth Should Know About Their Legal Rights, by Lisa Keen

Come Out and Win: Organizing Yourself, Your Community, and Your World, by Sue Hyde

BOOKS IN THE QUEER IDEAS SERIES

Love's Promises: How Formal and Informal Contracts Shape All Kinds of Families, by Martha M. Ertman

Gaga Feminism: Sex, Gender, and the End of Normal, by J. Jack Halberstam

God vs. Gay? The Religious Case for Equality, by Jay Michaelson

Queer (In)Justice: The Criminalization of LGBT People in the United States, by Joey L. Mogul, Andrea J. Ritchie, and Kay Whitlock

Beyond (Straight and Gay) Marriage: Valuing All Families Under the Law, by Nancy D. Polikoff

From the Closet to the Courtroom: Five LGBT Rights Lawsuits That Have Changed Our Nation, by Carlos A. Ball

At the Broken Places: A Mother and Trans Son Pick Up the Pieces, by Mary Collins and Donald Collins

The QUEERING of CORPORATE AMERICA

How Big Business Went from LGBTQ Adversary to Ally

CARLOS A. BALL

QUEER ACTION/QUEER IDEAS
A Series Edited by Michael Bronski

BEACON PRESS, BOSTON

BEACON PRESS
Boston, Massachusetts
www.beacon.org

Beacon Press books
are published under the auspices of
the Unitarian Universalist Association of Congregations.

22 21 20 19   8 7 6 5 4 3 2 1

This book is printed on acid-free paper that meets
the uncoated paper ANSI/NISO specifications for
permanence as revised in 1992.

Text design by Michael Starkman
at Wilsted and Taylor Publishing Services

*Library of Congress Cataloging in Publication
Control Number: 2019033096*

For my children, Sebastian and Ema

Contents

Note from Series Editor

IN APRIL OF 2019 President Donald Trump's White House ban on transgender troops—enforced against the advice of the Pentagon and many major military personnel—went into effect, reversing gains for the LGBTQ community that had advanced under Barack Obama's administration. Among the voices of protest was that of Erin Uritus, the CEO of Out & Equal: Workplace Advocates, a nonprofit that deals with LGBTQ workplace equality, who offered the following comment:

> President Trump likes to portray himself as a successful business man. But on this issue, he is completely at odds with American businesses. Corporate America has figured out that standing up for trans rights is not just the right thing to do, it is also good business. That's why a strong majority of the Fortune 500 companies offer protections based on gender identity and trans-inclusive healthcare options. The Trump Administration is trying to take America backwards. The good news is that Main Street won't let him succeed.[1]

If you were to ask anyone involved in the gay liberation movement or early LGBTQ rights movement of the early 1970s if the words "corporate America" would ever be used positively in a statement on LGBTQ rights, they would be shocked and probably appalled. Capitalism, corporate entities, and many aspects of consumerism were understood to be antithetical to liberation. But many things can change over half a century.

—

The LGBTQ movement in the United States has developed in stages over seventy years. While always a continuous movement, each stage had different political aims and tactics from the previous incarnation. Early homophile groups in the 1950s, such as the Mattachine Society and Daughters of Bilitis, called for social justice based on combating injustice, legal reform, and promoting healthy and affirming sexual identities. In 1969, after the Stonewall riots, the gay liberation movement emerged and embraced radical stances including feminism and combating social inequality, racism, imperialism, and capitalism. A few years after this, an LGBTQ rights movement emerged that was less radical but more broad-based and focused on legal reform, acceptance, and social equality.

Carlos Ball's *The Queering of Corporate America* finds its roots in each of these movements, although, for the most part, it is located in the contemporary LGBTQ rights movement of the last few decades. Ball's breathtaking thesis is that as the LGBTQ rights movement demanded equality in the corporate world—for political support, jobs, visibility, and basic human decency—it was capitalism, commerce, and advertising, that slowly morphed into entities that, in many ways, supported queer people and queer issues.

It is easy to label this as a case of "strange bedfellows making politics"—capitalism is usually not seen as a benefactor of progressive politics—but Ball makes the intriguing and vital argument that this merging of the interests of LGBTQ rights and commercial interests was not only productive for all concerned but logical and inevitable.

Charting the fascinating history of how activists within and outside major corporations lobbied and fought for changes in hiring, benefits, and nondiscrimination, Ball makes the case that—as at certain other times in US history—corporations were understood to be able to work for the common good, and even social justice, and not just the bottom line.

—

Ball's history—aside from being highly informative and entertaining—is an important examination of an aspect of LGBTQ history that has been, until now, completely overlooked. The history of the struggle for LGBTQ rights in the United States has been one of surprises and contradictions. *The Queering of Corporate America* is one more example of how the power of queerness dovetailed with other social forces to make America a better place for everyone.

Michael Bronski
SERIES EDITOR

Introduction

I N 1968, AN LGBTQ RIGHTS GROUP in San Francisco tried to place an ad in the Yellow Pages published by the Pacific Bell Telephone Company. The phone company refused to publish the ad, claiming that the firm had an obligation to protect its customers from a "filthy phone book" and that the word "homosexual" was "offensive to good taste." A few years later, Pacific Bell, which was then the largest private employer in California, responded to complaints of discrimination by queer activists by issuing a statement explaining that "we do not knowingly hire or retain in our employment persons—and this would include homosexuals—whose reputations, performance, or behavior would impose a risk to our customers, or employees, or to the reputation of the company. . . . We are not in a position to disregard commonly accepted standards of conduct, morality, or life-styles." The company later disclosed that it stamped a special code on applications of suspected gay, lesbian, and bisexual job candidates as a way of internally flagging individuals who should be rejected due to their sexual orientation.[1]

Almost fifty years later, the Arkansas legislature approved a measure that would have made it easier for businesses and others to discriminate against LGBTQ people as long as they did so for religious reasons. That same day, the CEO of Walmart, the largest private employer in Arkansas (as well as in the country and the world), issued a statement demanding that the Republican governor veto the legislation. The CEO explained that the proposed law encouraged discrimination and was therefore inconsistent with "our core basic belief of respect for the individual . . . and does not reflect the values we proudly uphold." Two days later, the conservative governor and state legislature, under intense pressure from Walmart and other large businesses, modified the law in ways that no longer condoned discrimination against sexual minorities and transgender individuals.[2]

Although these corporate responses by Pacific Bell and Walmart to LGBTQ issues represent only two of the hundreds of times big businesses have addressed matters related to sexual orientation and gender identity equality over the last several decades, they illustrate the ways in which corporate priorities and values, as they relate to issues important to queer people, have changed radically through the years. This book tells the story of how and why that corporate revolution has occurred.

Corporations are interested, above all else, in increasing revenues and protecting their individual bottom lines. As a result, a crucial reason for the queering of corporate America has undoubtedly been the recognition by large companies that, as the country changed, adopting and supporting LGBTQ rights positions could help them maximize profits by reaching new customers while hiring and retaining the most qualified employees. But an account of the queering of corporate America that focuses only on these bottom-line considerations misses other important and compelling aspects of the story. One of those is the crucial role that LGBTQ rights activism, through the decades, has played in encouraging and pressuring corporations to adopt LGBTQ-friendly policies. Another is the extent to which some corporate executives and board members have come to embrace, through the years, LGBTQ equality positions on different issues of importance to queer people, not only because it helps their companies compete in the marketplace, but also because it is, quite simply, the right thing to do.

It may seem obvious to many readers that LGBTQ equality

measures are good for both businesses and the nation as a whole. But in the decades following the Stonewall riots, corporate leaders had to be *persuaded* of both of those points. LGBTQ rights activism aimed at internal corporate policies was a crucial contributor to that process of persuasion. And after many corporate leaders became persuaded that LGBTQ rights proponents were, in effect, on the right side of history, they joined queer groups and activists in trying to convince the public as a whole to embrace LGBTQ equality policies and to reject anti-LGBTQ rights measures.

It may also seem to some readers that, under our era's prevailing capitalist values and norms, corporations should be understood only as profit-maximizing entities whose exclusive goal is to create wealth for their shareholders. But many in our country, during its earliest days, and then again later at different times and on different issues, have expected corporations to be meaningful contributors to the attainment of specific public objectives rather than to simply pursue profits to the exclusion of all other considerations. Queer activists articulated and promoted that alternative understanding of corporations in the last decades of the twentieth century when they demanded that big businesses account for the presence and interests of their LGBTQ employees within company walls, and of queer people more generally outside those walls.

LGBTQ activism aimed at corporations during the 1970s, 1980s, and 1990s was varied, extensive, and effective; indeed, some of the earliest, most important, and most successful LGBTQ rights activism focused on the actions of corporations. The activism included, for example, the street protests and "zap actions" of the early 1970s targeting high-profile discriminatory companies such as television networks and regional telephone companies, the boycott of the Coors Brewing Company in the late 1970s, the AIDS activism targeting pharmaceutical companies in the 1980s, and the concerted push for corporate LGBTQ nondiscrimination policies and domestic partnership benefits in the 1990s. Queer activism aimed at corporate America helped turn large businesses from, at worst, entities firmly opposed to LGBTQ equality and, at best, enterprises wholly indifferent to LGBTQ equality into reliable, powerful, and effective supporters of LGBTQ rights.

Most historical accounts of the LGBTQ movement have focused on activism directed at government actors, with the aim of explaining how the movement sought either to end discrimination by the government itself or to persuade public officials to prohibit private-sector discrimination. But it is not possible to have a complete and accurate picture of what the American LGBTQ rights movement has been able to achieve since the Stonewall riots without understanding how and why the movement targeted large corporations as a means to advance LGBTQ civil rights.

One of the most important consequences of LGBTQ activism aimed at corporations at the end of the last century was that it helped, after the new century, to turn big businesses from *targets* of political activism on behalf of queer equality to *sources* of that activism. This transformation is reflected in the ways in which corporate America has pushed for the adoption of LGBTQ antidiscrimination laws and marriage equality while vigorously opposing so-called religious freedom laws and transgender bathroom laws that condone or encourage discrimination against queer people.

The LGBTQ movement has achieved remarkable successes in gaining nationwide marriage equality and in persuading a growing number of states and local governments to enact laws protecting sexual minorities and transgender individuals from discrimination. Many factors have contributed to those gains, including corporate political activism on behalf of LGBTQ equality. That a growing number of large corporations were willing initially to embrace LGBTQ equality measures internally, and later to advocate externally on behalf of public policies promoting that equality, went a long way toward normalizing and mainstreaming a whole series of LGBTQ rights positions. In short, corporate advocacy on behalf of public policies aimed at promoting LGBTQ equality has been one of several important factors that both reflects and accounts for changes in how American society views queer people, their relationships, and their families.

Corporate political activism on behalf of LGBTQ equality has also played a crucial role in protecting equality gains from conservative backlash. After marriage equality started to spread across the country, social and religious conservatives began demanding that Republican-controlled state legislatures adopt so-called religious freedom laws that would immunize religious employers, landlords, and businesses from antidiscrimination liability for treating same-sex couples differently from heterosexual couples. And, in response to the growing number of state and local governments that were adopting gender identity antidiscrimination laws, right-wing activists began demanding that conservative states enact laws requiring transgender individuals to use public bathrooms that matched their biological sex as opposed to their gender identity.

Conservative activists initially persuaded Republican-controlled legislatures in several states to consider and, in some instances, to enact such laws. But strong and vociferous corporate opposition led to the eventual defeat or weakening of most of those measures. This occurred in states where progressive groups and advocates lacked the political strength to defeat the provisions on their own. Many corporations and business executives that took the lead in opposing the anti-LGBTQ measures were important supporters and funders of Republican candidates and, as such, had considerable clout with GOP elected officials. In deep-red states like Arizona, Arkansas, Georgia, Indiana, and Texas, corporate opposition to anti-LGBTQ laws overwhelmed the push for such measures by social and religious conservatives. It is not an exaggeration to say that there would be many more anti-LGBTQ statutes on the books today were it not for the strong corporate opposition to those provisions.

This book generally presents in positive terms large corporations' growing engagement with issues related to queer equality. For that reason, it is important to make three points about the *limits* of corporate support for progressive causes. First, despite corporate America's apparent commitment to equality principles as manifested in its more recent support for LGBTQ rights laws and opposition to anti-LGBTQ measures, the racial, gender, and sexual orientation composition of management positions at many large companies remains disturbingly homogeneous and does not come close to reflecting the nation's diversity. Just because large companies *say* that they are committed to diversity, inclusion, and equality within their walls, and just because they engage in public advocacy on behalf of antidiscrimination principles and laws, does not mean that they have taken the necessary remedial steps to make sure that the actual composition of their workforce is truly diverse, inclusive, and equal.

Nothing in this book is meant to suggest that discrimination by corporate America against queer people has come to an end. That discrimination continues to this day and is manifested both in overt discrimination and in subtler forms of differential treatment that force LGBTQ employees to hide or cover their sexualities and gender identities.[3]

Second, corporations in the United States come in all shapes and sizes. The focus here is on large companies because they have more often served as both targets and sources of queer rights activism than have smaller companies. Although big businesses have generally come out in support of LGBTQ rights, the picture is significantly more mixed among medium- and small-sized companies. Many of those firms have not taken explicit positions on LGBTQ equality; some have been as supportive as larger corporations; and yet others have opposed LGBTQ rights. Some owners in the latter group of businesses have received significant attention by claiming that the government, through the enforcement of antidiscrimination laws, cannot constitutionally require their firms to provide wedding-related goods and services to same-sex couples in ways that are inconsistent with their religious views.[4]

Third, I do not contend that large American corporations can or should be counted on to be crucial contributors to the attainment of progressive objectives across the board. There are many issues that go beyond the book's scope in which the interests of big corporations and those of progressives diverge in fundamental ways.

Examples include corporate support for measures that weaken the ability of employees to form unions and that undermine the ability of unions to adequately represent their members; corporate opposition to important and reasonable safety, health, and environmental regulations; corporate support for the growing privatization of essential services and benefits that have traditionally been provided by the government; and corporate opposition to the types of higher taxes, and accompanying redistribution of wealth, necessary to address the nation's growing and troubling social and economic inequalities. It is undoubtedly and unfortunately the case that corporations, on many issues, have promoted their shareholders' interests in ways that are inconsistent with those of the broader society.

At the same time, it is important not to allow what is in many instances justified criticism and skepticism of corporate objectives and motives to blind us from the fact that some corporations on some issues have proved helpful in promoting progressive values and goals. One such instance has been corporate opposition to unduly restrictive immigration proposals.[5] Another has been corporate endorsement of international climate control agreements.[6] And yet another has been corporate support for LGBTQ equality.

In my view, it is a mistake either to automatically embrace or to categorically reject the prospect of working with corporate interests to attain progressive goals and reforms. Instead, it is better to closely explore these issues one by one. When corporations obstruct the attainment of social reform and justice objectives, they should be opposed and criticized. But when activists persuade companies that attaining those objectives is consistent with their priorities and interests, progressives should proceed to work with them in forming the types of broad political coalitions that are necessary to effectively produce change in contemporary America.

The Supreme Court's controversial opinion in *Citizens United v. Federal Elections Commission*, in which a bare majority of justices struck down reasonable limits on the ability of corporations to spend company funds with the objective of influencing election results, has justifiably heightened the skepticism among many about the outsized power and influence of corporations in American society.[7] Strong corporate support for LGBTQ equality complicates the view that corporate participation in matters of politics and public policy is intrinsically suspect and invariably detrimental to the attainment of social welfare and justice reforms. Issues associated with the proper role of corporations in our democracy are complicated and multifaceted and, as such, are not amenable to easy or categorical conclusions.

CHAPTER I

A (Very) Brief History
of Corporations in America

MANY PEOPLE IN OUR CAPITALIST SOCIETY are quick to assume that the exclusive function of corporations is to maximize profits with the sole objective of creating wealth for their shareholders. But the reality is that there is currently significant disagreement, as there has been throughout much of American history from the colonial period until today, over the appropriate roles of business corporations in society. Large numbers of Americans, at different times and on different issues, have expected corporations to be important participants in the attainment of public and social objectives. In fact, the role played by large businesses in promoting LGBTQ equality has been only one of many involvements by corporations in matters that go beyond issues strictly limited to questions of profits and the so-called bottom line.

Another historical example of corporate engagement with social issues is the way in which big businesses grappled with matters of racial justice in the decades following World War II. As with LGBTQ equality concerns, racial justice issues raised questions of discrimination, fairness, and equal opportunity. Large corporations played multifaceted roles in the racial integration of the workplace from the 1940s through the 1980s. As with queer equality, major firms were initially slow to embrace racial equality and the need for antidiscrimination laws. But big corporations eventually came to defend and promote racial equality ideals. Several decades later, large companies followed a similar path in matters related to LGBTQ equality.

Corporations and the Public Good

The colonists and early Americans largely viewed corporations as entities whose function was to help society achieve specific public ends. Those ends included the provision of education (America's oldest corporation, Harvard University, was chartered in 1636), the provision of credit (the nation's first banks were created by government officials), and the building of roads, bridges, and canals. Colonial and early state governments legally recognized particular corporations in order to attain specific public objectives. The state granted corporations certain legal privileges, such as the ability to accumulate relatively large amounts of wealth, have a perpetual life, and enjoy limited liability for their owners, in return for the corporations' agreeing to help the government attain particular social goals. The prevailing view of corporations was not that of today, in which they are expected to compete with each other in order to promote market efficiencies and maximize profits. Instead, the goal was to empower particular corporations with the necessary legal authority and financial means to allow them to accomplish particular public objectives.[1]

As a result, early corporations in the United States were, in effect, semipublic entities individually chartered, and frequently partially funded, by state legislatures with the goal of providing specific public goods. During this period, it was not always easy to distinguish between government and corporate activities, given that public officials relied heavily on corporations to attain crucial public objectives. In addition, governments kept corporations on tight leashes. Before the middle of the nineteenth century, it was not possible in most states to create a corporation without the legislature's explicit permission. And government officials frequently revoked corporate charters when they believed corporate owners were not meeting their public obligations. Two historians have explained that, in the nation's early decades, "the corporation was conceived as an agency of government, endowed with public attributes, exclusive privileges, and political power, and designed to serve a social function for the state."[2]

Before the development of stock markets and the emergence of private banks, government-created banks provided credit to businesses and farmers. These early banks, as one commentator notes, "showed more interest in public service than in maximizing profits." This is what Alexander Hamilton, the moving force behind the creation of the Bank of the United States, had in mind when he reasoned that "public utility is more truly the object of public banks than private profit."[3]

In addition, before private railroads changed the nation's transportation and economy in fundamental ways, it was government-approved corporations that built much of the country's basic infrastructure, such as turnpikes, bridges, and canals, including the famous Erie Canal, which links Lake Erie to the Hudson River. It was these corporations acting in the public service "that began to stitch together the independent colonies into one nation with a single, national economy."[4]

The prevailing understanding of corporations as entities formed to attain particular social ends began to change around the middle of the nineteenth century and accelerated rapidly after the Civil War. During this period, a growing number of Americans began to view corporations as primarily profit-maximizing institutions that appropriately prioritized private gains over public objectives. At the same time, many Americans came to see the provision of public goods (such as building basic infrastructure) as indirect by-products rather than the primary objective of corporate activities.

There were several reasons for this shifting understanding of the role of corporations in society. The US Supreme Court's 1819 decision in *Dartmouth College v. Woodward*, in which it viewed corporations as private institutions with vested contract rights protected by the Constitution in ways that limited the authority of states to regulate them, was an early instigator of this change. Another factor was the rapid spread of private railroads across the country and the emergence of new and socially transforming technologies (such as electricity and the telegraph) largely controlled by private hands.

In addition, the proliferation of general incorporation laws in the mid-nineteenth century made the benefits of incorporation widely available without a special grant from the legislature—and without a requirement that the newly formed corporations pursue particular social objectives. Furthermore, by the end of the century, a number of states, led by New Jersey, began to compete with each other to attract tax revenue from corporate franchises, in part by revising their general incorporation laws to allow corporations to be formed for any lawful purpose, to hold stock in other corporations, and to be of unlimited size. As a result of these and other developments, the social understandings of corporations began to change from that of quasi-public institutions whose primary purpose was to pursue the common good to wholly private entities whose main function was to create profits for their owners.[5]

When government stepped back from chartering and regulating particular corporations in order to attain specific social objectives, a handful of firms in many crucial sectors of the economy, including transportation (for example, railroads), manufacturing (for example, steel), and natural resources (for example, oil), soon grew so big that they dominated their respective markets, scared competitors away, and accumulated vast amounts of wealth. In the early part of the nineteenth century, governments had *created* corporate monopolies in order to pursue specific public objectives, while placing significant limits on the amount of wealth the entities could amass. In contrast, governments in the later part of the century *allowed* new monopolies to form without any meaningful legal limits, leading to the formation of large corporate trusts (such as John D. Rockefeller's Standard Oil) and to concentrations of wealth never seen before in the nation's history.[6]

The country during this Gilded Age experienced remarkable rates of economic growth. By the start of World War I, the United States produced 36 percent of the world's industrial output, more than the two next largest economies (Germany and Britain) combined. But the growing monopolies and huge concentrations of wealth led to increased calls during the Progressive Era for legal and policy reforms intended to curb corporate power. The government during this period adopted new regulations aimed at reining in the power of monopolies and protecting the health and safety of workers and consumers. The Progressive Era was also characterized by political and social activism directed at encouraging large corporations to act in socially responsible ways. This public pressure induced several of the richest corporate families (such as the Carnegies and the Rockefellers) to create charitable foundations to redistribute some of the enormous wealth they had accumulated through the decades.[7]

Public pressure and employee activism also encouraged some corporations to implement the nation's first employee benefit plans and pension systems. For example, Procter & Gamble in 1915 implemented the first corporate disability benefits and retirement programs for workers. A few years later, the company instituted an eight-hour workday while guaranteeing its employees work for at least forty-eight weeks a year. At around this time, US Steel spent about $10 million a year on employee benefits programs and International Harvester implemented a profit-sharing plan for its workers. By the mid-1920s, about 80 percent of the nation's largest companies had corporate welfare policies that sought to improve working conditions, provide some recreational and educational services for workers and their families, and establish savings and insurance plans.[8]

However, there were legal limits to how far corporations could go in advancing the interests of individuals who were not their owners—when conflicts arose between the interests of employees and consumers, on the one hand, and maximizing profits to the benefit of shareholders, on the other, companies were often legally required to choose the latter. Henry Ford learned this lesson after he announced in 1916 that his automobile company would stop paying special dividends to stockholders and use the money instead to build a new manufacturing plant as a way of improving the lives of the working class. As law professor Kent Greenfield notes, the company took the position that it "was motivated by a desire to do social good for the company's employees and customers, arguing that shareholder gain was not the purpose of a successful business but its byproduct."[9] Spending corporate money in the new plant rather than distributing it to shareholders, the company argued, was the better choice because it would create more jobs while lowering the prices of automobiles for the paying public. As Henry Ford explained, "My ambition is to employ still more men; to spread the benefits of this industrial system to the greatest possible number, to help them build up their lives and their homes."[10]

But after shareholders challenged Ford's refusal to pay the dividends, the Supreme Court of Michigan famously ordered the company to do so. In doing so, the court held that the primary purpose of corporations was to pursue profits on behalf of shareholders. The court added that while company directors had considerable discretion in how they achieved that end, they lacked the legal authority to modify the profit-maximizing objective itself.[11]

Nonetheless, the adoption of employee benefits policies, which can be understood as early forms of "corporate social responsibility" measures, by companies such as Procter & Gamble and US Steel helped improve the lives of some workers, even if the ultimate goal was to reap greater corporate profits. However, these types of corporate welfare policies proved wholly inadequate in ameliorating the economic and social devastation wrought by the Great Depression. In fact, the governmental activism that defined the New Deal period was premised on the view that large government social welfare programs, alongside vigorous public oversight and regulation of the private sector, were essential means to address the harmful consequences of unrestrained and unregulated competition by private businesses. As a result, during the 1930s the scope and influence of the public sector grew significantly while that of the corporate sector shrank accordingly.

The country's subsequent entry into World War II required new forms of cooperation between the federal government and corporations to help the nation defend itself against its enemies. The war effort also had other crucial social and economic consequences, starting with the ways in which government and private investments necessitated by that effort helped end the Great Depression. Furthermore, the internal mobilization required by the war made it more difficult to ignore questions of racial segregation and discrimination in public and private workplaces.

The postwar period was characterized by continued cooperation between the federal government and large corporations, with the former frequently turning to the latter's top executives to fill cabinet and other leadership positions and to join government-created special commissions and working groups. There was also a return to corporate bigness—while the postwar economy was not, as it had been earlier in the century, dominated by only a handful of powerful monopolies, most economic sectors in the postwar period included huge corporate participants, such as General Motors and Ford in the automobile industry and Xerox and IBM in the information and technology sector.

The postwar period also saw growing disagreements about the roles and responsibilities of corporations. On one side of the debate were individuals like the libertarian, Nobel Prize–winning economist Milton Friedman, who contended that the only responsibility of corporations was to make profits for their stockholders. But there were others who questioned this view by arguing that companies also had duties to society in general and to their employees, customers, and local communities in particular. Although at first it was primarily academics and others outside the corporate world who expressed such views, a growing number of corporate executives by the 1970s began to recognize publicly that society expected more of their firms than the mere maximization of shareholders' wealth. As the Committee for Economic Development, a group composed of business people and educators, put it in 1971, "Business is being asked to assume broader responsibilities to society than ever before and to serve a wider range of human values. Business enterprises, in effect, are being asked to contribute more to the quality of American life than just supplying quantities of goods and services. Inasmuch as business exists to serve society, its future will depend on the quality of management's response to the changing expectations of the public."[12]

The 1970s were also characterized by the declining power of labor unions, entities that had served for decades as corporations' main political opponents. On the one hand, the decline of organized labor permitted corporations to increase their political and social influence. On the other hand, other groups emerged that sought both to limit corporate power and to channel its exercise in ways they believed were socially useful and just. Prominent among these groups were civil rights organizations, feminist groups, and environmental organizations. With the support of these groups and others, a corporate social responsibility movement emerged in the 1970s and has grown stronger in the decades since.[13]

Prior to the 1980s, supporters of limiting corporate power succeeded in persuading the government to adopt environmental, consumer, and other forms of laws that constrained corporate discretion in the pursuit of profits. Examples of such laws included the Clean Air Act, the Clean Water Act, the Consumer Product Safety Act, and the National Environmental Policy Act. In contrast, after Ronald Reagan came into office, the federal government became significantly less likely to adopt regulations limiting corporate power. Nonetheless, a growing number of corporations in the last few decades have adopted internal policies and measures, which sometimes go beyond what is required of them by law, aimed at promoting specific social objectives. Examples of such objectives include protecting the environment, promoting diversity and equal opportunity, and avoiding abusive uses of foreign labor. In the last few decades, it has become important for a growing number of large corporations to demonstrate to an increasingly demanding public that they can pursue profits while acting as good social citizens.

The fact that a significant number of big corporations in the late twentieth century adopted sexual orientation antidiscrimination policies before government entities prohibited them from discriminating against sexual minorities is one example of how some corporations sought to demonstrate a commitment to socially responsible actions even in the absence of legal mandates. But before corporations began grappling with discrimination against queer people in their workplaces, they had to contend with issues of racial discrimination. The roles of different corporations in resisting and assisting racial integration presaged the varying roles that big businesses would later play in questions related to LGBTQ equality.

Corporations and Racial Equality

There were several reasons why World War II increased the political and social salience of the pervasive forms of racial segregation and discrimination that had existed across the United States since the nation's founding. First, African American service members played a crucial role in winning the war, contributing to President Harry Truman's path-breaking order in 1948 calling for the military's racial integration. Second, the industrial output necessitated by the war effort created millions of new jobs, which, among other things, induced a large northern migration by African Americans. And third, the war effort increased the power and reach of the federal government, eventually leading it to take a more active role in combating racial segregation and discrimination.

After the war started in Europe, but before the United States entered the conflict, the federal government pushed to increase industrial production with the objective of assisting Britain's fight against Germany. Organizations such as the National Association for the Advancement of Colored People (NAACP), the National Urban League, and the Brotherhood for Sleeping Car Porters (an African American union) used the national emergency as an opportunity to pressure the Roosevelt administration to take steps to promote equal employment opportunities. A threatened march on Washington by thousands of African Americans led President Franklin Delano

Roosevelt in 1941 to sign an executive order mandating that manufacturers with Pentagon contracts not discriminate on the basis of race, creed, or national origin. The executive order also created a federal entity, the Fair Employment Practices Committee (FEPC), whose responsibility it became to oversee equal opportunity among defense contractors. Although the FEPC had no enforcement power and was able to help only a small number of African American workers land defense industry jobs, the mere fact of its existence, as the historian Nancy MacLean puts it, "taught a clear lesson: that progress would come from a combination of grassroots organizing and federal action against recalcitrant employers."[14]

During this time, most corporate leaders and managers objected to racial equality in the workplace. A survey taken for the National Association of Manufacturers (NAM) in 1944 found that 74 percent of owners, managers, and white-collar workers opposed opening so-called white jobs to African Americans. And even corporate owners and executives who were not themselves opposed to equal opportunity had significant concerns that integration would lead to lower productivity among resisting white workers and greater costs because of the need to train new black employees.[15]

Many of the half a million African Americans who served in the military during the war returned to civilian life determined to avoid the type of dead-end jobs to which they had been relegated before the conflict. Troubled and angered that the same rampant discrimination in employment that limited their opportunities in life before the war remained firmly in place after it, many veterans joined organizations (such as the NAACP and the National Urban League) and unions (such as the Congress of Industrial Organizations) that were increasingly committed to racially integrating the nation's workplaces. The demand for greater workplace equality and opportunities was particularly strong in northern and western states where African Americans already enjoyed formal legal equality. A research report commissioned by NAM noted that equal employment opportunity was "rated the No. 1 goal" by "young Negroes."[16]

The civil rights movement of the 1950s brought together the

southern struggle for freedom, led by Dr. Martin Luther King Jr., with the northern struggle for better jobs and economic justice, led by activists such as civil rights strategist Bayard Rustin and trade unionist A. Philip Randolph. After thousands of African Americans participated in the Montgomery bus boycott as a dramatic way of demanding dignity and equal treatment, a variety of civil rights organizations worked in multiple ways to make better jobs available to black Americans—for example, the Negro American Labor Council emphasized union activism, the NAACP focused on legal challenges, the Congress of Racial Equality (CORE) emphasized community-based direct action, and the National Urban League organized job training programs while exhorting companies to hire workers who completed them. The historic march on Washington in 1963 was organized around a call for "jobs and freedom." As historian MacLean notes, "The black trade unionists who conceived the event and the marchers who answered the call believed that access to good employment on both sides of the Mason-Dixon line was vital to full inclusion in a fair America."[17]

As would happen decades later in the context of LGBTQ rights, civil rights activists targeted corporations directly. For example, in the late 1940s, Rustin and CORE activist James Peck bought shares in the Greyhound Bus Company with the objective of using shareholder meetings as a forum to bring attention to racial discrimination in the private sector. For the next few years, the two men battled with the bus company in an effort to persuade it to stop racially segregating its customers along its southern routes. A few years later, civil rights and community activists used a similar strategy to disrupt Eastman Kodak's annual shareholder meetings to publicize that company's lack of hiring and promotion of racial minorities.[18]

Although Roosevelt's wartime executive order constituted an important first legal step in promoting equal opportunity, civil rights activists expected a great deal more from the government. In particular, activists in the postwar period began demanding federal legislation prohibiting private employers from discriminating on the basis of race. Unfortunately, it would take almost twenty years after the end of World War II for Congress to enact such a law. There were several reasons for that long delay. One factor was the opposition of powerful Southern Democrats in the US Senate who repeatedly used the filibuster to quash civil rights bills. Another reason was that many business leaders, though not all, opposed antidiscrimination laws, viewing them as both coercive and unnecessary. For example, NAM questioned whether toleration could be legislated, while insisting that civil rights laws would engender backlash, greater racial division, and freewheeling government bureaucracies. The better approach, NAM and other corporate groups and leaders contended, was to rely on companies taking voluntary and gradual steps, depending on their needs and the workforce resources available to them, to increase equal opportunities for African Americans. From this perspective, the private sector had a responsibility to address issues of racial discrimination, but it should be allowed to do so with little or no governmental interference and oversight.

With few prospects for federal legislation, civil rights activists pushed for antidiscrimination laws at the state level with some success. New York in 1945 became the first state to enact a law prohibiting racial discrimination in employment. By 1950, the number of states with such laws increased to seven, and by 1960, to twenty-eight. Most business groups and leaders vigorously opposed these laws, an opposition that sometimes helped defeat civil rights bills. And when corporate lobbying failed to kill the antidiscrimination measures altogether, it frequently succeeded in weakening them significantly.

One limiting feature of most early state laws prohibiting employment discrimination was that they emphasized conciliation and education rather than the imposition of legal liability on employers that discriminated. As such, the statutes did not generally allow the government to sue employers and instead required African American plaintiffs to bring individual and costly lawsuits, while imposing on them the difficult evidentiary burden of proving that their employers had intentionally discriminated against them because of their race. Despite the state laws' significant limitations, the mere fact of their enactment legitimized the government's promotion of racial equality and made employers more conscious of the social importance of equal opportunity.[19]

Responding to pressure by civil rights activists, President Truman in 1951 created the President's Committee on Equal Employment Opportunity. Despite the group's rather grandiose name, it did little other than appeal to corporations to provide greater opportunities to African Americans, a request that companies largely ignored. When the NAACP in 1958 complained to the Department of Defense that its largest contractors were doing nothing to address the rampant racial discrimination that festered inside their companies, the department refused to do anything meaningful about it. A 1961 study of almost three hundred federal contractors in North Carolina found that one-fifth refused to hire African Americans in any capacity and that four-fifths refused to hire black women. And the surveyed companies that did hire African Americans limited their positions to unskilled jobs. Also in 1961, security guards at General Motors' large manufacturing plant in Atlanta prevented African Americans *from even entering the facility*, making it impossible for black individuals to apply for jobs. For its part, Western Electric that year employed 14,708 supervisors and managers; only one was African American.[20]

Into the 1960s, many American companies limited racial minorities and women to a handful of low-level career tracks. Personnel managers seemed to operate under the delusion that the sorting of employees according to their race and gender was somehow a consequence, as one sociologist puts it, "of self-selection, or of natural proclivities."[21] But the reality was that many employers had formal hiring and promotion rules that excluded African Americans and white women from a wide range of jobs. And the companies that lacked such explicit rules usually left filling entry-level positions to the discretion of white supervisors and foremen, who chose other white men for most positions, leaving blacks and white women with little chance of getting anything other than the most menial of jobs, if they even had the opportunity to get any positions at all.[22]

Not all corporations ignored the blight of racial discrimination within their firms. Some companies led the way in promoting equal opportunity in the workplace starting as early as the 1940s. For example, International Harvester, a manufacturer of farm equipment, implemented a nondiscrimination policy in 1941 at its twenty-three plants. In its southern facilities, the company organized meetings with white employees to explain the new policy, worked with local National Urban League chapters to identify potential African American employees, offered training programs for black workers, and kept statistics regarding the racial composition of its workforce. After the war, General Electric hired a small number of black engineers and administrators. The Radio Corporation of America (RCA) also embraced equal opportunity policies in the 1940s. Although most business leaders remained adamantly opposed to antidiscrimination laws, representatives of some of these pioneer companies testified before Congress in the postwar period in support of laws mandating equal opportunity for racial minorities in the workplace.[23]

At first, the number of corporate executives who were willing to institute fair employment practices, which made it possible for African Americans to begin landing positions previously limited to white employees, was small. But that number gradually grew so that by the middle of the 1960s, as historian Jennifer Delton explains, "the climate of opinion among corporate executives . . . was favorable to equal employment opportunity. It would of course take much more than a favorable climate of opinion to change discriminatory employment practices, but a supportive atmosphere was a necessary precondition."[24]

In 1961, President John F. Kennedy signed an executive order requiring all government contractors (not just those paid by the Department of Defense) to take "affirmative action to ensure that applicants are employed, and that employees are treated during employment, without regard to their race, creed, color, or national origin."[25] Shortly thereafter, about three hundred companies with federal government contracts formed an organization called the Plans for Progress (PFP). The PFP pledged to eliminate corporate practices that excluded racial minorities and women from the firms' workplaces and to take affirmative steps to increase equal opportunity.

The PFP collected and analyzed statistics on minority employment, sponsored hundreds of conferences and workshops aimed at helping companies to racially integrate, developed scholarship and training programs for underserved youth, and sponsored vocational guidance seminars at black high schools. The PFP also encouraged its member companies to adopt explicit policies aimed at reducing workplace racial segregation and discrimination. Dozens of PFP companies responded by taking steps aimed at partially integrating some parts of their workplaces. These steps included conducting outreach to black community organizations, recruiting at historically black colleges, and evaluating and revising job and training program criteria, all with the objective of increasing the racial diversity of the companies' applicant pools. These actions had some beneficial results, albeit modest ones. For example, a survey of one hundred PFP companies found that, between 1961 and 1964, the number of their African American salaried workers increased from 28,143 (1.5 percent of the total number of employees) to 47,134 (2.5 percent of the total number of employees).[26]

Despite these gains, most civil rights activists believed that only strong civil rights laws could effectively address the long-standing and systemic racial discrimination that existed in both the public and the private sectors across the country. And given that it was unlikely many additional states, especially southern ones, would enact such laws anytime soon, the only realistic solution to the problem was to adopt comprehensive federal civil rights legislation.

The Civil Rights Act of 1964 grew out of a proposed bill that President Kennedy had sent to Congress the previous summer. Kennedy's bill primarily addressed discrimination by businesses, such as stores and theaters, in their selling of goods and services to the general public and did not include a provision prohibiting employment discrimination in the private sector. But liberal members of Congress pushed to amend the bill to address employment discrimination by private employers. Corporate support in the early 1960s for such a law varied greatly. For example, in a letter to a congressional committee, the US Chamber of Commerce opposed the bill, "because the problems involve so many considerations that any bill comprehensive enough to cover all of them would, in all probability, do more harm than good." At a later point, the group went so far as to absurdly claim that the proposed law was a prelude to dictatorship. For its part, the corporate-friendly magazine *U.S. News and World Report* complained that the legislation, which "compels employers to hire Negroes, and treat them the same as whites," constituted nothing more than the "forced hiring of Negroes." Other corporate groups, such as NAM, refused to take a position on the bill, while a handful of pioneering corporate leaders publicly supported a comprehensive federal civil rights law.[27]

Despite this mixed record of corporate support, it bears emphasizing that by the time Congress enacted the Civil Rights Act of 1964, dozens of large corporations, especially those with government contracts, were already taking some steps to promote equal opportunity in their workplaces. At the same time, there remained large and important economic sectors, such as southern textile manufacturing and northern construction, in which there was almost no corporate support for racial integration and, as a result, there had been little movement in that direction prior to the law's enactment. It was in these sectors that the passage of the Civil Rights Act had the greatest impact. Civil rights groups filed dozens of lawsuits in the 1960s seeking to enforce the statute's equality mandates, especially in those parts of the economy in which corporations had done little on their own to address racial discrimination. The general success of these lawsuits made clear to corporate leaders across the country that they had no choice but to begin or continue racially integrating their workplaces.[28]

The racially motivated urban unrest of the second half of the 1960s, coupled with the persistently high unemployment rate among racial minorities, also led a growing number of corporations to publicly embrace equal opportunity policies. Specifically, for the first time, some companies assumed responsibility for training the so-called hard-core unemployed in what one historian has labeled "a short-lived burst of social responsibility."[29] Corporations also increased their donations to groups such as the National Urban League and the NAACP. And, perhaps most important, a growing number of large employers began reformulating hiring criteria in order to promote the racial integration of their workplaces. This was particularly true of corporate hiring of blue-collar workers and other unskilled employees; for those jobs, some companies dispensed with requiring high school diplomas and previous job experience in order to increase the number of African American and other racial minority applicants. Although the Equal Employment Opportunity Commission (EEOC) would eventually interpret Title VII of the Civil Rights Act of 1964 to require employers to make sure their hiring criteria did not disproportionally impact racial minorities, a legal position upheld by the Supreme Court in 1971, many large companies by then had already made changes to such criteria with the objective of promoting the racial integration of their workplaces.[30]

In 1968, President Lyndon Johnson formed the National Alliance of Businessmen (NAB) with the purpose of encouraging large employers to hire society's most economically disadvantaged individuals. The NAB was headed by Henry Ford II (president of the Ford Motor Company) and included top executives from large corporations such as Alcoa, Coca-Cola, McDonnell Douglas, and Mobil. The federal government also created a program, known as the Job Opportunities in Business Sector (JOBS), to subsidize private-sector hiring and training of the long-term unemployed. In the late 1960s and early 1970s, tens of thousands of previously unemployed individuals were hired under the auspices of the NAB and JOBS programs. Although some corporate executives continued to insist that corporations should only be in the business of maximizing profits for their shareholders, others took the position that private-public programs such as NAB and JOBS were necessary to address the needs of society's most disadvantaged members. At the time, surveys showed that a majority of large corporations had instituted programs to assist individuals who failed to complete high school in finding jobs, to retrain workers whose previous jobs had been eliminated due to automation, and to improve the career opportunities of racial minority employees.[31]

The public-private job programs of the late 1960s and early 1970s were short lived—they soon fell victim to growing government deficits, the persistence of high unemployment rates, and the relentless ideological critiques of government spending by political conservatives. However, the existence of the programs demonstrated that at least some corporate leaders at the time were willing to grapple with the complexities of economic and racial inequality in the United States.

It was not just outside forces, such as pressure from government officials and civil rights activists, that encouraged many large corporations in the 1960s and 1970s to take affirmative steps to promote racial equality; some of the pressure also came from human resources personnel inside corporations. That pressure grew especially strong after Congress in 1972 amended the Civil Rights Act of 1964 to grant the EEOC the authority to enforce Title VII by directly suing employers. After that statutory change, it became increasingly common for corporate human resource departments to advise their companies to institute internal discrimination grievance procedures to demonstrate both to minority employees and to the EEOC that the firms were acting proactively and in good faith to address discrimination. Personnel experts also frequently recommended that corporations adopt specific mechanisms to prevent discrimination, including the formalization and wide dissemination of job descriptions and requirements, the adoption of open bidding systems for jobs, and the implementation of salary classification systems that tied wages to particular skills and responsibilities.[32]

After Ronald Reagan became president in 1981, the federal government dramatically changed gears from encouraging and, in some instances, requiring private-sector affirmative action programs to opposing all policies that took race into account as a way of ameliorating systemic and persistent racial and economic inequalities.

By that time, however, many corporate executives had become strong supporters of affirmative action. Much to the chagrin of the business-friendly Republican administration, executives generally fought the federal government's efforts to cut back on affirmative action programs by filing amicus briefs in the courts in support of such programs, sending telegrams to the White House complaining about affirmative action cutbacks, and testifying before Congress about the benefits of affirmative action and equal opportunity policies for their corporations. Surveys conducted in the 1980s showed that clear majorities of large companies intended to retain their affirmative action policies regardless of federal employment mandates.[33]

The critiques of affirmative action by Reagan administration officials and conservative activists did have one effect on internal corporate antidiscrimination policies: corporate America began distancing itself from the term *affirmative action*, and instead moved to embrace *diversity*. Personnel experts within companies, and former corporate human resources employees who now worked as outside equal opportunity consultants, responded to the attacks on affirmative action by pressing for "diversity" management, training, and education. A survey of more than four hundred leading US companies in 1991 found that three out of every five had diversity training programs in place and many others intended to implement them soon.[34]

Those who pushed for corporate diversity programs relied on two basic arguments. First, that such programs were needed to tap into the full potential of racial minority and female employees while securing their successful integration into the workplace. Second, that a diverse workforce, with its broader set of viewpoints and life experiences, would help companies to more effectively design, produce, and market goods and services for a customer base that was itself becoming more diverse.[35]

Many corporate employment policies that had been understood earlier to constitute forms of affirmative action were now, in effect, rebranded as diversity practices. However, the shift was more than just semantic in nature. In the 1960s and 1970s, corporations (and other important social institutions such as universities) had focused not only on increasing workplace opportunities for racial minorities, but also on *remedying* past discriminatory wrongs. In other words, the impetus behind affirmative action programs had been largely backward looking: it was the past systemic discrimination against racial minorities that required, as a legal and moral matter, the implementation of new and expansive policies aimed at integrating America's workplaces. In contrast, diversity was forward looking: corporate diversity policies were primarily about creating a better and more successful future for the corporate entities themselves, for their racial minority and female employees, and for society at large.

In some ways, therefore, the earlier "affirmative action" policies had been more intimately connected to questions of social justice and structural inequality than the later "diversity" programs. And yet, from a progressive civil rights perspective, the corporate embrace of diversity had one important benefit: while affirmative action programs had focused primarily on addressing discrimination against African Americans, the concept of diversity came to encompass other racial and ethnic groups, as well as groups defined by traits other than race and ethnicity. It was now generally understood by many corporate leaders that truly diverse workplaces were those that welcomed not only African Americans, but also women, Latino Americans, Asian Americans, recent immigrants, people with disabilities, and, eventually, LGBTQ individuals as well. As historian Delton explains, "Diversity, precisely because it is broader and more inclusive, has facilitated a more definitive change in corporate culture. . . . Inclusiveness in all of its forms became a new corporate virtue. Even if true integration in the workplace remains elusive, the corporate culture and personnel structures—with their emphases on inclusion, 'difference,' and pluralism—are now prepared to accommodate and encourage it."[36]

Despite the growing commitment shown by corporate America to equal opportunity in the decades following World War II, the process of racially integrating large corporations, especially at the executive and managerial ranks, has been a slow and difficult one that

continues to this day. But notwithstanding the slow-moving progress, corporate America, after initially opposing efforts to racially
integrate its workplaces, eventually embraced the ideals behind (if
not always, the practice of) equal opportunity, affirmative action,
and, more recently, diversity. The fact that corporate America by the
1990s had embraced the ethos of equal opportunity and diversity
helped turn large corporations into LGBTQ allies. This allowed the
LGBTQ movement to make significant gains in the private sector at
a time when it was enjoying only limited success in the governmental
sphere. But before large corporations generally became allies of that
movement, there was significant corporate resistance to queer equality in the 1970s and 1980s. That resistance engendered some of the
earliest, strongest, and most important activism in the history of
the LGBTQ rights movement.

CHAPTER 2

LGBTQ Corporate Activism in the 1970s

T HERE WERE THREE MAIN REASONS why LGBTQ rights supporters, in the years following the Stonewall riots, chose corporations as targets for activism. First, some corporations had explicit anti-LGBTQ policies and practices for everyone to see. In 1970, for example, a Los Angeles bank made clear in its job application forms that it would not hire alcoholics, drug users, or "homosexuals." At around the same time, the Pacific Bell Telephone Company, the largest private employer in California, announced that it would not hire open "homosexuals," because doing so would "disregard commonly accepted standards of conduct, morality, or life-styles." Until 1978, the Coors Brewing Company routinely asked job applicants, while attached to lie detector machines, whether they had engaged in same-sex sexual conduct and denied them jobs if they had. (The company's testers also inquired whether applicants were thieves or communists.) For their part, broadcast networks consistently portrayed sexual minorities on their television shows as criminally inclined or psychologically disturbed (or both). In short, some corporations, like other powerful institutions in American society, routinely and openly discriminated against queer people while promoting stereotypical understandings of their lives and relationships. Given the prominent economic, political,

31

and social roles of large corporations in the United States, meaningful equality for queer people was simply not attainable in the face of corporate-sponsored discrimination and stereotyping.[1]

A second principal reason why post-Stonewall LGBTQ activism focused on large corporations was that the firms' interests in promoting and protecting their brands made them particularly sensitive to the negative publicity that came with exposing discrimination. Large corporations spend millions of dollars every year developing and marketing their brands and are, as a result, highly sensitive to criticisms that might tarnish those brands. Queer activists through the decades have sought to use that susceptibility to pressure companies to change their policies and practices as they relate to sexual minorities and transgender individuals.

Interestingly, the need to protect corporate brands from negative publicity made companies more willing to change explicit anti-LGBTQ policies than government entities. Indeed, it was more likely, during the 1970s and into the 1980s, that a large corporation targeted by queer activists would cease explicitly discriminating against sexual minorities than, for example, a government agency would stop discriminating against queer people or, just as important, a state or local legislative body would adopt sexual orientation antidiscrimination laws. To enact such laws, queer activists had to persuade a majority of elected officials in a given jurisdiction to support adding sexual minorities to civil rights laws; outside of a few liberal municipalities, this was an extremely difficult task for the embryonic LGBTQ rights movement to accomplish in the years following Stonewall. In contrast, to persuade a corporation to rescind a ban on hiring open LGBTQ individuals, it was only necessary to convince a handful of executives that the company had more to lose financially from the negative publicity engendered by criticism of and protests against their discriminatory policies than from tolerating out-of-the-closet sexual minorities in the workplace.

Finally, the fact that corporate America had tens of thousands of LGBTQ employees (most of whom were, admittedly, firmly in the closet) made corporate workplaces obvious and natural targets of

LGBTQ rights activism. Whether they knew it or not, corporate leaders and heterosexual coemployees were already working alongside sexual minorities and transgender individuals, in many cases developing the cooperative bonds, mutual trust, and even lasting friendships that the pursuit of common objectives, including corporate ones, frequently engenders.[2] In this sense, LGBTQ individuals, as a group, were not outsiders and "strange others" to corporate America; instead, they were integral members of corporate workplaces. And many of them were likely to come out of the closet and share the joys and challenges of their personal lives with their fellow workers (as heterosexual employees did all the time) if they could be guaranteed a modicum of job security and protection against discrimination.

Jack Baker, a gay law student at the University of Minnesota, was an early LGBTQ activist who understood that the movement had much to gain from targeting corporations and their internal practices. After realizing in 1969 that his university lacked policies governing corporate recruiters on campus, Baker pushed administrators to form a committee to draft such policies and made sure that he was named a member. Baker knew there was little chance that the university would explicitly prohibit recruiters from discriminating on the basis of sexual orientation. But the antidiscrimination protection could be provided indirectly if the university adopted a policy requiring recruiters to hire only on the basis of actual job qualifications. This would implicitly prohibit hiring not only on the basis of irrelevant criteria such as race and religion, but on sexual orientation as well. After Baker and others pushed for such a policy, the university, following almost two years of internal deliberations, adopted it.[3]

After the policy was in place, the university's gay student group wrote to twelve large companies based in the Twin Cities inquiring whether they discriminated on the basis of sexual orientation. The letter warned recipients that the group was prepared to bring public attention to companies that discriminated against queer people. Three corporations—General Mills, Pillsbury, and Dayton's department store—responded by claiming they did not discriminate against gay people. In contrast, a Honeywell Corporation vice president wrote back brazenly explaining that the company "would not knowingly hire a homosexual person" and adding, rather cryptically, that "our practice is the result of actual adverse prior experience." (The other eight companies did not bother to respond.)[4]

Gay students eventually filed a complaint with the University of Minnesota, asking it to bar Honeywell from recruiting on campus, given that the company hired individuals on the basis of a criterion (sexual orientation) that had nothing to do with job qualifications, in violation of the university's new policy. Honeywell, suddenly facing the troubling possibility that the state's largest university might prohibit it from recruiting students on campus, announced a few months later that it would no longer discriminate on the basis of sexual orientation.[5]

Queer activists aimed their sights at other corporations throughout the 1970s. One such campaign targeted two so-called Baby Bell (or regional) phone companies that had explicit anti-LGBTQ policies. Another campaign was aimed at the three major television networks, given that their news and entertainment programs routinely portrayed LGBTQ people in stereotypical and negative ways. Furthermore, LGBTQ groups joined with other progressive organizations in a broad grassroots push to boycott the products of the Coors Brewing Company, a corporation with a particularly problematic and controversial track record on labor and equal opportunity issues.

Before delving into the details of these LGBTQ rights campaigns, it is worth emphasizing that discrimination by corporations was by no means limited to sexual minorities. During this time, advocates for racial and gender equality also repeatedly complained about the many ways in which corporations failed to provide equal treatment and opportunities to racial minorities and women. The difference was that while federal law rendered much racial and sex discrimination in the private sector illegal, and while federal agencies, along with some of their state and local government counterparts, were beginning to be more assertive in holding corporations accountable for such discrimination, none of this applied to discrimination on the basis of sexual orientation. For example, female employees of AT&T in the early 1970s brought a class action lawsuit under the Civil Rights Act of 1964 that led to a groundbreaking $38 million settlement with the company. The fact that queer people could not similarly turn to the courts or to the government to seek protection against discrimination meant that the only way LGBTQ activists could bring about changes in corporate policies and practices was through grassroots protest campaigns. In doing so, queer people took advantage of the only meaningful source of legal rights they enjoyed at the time: the First Amendment's protections of the right to speak, organize, mobilize, and agitate.[6]

Although there were obvious disadvantages to not having the option of suing corporate employers for violating antidiscrimination laws, there was one unanticipated advantage: it forced LGBTQ activists to engage in highly public campaigns to bring notice to the rampant discrimination against sexual minorities that prevailed across corporate America. This activism helped not only to bring public attention to discrimination by corporations, but also to heighten the visibility of sexual minorities more generally in ways that went beyond what could have been accomplished through antidiscrimination litigation in the courts. For LGBTQ people in particular, overcoming invisibility was a crucial first step in achieving basic civil rights. The fact that the law denied queer people basic equality rights encouraged sexual minorities to take to the streets and engage in the types of visible and effective grassroots organizing and protesting that eventually led to crucial reforms both in the private sector and in government policies.

Targeting the Phone Companies

Gay activists in San Francisco in 1964 formed an organization called the Society for Individual Rights (SIR). In the inaugural issue of its monthly magazine *Vector*, the group's president wrote, "By trying to give the individual a sense of dignity before himself and within his Society, SIR is dedicated to [the] belief in the worth of the homosexual and adheres to the principle that the individual has a right to his own sexual orientation." The organization aimed, as an editorial in *Vector* explained, "to present the homosexual as he is— by far and large a responsible and moral member of his community and one seeking only the equal protections of the laws guaranteed by the 14th Amendment to the Constitution of the United States."[7]

In pursuing its objectives, SIR engaged in a wide variety of activities, including holding voter registration drives, hosting forums for candidates running for local offices, and organizing social events. It also distributed a pocket-sized publication (called the *Pocket Lawyer*) informing queer people of their rights if they were harassed or arrested by the police in or near gay bars. The group's outreach to broad sectors of the LGBTQ community led it to become, by the late 1960s, the biggest gay group in San Francisco (and the nation) with a membership of almost a thousand.[8]

As part of its efforts to increase membership and spread its message, SIR in 1968 attempted to place an ad in the Yellow Pages published by Pacific Bell. That firm, one of several regional telephone companies, provided telephone services to most Californians. Before the internet, the Yellow Pages was a widely used advertisement publication through which organizations of all kinds, both for-profit and nonprofit, advertised their goods and services to the general public. The ad that SIR wanted to place in the Yellow Pages included its address and phone number and read as follows: "HOMOSEX-UALS—Know and protect your rights. If over 21, write and visit SIR." Pacific Bell rejected the ad, claiming that the company had an obligation to protect its customers from a "filthy phone book," that the word "homosexual" was "offensive to good taste," and that the advertisement "would offend subscribers."[9]

SIR responded by filing a complaint with the California Public Utilities Commission, the regulatory agency that oversees utility companies in the state. The commission rejected SIR's complaint, concluding that the gay group had failed to show that Pacific Bell had acted in an arbitrary and capricious manner. It was only after SIR appealed the commission's ruling to the California Supreme

Court, that Pacific Bell backed down and accepted the advertisement, three years after it first refused to publish it.

In the meantime, SIR and other LGBTQ groups continued to tangle with Pacific Bell because of another issue: its refusal to hire openly gay, lesbian, and bisexual individuals. At the time, the company was one of the largest employers in the country, with a workforce of more than ninety thousand employees. In 1970, SIR wrote to Pacific Bell asking about its personnel policies as they related to sexual orientation. In response, an assistant vice president wrote back explaining that "we do not knowingly hire or retain in our employment persons—and this would include homosexuals—whose reputations, performance, or behavior would impose a risk to our customers, or employees, or to the reputation of the company. . . . We are not in a position to disregard commonly accepted standards of conduct, morality, or life-styles."[10]

Although Pacific Bell was by no means alone among corporations in refusing to hire openly gay, lesbian, and bisexual individuals, the bluntness of its response to SIR's letter angered LGBTQ activists. Starting in 1971 and continuing for several years, groups such as the San Francisco Gay Activists Alliance regularly picketed outside the company's headquarters in San Francisco. During one of those protests, held on Good Friday in 1973, a young gay man sporting a white robe and a shaggy beard dragged a heavy telephone pole on his back, intended to resemble Christ's cross, to the cheers of a large group of LGBTQ protestors.[11]

San Francisco enacted an ordinance in 1972 prohibiting city contractors from discriminating on the basis of sexual orientation. LGBTQ activists quickly filed a complaint with the city's Human Rights Commission, arguing that Pacific Bell was subject to the ordinance because it had contracts with the city to provide public pay phones. The company responded by contending that, as a utility, it could only be regulated by the state and that therefore the local ordinance did not apply to it.

The filing of the complaint provided activists with access to relevant internal company documents. One document explained Pacific

Bell's official policy regarding sexual minorities. Titled "Employment of Homosexuals," the policy stated that "we do not give favorable consideration [in employment matters] to anyone who, in our judgment, may create conflicts with existing employees or the public we serve. This includes, but is not limited to, any manifest homosexual." It was later learned that the company stamped "Code 48" on applications of suspected gay, lesbian, and bisexual job candidates as a way of internally flagging individuals who should be rejected due to their sexual orientation.[12]

As LGBTQ activists continued to press the company to rescind its discriminatory policy, Pacific Bell defended itself by claiming that it only barred from employment individuals who "flaunted" their same-sex sexuality, a position that, not surprisingly, did not satisfy the activists. In the two years following the enactment of the city's antidiscrimination ordinance, government officials, company representatives, and queer activists held several meetings aimed at resolving their differences, but the disagreements over the legality and appropriateness of the company's policy remained.[13]

Pacific Bell was not the only regional phone company that found itself in the crosshairs of LGBTQ activists. Northwestern Bell in 1973 admitted on the front page of the newspaper *Minneapolis Star* that it would not hire "admitted homosexuals." As the company's public relations chief explained, "Until society recognizes homosexuality as socially acceptable behavior, we believe that employing known homosexuals would tend to have an adverse effect on how our company is regarded by other employees and the general public."[14]

Northwestern Bell had been forced to address its employment policy regarding sexual minorities after activists publicized that it had rescinded a job offer to a young man, who had applied to be a bicycle messenger, after he told a company nurse during a preemployment physical that the army had rejected him because he was gay. Responding to the company's announcement and defense of its antigay policy, Twin Cities LGBTQ activists, in groups that ranged from a handful to around two dozen individuals, distributed leaflets and picketed in front of the company's headquarters in Minneapolis every workday for several weeks. In response, the Minnesota chapter of the liberal group Americans for Democratic Action, a state senator, and a local television station came out in favor of laws prohibiting discrimination against sexual minorities. For its part, the Minnesota chapter of the ACLU filed a federal lawsuit against the phone company on behalf of the gay bike messenger, arguing that its status as a monopoly rendered it a quasi-governmental entity subject to equality obligations under the federal Constitution. In addition, LGBTQ students at the University of Minnesota filed a complaint with the school asking that the company be prohibited from recruiting on campus until it lifted its ban on sexual minority employees.[15]

The following year (1974), Minneapolis amended its civil rights ordinance to prohibit discrimination in employment, in housing, and by places of public accommodation on the basis of "affectional or sexual preference." Three days after the amendment became effective, Northwestern Bell announced that rather than fight the new law in the courts, as it had earlier threatened to do, it would rescind its exclusionary hiring policy aimed at sexual minorities. It also announced that it had settled the ACLU lawsuit by agreeing not to engage in any further discrimination against gay individuals and by paying the plaintiff $900 in back wages.[16]

At the time, AT&T, the parent company of local Bell subsidiaries such as Pacific Bell and Northwestern Bell, was facing significant public scrutiny for its differential treatment of racial minorities and women. The corporation had recently reached a landmark settlement of $38 million in a class action lawsuit brought by female employees alleging systemic discrimination within the company.[17] AT&T, shortly after Northwestern Bell rescinded its antigay policy, announced in an employee newsletter that it would not discriminate against gay workers. The announcement explained that an "individual's sexual tendencies or preferences are strictly personal and information about these maters shouldn't be sought out by company personnel." Bruce Voeller, the executive director of the National Gay Task Force (NGTF), hailed AT&T's announcement as "a very important beginning," while the *Advocate* magazine opined that "this move by AT&T could be the breakthrough that [might] persuade other major businesses to lift the corporate barrier gay people in business find inhibiting their careers and life-styles."[18]

The announcements by AT&T and Northwestern Bell constituted the first time that large American companies took explicit and public steps to address the issue of sexual orientation discrimination in their workplaces. The companies' actions demonstrated to LGBTQ rights activists, only five years after Stonewall, that public pressure campaigns could be effective in persuading at least some large corporations to start addressing issues of sexual orientation equality in the workplace.[19]

Hoping to build momentum from the telephone companies' announcements that they would no longer discriminate against sexual minorities, the NGTF wrote to eighty-six large corporations asking about their sexual orientation policies. About half the companies responded to the survey. The majority of the respondents, including DuPont, Exxon, and Procter & Gamble, skirted the issue by claiming that they did not ask their employees or job applicants about their sexual orientation. But several other companies, including American Airlines, Bank of America, and IBM, responded by assuring the LGBTQ group that they did not discriminate on the basis of sexual orientation.[20]

Activist groups did not have the resources needed to organize campaigns against the dozens of large corporations that explicitly or implicitly discriminated against sexual minorities. It was also not possible in most parts of the country to use litigation as a tool for reform because, outside of a handful of ordinances enacted by liberal municipalities, there were no laws that explicitly prohibited discrimination on the basis of sexual orientation. (The first state to enact such a law was Wisconsin in 1981; the second, Massachusetts, did not do so until nine years later.) All this meant that LGBTQ activists had to be strategic in choosing which corporations to target in public campaigns. Important factors in that determination included the company's size and visibility—the bigger the company, and the more visible it was to the general public, the more likely it would respond positively to LGBTQ rights campaigns aimed at changing its policies toward sexual minorities.

Another criterion that determined which corporations to target, interestingly enough, was a company's willingness to admit that it discriminated. When LGBTQ activists in the 1970s wrote to corporations asking whether they discriminated against sexual minorities, many firms refused to answer, and most of the ones that did reply skirted the issue by responding, usually falsely, that they did not care about the sexual orientation of their employees. But a handful of companies were honest enough to openly admit that they discriminated against sexual minorities. Interestingly, queer activists were helped when companies like Northwestern Bell (for a brief period) and Pacific Bell (for more than a decade) dug in their heels by insisting publicly that there was nothing wrong with firing or refusing to hire individuals because of their same-sex sexual orientation. Although the Civil Rights Act of 1964 did not explicitly protect employees from discrimination on the basis of sexual orientation, the enactment of that law and of other civil rights statutes (such as the Fair Housing Act of 1968) passed in its wake, helped cement in the minds of many Americans that discrimination was not only legally prohibited in many instances, but also morally wrong. This made it possible for queer activists to embrace the language of equal opportunity and justice, while painting discriminatory companies as being out of step with contemporary American ideals and values.

In the particular context of telephone companies, the fact that public utilities were subject to more rigorous forms of government regulation than most other corporations helped the LGBTQ rights cause. In California, Pacific Bell learned this lesson the hard way. Although its parent company, AT&T, had officially eschewed discrimination against sexual minorities, Pacific Bell continued to refuse to lift its ban on gay employees. (The regional telephone companies had significant discretion to set many of their own policies, including some employment policies, independently of the parent corporation.) In 1975, a group of gay plaintiffs brought a class action lawsuit against Pacific Bell in state court, challenging its exclusionary policy under both California's civil rights laws and public utility regulations.

One plaintiff was a job applicant who had been denied a position by Pacific Bell when he revealed during the application process that he was a member of the Metropolitan Community Church, a religious denomination composed primarily of sexual minorities. Another plaintiff was a former telephone company employee who had resigned his position in the face of pervasive antigay harassment by several of his coworkers.

Pacific Bell moved to dismiss the lawsuit, arguing that California law did not prohibit discrimination on the basis of sexual orientation. The California Supreme Court in 1979 agreed that the state antidiscrimination statute did not protect sexual minorities as such. But the court refused to dismiss the lawsuit altogether, ruling instead that since public utilities were analogous to state agencies, the state constitution applied to them. The court added that the constitution prohibited entities subject to its mandates, including privately owned utilities, from arbitrarily excluding classes of individuals from employment. The ruling constituted the first time that a state appellate court held that a private company violated state law when it discriminated against sexual minorities. The supreme court returned the case to the lower court for a factual determination of whether Pacific Bell had engaged in discrimination against LGBTQ individuals.[21]

The court's ruling energized the LGBTQ rights campaign aimed at Pacific Bell. Facing growing criticism not only from queer activists, but also from some elected officials and media outlets, the company, a year after the court's ruling, adopted a policy of nondiscrimination on the basis of sexual orientation. Nonetheless, the lawsuit dragged on for several more years because Pacific Bell refused to admit that it had impermissibly discriminated against lesbians, gay men, and bisexuals in the past. The company finally settled the case in 1986, agreeing to pay $3 million to about 250 former employees and job applicants who charged that they had been discriminated against because of their sexual orientation. Although, as is common in such settlements, the company did not admit wrongdoing, the agreement, at the time, constituted the largest settlement in a sexual orientation discrimination case.

By the time Pacific Bell settled the lawsuit, the federal government, aiming to encourage competition and innovation in the telephone business, had broken up AT&T. According to an article published in the *Harvard Business Review* in 1989, the need to survive in a new and more competitive marketplace forced Pacific Bell to change its conservative corporate culture in two important ways. First, the firm now focused, in ways it had never done before, on seeking to satisfy investors' expectations by placing greater emphasis on financial success. Second, the company started adopting corporate policies that were responsive "to new constituencies that were socially conscious, where the company had always been seen as socially and politically backward." Pacific Bell's idea of social engagement, the article explained, had traditionally been "to join all the Rotary Clubs in California. While that approach might have worked in the 1950s, in the 1980s California's shifting coalitions of interest groups—blacks, Hispanics, consumer-oriented organizations—increasingly wielded political power. Pacific Bell had long treated these groups as if they were the enemy. Now, however, these same groups were major purchasers of telecommunications services. . . . For the phone company to prosper on its own, it somehow had . . . to reach a mutually workable level of understanding and accommodation" with these segments of the population.[22] As the company was now forced to recognize, LGBTQ individuals constituted one of these increasingly important population segments.

It might have been possible for Pacific Bell, in earlier years, to ignore both the demands of queer activists and the fact that a significant proportion of its employees and customers were sexual minorities. But by the mid-1980s, the company could no longer afford to turn a blind eye to the increased political power of the LGBTQ movement in California in general and in its big cities in particular. It also could no longer afford to blithely ignore the interests and demands of its increasingly visible and vocal LGBTQ workforce and customer base.

One way in which Pacific Bell's new corporate culture manifested itself was in the firm's willingness to respond proactively and sensibly to the AIDS crisis. In doing so, Pacific Bell became one of the first companies to implement policies accommodating HIV-positive employees in the workplace, to improve health insurance coverage with the objective of helping its workers with AIDS, and to educate its employees about the disease and how it spreads. The company's implementation of these policies led the authors of a 1988 book on AIDS in the workplace to call Pacific Bell a "role model" among large American corporations.[23]

The company also took the lead among California corporations in successfully opposing a measure, placed on the 1986 state ballot after it received the support of almost seven hundred thousand signatories, which called for the mandatory HIV testing of all state residents, the reporting of positive test results to government officials, the barring of HIV-positive individuals from schools and jobs in restaurants, and even authorizing their being quarantined. In addition, the company helped defeat a 1988 voter proposal that would have abolished anonymous HIV testing in the state. A few years later, Pacific Bell extended its bereavement leave to employees with domestic partners and included sexual orientation issues in its diversity training programs.[24]

In short, Pacific Bell was one of the first companies to change, in a relatively brief period of time, from publicly opposing LGBTQ equality to adopting internal practices and promoting public policies that corresponded with the interests and objectives of the LGBTQ rights movement. Several factors accounted for this corporate transformation, including pressure from queer activists on the streets, in the media, and in the courts, as well as changes in the company's internal culture instigated by more competitive market conditions and by what growing segments of the public were increasingly expecting from leading corporations. The phenomenon of large corporations changing from being either opposed to or uninterested in LGBTQ equality issues to becoming important allies of the LGBTQ rights movement was one that repeated itself, time and time again, in the last quarter of the twentieth century.

Television Networks and Homophobic Programming

As already noted, it was not possible for LGBTQ activists in the years following Stonewall to target all, or even most, of the large corporations that discriminated against queer people. Instead, resource limitations and other practical considerations required activists to pick and choose which corporations to target as part of public campaigns aimed at promoting LGBTQ rights and raising the visibility of sexual minorities. The three major broadcast networks (ABC, CBS, and NBC) constituted appealing corporate targets because they produced the vast majority of news and entertainment programs shown on television and, as such, had enormous influence on American society, politics, and culture.

While a handful of gay characters began appearing in some scripted television shows in the mid-1960s, the programs almost always portrayed sexual minorities as either violent or psychologically disturbed (or both). The networks' news divisions also started paying greater attention to sexual minorities in the 1960s; unfortunately, LGBTQ people generally fared no better in news shows than in scripted ones. In 1967, for example, CBS broadcast a one-hour program, part of its news series *CBS Reports*, titled "The Homosexuals," hosted by television journalist Mike Wallace. On the positive side, the show constituted the first time that millions of Americans (the episode was watched by about a third of television viewers) heard directly from LGBTQ people (in this case, gay men) about their lives. But the show's editorial perspective was exceedingly negative, presenting gay men as promiscuous, emotionally unfulfilled, and lonely. At one point during the show, Wallace used a concerned voice to tell his viewers that "the average homosexual, if there be such, is promiscuous. He is not interested or capable of a lasting relationship like that of a heterosexual marriage. His sex life, his love life, consists of a series of one-chance encounters at the clubs and bars he inhabits. And even on the streets of the city—the pickup, the one-night stand, these are characteristics of the homosexual relationship." Wallace concluded the show by stating that this is "the dilemma of the homosexual: told by the medical profession he is sick; by the law that he's a criminal; shunned by employers; rejected by heterosexual society—incapable of a fulfilling relationship with a woman, or for that matter with a man. At the center of his life he remains anonymous. A displaced person. An outsider."[25]

Although there was some scattered criticism of CBS for airing such a negative portrayal of gay people, the homophile movement (as the LGBTQ rights movement was called prior to Stonewall) did not have the organizational strength to engage in successful protest campaigns against television networks. But that changed in the 1970s as an energized and increasingly confrontational gay liberation movement realized that meaningful equality for queer people was impossible unless the heterosexual majority viewed sexual minorities as their moral equal. And there was little chance of that occurring as long as television networks and other media outlets depicted LGBTQ people as dangerous, ill, lonely, and despairing individuals.

One early example of activists' willingness to challenge the media's portrayal of queer people took place in 1970 when members of the Gay Activists Alliance (GAA) engaged in a "zap action" by loudly descending on the New York City offices of *Harper's* magazine. The monthly had published a deeply homophobic article in which the author had stated, "If I had the power to do so, I would wish homosexuality off the face of the earth."[26] Shortly after the zap action, GAA member Marty Robinson appeared on *The Dick Cavett Show* on ABC to explain the reason for the protest: "Heterosexuals live in a society without any scorn—they live openly, their affection is idealized in movies [and] theater. Homosexuals want the same thing: to be open in this society, to live a life without fear of reprisal from anyone for being homosexual—to live a life of respect."[27]

The GAA, and later the NGTF, took the lead in pressuring television networks to change the ways in which they reported on and portrayed LGBTQ people. In 1973, a gay employee at ABC provided activists with a copy of a script for an upcoming episode of the popular show *Marcus Welby, M.D.* The episode's guest character was a depressed and alcoholic married man who was counseled by the sage television doctor to repress his "homosexual tendencies." GAA members met with ABC executives to demand that they make changes to the show so that viewers would not link having a same-sex sexual orientation with mental depression and substance abuse. A few days after the network representatives refused to do so, about twenty-five GAA members conducted a zap action at ABC's New York City headquarters by occupying the offices of the company's top executives. After the activists refused to leave, the police arrested them for trespassing. On the day the episode aired, two dozen protestors picketed outside ABC's Los Angeles station.[28]

Later in 1973, a gay activist went onto the set of the *CBS Evening News* and stood behind the famous newscaster Walter Cronkite—who was reading the news to a live audience—holding a sign that read, "Gays Protest CBS Bigotry." Although the screen quickly went black, the zap action was itself news, covered widely by media outlets across the country. Cronkite rejected the accusation that CBS was biased against LGBTQ people. But the following spring he did his first positive story on the subject of sexual minorities, explaining to viewers how LGBTQ rights activists had succeeded in persuading several municipalities across the country to enact ordinances prohibiting sexual orientation discrimination.[29]

In 1974, ABC shared with NGTF a script of another upcoming *Marcus Welby, M.D.* episode that included a gay character. (The network decided to share the script with activists because it suspected, probably correctly, that one or more of its gay employees would eventually do so anyway.) The gay character in this particular episode was a high school teacher who sexually abused one of his male students. Representatives of NGTF urged the network not to air the show, given that it promoted the pervasive and insidious stereotype of gay men as child molesters. But ABC agreed to make only minor changes to the show's script, leading NGTF and GAA activists to organize a multipronged grassroots campaign against the network. Activists persuaded the American Psychological Association (which the year before had removed "homosexuality" from its list of mental illnesses), the National Organization of Women, and the National Educational Association to condemn the program; a handful of corporations to withhold their advertisements from the show; and five local ABC affiliates not to air the episode.[30]

Also in 1974, about two hundred demonstrators picketed outside CBS's New York City headquarters to protest the depiction of gay men as pedophiles in shows like *Kojak* and antigay slurs in shows like *M*A*S*H**. That same year lesbian groups targeted NBC for its planned airing of an episode of *Police Woman* titled "Flowers of Evil," about three lesbians who robbed and killed the residents of the nursing home they owned before they were stopped by the show's enterprising female detective. At the end of the episode, after the television detective saved the day by arresting the three lesbians, she somberly told them that she was aware of "what a love like yours can do to someone."[31]

NBC's scheduled airing of the *Police Woman* episode led the Lesbian Feminist Liberation to unfurl a giant banner reading "Lesbians Protest NBC" from a building across from the network's New York City headquarters in Rockefeller Center, while demonstrators below chanted "NBC works against lesbian civil rights." Several activists, receiving help from sympathetic LGBTQ network employees, made their way into the headquarters and occupied executives' offices.

The protests led NBC representatives to meet with NGTF members, who forcefully expressed their grievances about the network's anti-LGBTQ programming. The activists also demanded that NBC's nondiscrimination policy be expanded to include sexual orientation. A few months later, the NGTF's media director became the first open LGBTQ person to testify before the Federal Communications Commission, explaining to the regulatory agency the ways in which the networks' repeated stereotypical and negative portrayals of LGBTQ people harmed sexual minorities.[32]

The pressure that LGBTQ activists put on the networks soon began to bear fruit. ABC and NBC agreed not to show reruns of the "gay rapist teacher" (ABC) and "killer lesbians" (NBC) episodes. The three major networks also agreed to share scripts with the Gay

Media Task Force, a group led by the gay activist Newton Deiter, in order to receive feedback from members of the LGBTQ community during the development of shows with gay and lesbian characters. This consultative process led to some positive portrayals of gay and lesbian individuals on television during the second half of the 1970s.[33]

It bears noting that the LGBTQ activism aimed at the networks did not end the stereotypical and negative depictions of sexual minorities on television. But the activism did succeed in permitting the viewing public (almost the entire nation), every once in a while, to see more balanced and accurate representations of the lives, relationships, and aspirations of LGBTQ people on their television screens.

Another tangible benefit arose from LGBTQ activism aimed at the major television networks: pressured by activists, all three companies in 1975 announced the adoption of sexual orientation nondiscrimination policies. And, the following year, again at the urging of activists, CBS agreed to revise its job application form to explicitly state that the company did not discriminate on the basis of "sexual preference." This meant that the television industry, only a few years after Stonewall, became the first corporate sector to widely adopt sexual orientation nondiscrimination policies.[34]

It was not exactly a secret that the television industry, like other parts of the entertainment business, attracted a large contingent of LGBTQ individuals interested in the work. But to come out as an open LGBTQ person, even in the relatively liberal entertainment field, at best limited careers and at worst ended them. In 1970, for example, CBS fired five employees when it learned that the military had earlier discharged them for "homosexual tendencies."[35] When the three major television networks, only five years later, adopted nondiscrimination policies, the many LGBTQ employees working in the television industry did not suddenly bolt from the closet. But the networks' adoption of those policies initiated change in their corporate cultures in ways that encouraged a small, and with time a growing, number of LGBTQ employees to be open about their sexual orientation at work. The presence of open LGBTQ employees, in turn, affected programming: it was more difficult for networks to produce homophobic shows after learning that many employees who worked on them were LGBTQ themselves.

In the end, early LGBTQ rights activism aimed at television networks was remarkably successful. In the years that followed, positive portrayals of LGBTQ people on television began to outnumber stereotypical and negative ones. In the 1990s, the networks for the first time created entire shows (such as *Will & Grace* and *Ellen*) around well-adjusted LGBTQ characters who were at ease with their sexual orientation (and eventually, in the case of transgender characters, with their gender identity). LGBTQ activism, of course, was not the only factor contributing to the changes in programming. Changes in the content of television shows, to a considerable extent, reflect changes in the wider society. As the country as a whole became more tolerant and accepting of LGBTQ people, it became easier, less controversial, and increasingly profitable for television networks to broadcast positive LGBTQ programming. But that was not the case in the years following Stonewall. During the 1970s and into the 1980s, LGBTQ activists had to repeatedly pressure television executives to account for the ways in which their entertainment and news shows portrayed sexual minorities to the viewing public.[36]

The Coors Boycott

One of the best-known examples of early LGBTQ rights activism aimed at corporations, the boycott of Coors beer, was not started by queer activists. Instead, the boycott was the brainchild of Latino activists in Denver in the late 1960s who were looking to politically energize Denver's growing Chicano community. Coors, the Colorado-based brewing company, was an appealing target because the firm was known for its vigorous opposition to labor unions and its poor track record in hiring racial minorities and women. In 1966, only about 2 percent of employees in the company's brewery plant in Golden, Colorado, were Latino. Indeed, with the exception of some clerical and low-skilled positions, the company, well into the 1970s, was overwhelmingly male and white. The company was also an appealing target because its wealthy owners were outspoken supporters of conservative causes and leading funders of hard-right political groups.[37]

Inspired by the grape boycott organized by Cesar Chavez's and Dolores Huerta's United Farm Workers (UFW), and angered by the Coors family's support of grape growers in their fight against organized labor, Colorado Latino activists in 1967 called for a boycott of Coors beer. Activists took out ads in Colorado newspapers publicizing the company's poor track record in hiring Latinos and filed a complaint with the Equal Employment Opportunity Commission (EEOC). National Latino groups, such as the National Council of Hispanic Citizens and the American GI Forum (a Latino veterans group), joined the call for a boycott. Two years later, a group of Chicano students at Southern Colorado State College (now Colorado State University–Pueblo) were arrested while demonstrating on campus in favor of the boycott.

Although unions representing Coors workers had in the past called for boycotts, such calls had arisen in the context of strikes and other workers' actions that pursued specific collective bargaining goals. The new boycott of Coors called for by Latino groups was different because its objective, like that of the Montgomery bus boycott of the 1950s and the more recent UFW-organized boycott of grapes, was to bring attention to issues of racial injustice and discrimination.[38]

In 1973, Coors angered union activists when its beer distributor in the San Francisco area refused to agree to a contract with the Teamsters Local. After a Teamster official by the name of Allan Baird learned of the Latino-sponsored boycott of Coors, he urged his union to join in. Baird also traveled around the Bay Area exhorting minority groups, such as the Black Panther Party and the Native American Labor Advisory Council, to boycott Coors. In addition, Baird reached out to leaders of the LGBTQ community, including Harvey Milk, asking them to join the boycott.[39]

For many LGBTQ activists, first in San Francisco and then in other cities such as Los Angeles and Houston, joining the boycott was appealing for two main reasons. First, Coors was well known among gay activists because of its polygraph testing policy. Coors in the late 1950s had insisted that its union contracts include a provision allowing it to fire employees who engaged in conduct that "violates the common decency or morality of the community." A few years later, the company began requiring many of its job applicants to answer questions while attached to a polygraph machine. The questions asked about past criminal activity, support for radical (left-wing) causes, and sexual conduct. Male applicants were routinely asked whether they were gay or had ever engaged in same-sex sexual conduct.[40]

Second, the Coors boycott offered a unique opportunity for LGBTQ activists to work in concert, and create grassroots and organizational links, with racial minority groups and labor unions. In San Francisco, Milk and other gay activists asked the Teamsters, in return for their support of the boycott, to push for the hiring of gay workers for beer delivery jobs, in the same way that racial minority groups demanded that the union add affirmative action programs to its list of demands. The LGBTQ activists reasoned that supporting the boycott would not only bring jobs to their community, but it would also encourage labor activists to reciprocate by supporting LGBTQ rights issues. As Milk put it, "If we want others to help us in our fight to end discrimination, we must help others." And, in fact, Baird and his Teamsters Local in 1974 publicly supported a bill introduced in the state legislature that would prohibit employment discrimination on the basis of sexual orientation and worked to add sexual orientation to the nondiscrimination provisions included in union contracts with employers.[41]

It turned out that the Teamsters' support for the boycott was short-lived; in the summer of 1975, officials from the national union prohibited the Bay Area local from further participating in it. The Teamsters would once again support the boycott, along with the AFL-CIO, later in the 1970s. By that time, the boycott had already spread throughout the LGBTQ community in San Francisco, leading many gay and lesbian bars in the city to refuse to sell Coors beer. And soon LGBTQ groups and activists in other parts of the country were urging gay and lesbian bars not to carry, and sexual minorities not to buy, Coors products.[42]

Two other factors contributed to the growing strength of the Coors boycott, fueled, as it was, by the corporation's discriminatory policies. First, the EEOC in 1975 filed a lawsuit against the company for discriminating against racial minorities and women. The government agency demanded that Coors provide appropriate back pay to those it discriminated against and institute an affirmative action program. Two years later, the company signed a settlement agreement with the federal agency that, while not acknowledging past wrongs, committed Coors not to discriminate on the basis of race, national origin, or sex. The company also agreed to set timetables for hiring racial minorities and women and to dedicate $250,000 for the training and recruitment of minorities.[43]

Second, the AFL-CIO in 1977, responding to the company's anti-union activities at its Golden manufacturing plant that had resulted in a strike, came out in support of the boycott. The following year, Coors announced a 12 percent reduction in its profits, with the company acknowledging that the boycott was a factor in that drop. Shortly thereafter the *Wall Street Journal* reported that the company's market share in California had dropped to 23 percent from 41 percent just five years earlier.[44]

Feeling the political heat, and wanting to put an end to the boycott, the company began hiring a greater number of Latinos while increasingly giving money to Latino community groups. Coors in 1978 stopped asking questions about sexual orientation in its polygraph testing of job applicants and added sexual orientation to the company's antidiscrimination policy, becoming the first brewing company in the United States to do so. In addition, the company in 1979 became the first major American corporation to advertise in a gay magazine (the *Advocate*), paying for a full-page ad showing a photograph of a well-groomed man (presumably gay) under the headline

"I've Heard Coors' Side and I Am Satisfied." Two years earlier, the company had welcomed a reporter for the *Advocate* to its Golden facility and encouraged him to speak to its employees, leading to the publication of an article in the gay magazine contending that Coors was not the antigay company that activists claimed it was.[45]

Although some in LGBTQ communities welcomed the gay-friendly steps taken by Coors and began calling for lifting the boycott, others insisted on continuing the boycott for several reasons. First, as the case of Pacific Bell would soon show, a firm's adoption of a nondiscrimination policy was not enough to satisfy most activists in the absence of an explicit recognition by the targeted company that it had, in fact, discriminated against sexual minorities in the past. Second, several members of the Coors family continued to give large amounts of money, derived mostly from the company's profits, to conservative groups and causes that were fighting the LGBTQ movement on several fronts. As Harvey Milk explained,

> Coors constantly has given money to right-wing organizations that, in turn, give money to organizations that are very antigay, antiwomen, and antiminority. For example, they have given money to the John Birch Society, and they were instrumental in setting up the Heritage Foundation. Those groups in turn give money to antigay organizations. It's commonly called laundering money. Every time you buy a bottle of Coors beer, part of that money is given to attack gay people and women in one form or another.[46]

Third, as indicated by Milk's comments, the Coors boycott was not just an LGBTQ rights cause; it was also the result of activism by a broad coalition of progressive groups (representing racial minorities, women, workers, environmentalists, and LGBTQ people) that came together to try to make the owners of the company pay a political and financial cost for their support of a range of practices and policies (for example, anti–affirmative action, anti–environmental protections, anti–worker protections, and anti-union) that were inconsistent with progressive objectives and values. In short, the fact that the company no longer asked applicants highly intrusive questions about their sexuality while attached to lie-detector machines and that it had adopted a sexual orientation antidiscrimination policy under pressure from the boycott was not enough to satisfy most boycott proponents, both within and outside LGBTQ communities.

In the years that followed, Coors continued to try to appease boycott supporters by, for example, giving money to groups such as the NAACP and the National Council of La Raza (a Latino rights organization), while committing itself to training and hiring more racial minorities and women. It also reached an agreement with the AFL-CIO not to orchestrate anti-union campaigns during labor organizing drives at its facilities. On the LGBTQ front, the company initially responded to the AIDS epidemic by announcing that it would not allow gay employees to hold jobs that would bring them into contact with beer while it was being brewed. But the company soon rescinded that ill-considered policy, and then proceeded to give significant amounts of money to AIDS and LGBTQ community organizations. In addition, the company in 1992 opposed an amendment to the Colorado constitution aimed at denying sexual minorities, and no others, the right to be afforded antidiscrimination protection by state and local laws. Furthermore, Coors in 1995 became one of the largest corporations (the biggest in Colorado and the first beer company) to offer domestic partnership benefits to its employees.[47]

These steps divided boycott supporters. Some activists who had previously supported the boycott now called for its lifting, given the company's financial support for progressive groups and causes. These activists were willing to distinguish between the company's new sense of corporate responsibility, on the one hand, and the extremely conservative views and political funding decisions of the Coors family, on the other.

But other progressives refused to give up on the boycott because they remained highly troubled by the Coors family's financial support for right-wing causes. As one commentator noted,

> For many people, granting health benefits to a handful of gay employees' partners is less significant than giving $150,000 a year to the Free Congress Foundation, which supports

candidates who consider homosexuality "an infamous crime against nature." For many people, finally naming a Mexican American to the board of directors is outweighed by enthusiastic support for the Heritage Foundation which backs anti-immigration and English-only initiatives. For many people, a black company vice president does not counterbalance millions given to fight affirmative action, welfare, and civil rights enforcement.[48]

The question of whether to lift the boycott continued to divide African American, Latino, and LGBTQ organizations and activists for years. Within queer communities as late as the 1990s, there were repeated and heated debates over whether Coors's funding of LGBTQ and AIDS organizations and its gay-friendly employment policies merited the lifting of the boycott. For example, a furor erupted after the West Hollywood City Council passed a resolution in 1997 commending Coors for "its record of outstanding relations with its lesbian and gay employees and for its outreach to the lesbian and gay community." Although some in the local LGBTQ community supported the city council's action, many vociferously criticized it. The city council the following year rescinded its Coors resolution in a 5–4 vote.[49]

Coors's decision, around the same time, to cosponsor LGBTQ pride parades in Los Angeles and San Jose, as well as a fund-raiser for the Lesbian and Gay Community Center Project in San Francisco, stoked similar passions and led to pitched rhetorical battles among LGBTQ activists on both sides of the issue. Proponents of lifting the boycott argued that their opponents were stuck in the past and that the company should be rewarded for becoming a good corporate citizen. For their part, boycott supporters accused opponents of selling out their values for a few dollars and of ignoring the Coors family's continued financial support of antigay right-wing organizations.[50]

Regardless of who had the better arguments on these issues, it is undoubtedly the case that the boycott activism led the company to approach LGBTQ issues in radically different ways. When the boycott began, the only interest the company had in queer people was manifested in its asking job applicants, while connected to lie detector machines, whether they had engaged in same-sex sexual conduct. Otherwise the very existence, to say nothing of the interests and aspirations, of sexual minorities was simply not on the company's radar screen. By the mid-1990s, after twenty years of boycott activism by LGBTQ groups and others, Coors had become a leader among large corporations in embracing LGBTQ rights positions; by that time, the company offered domestic partnership benefits, publicly opposed antigay laws and supported sexual orientation antidiscrimination laws, and generously funded AIDS and LGBTQ community organizations. In short, concerted and focused activism turned the corporation from a perpetrator of discrimination against sexual minorities to an active supporter of LGBTQ causes and organizations.

Although the 1970s LGBTQ activism aimed at corporations was generally successful, its overall impact was relatively limited because its primary objective was to try to end overt discrimination by "worst offender" corporations. Once LGBTQ activists succeeded in bringing attention to and encouraging public condemnation of the companies' discriminatory practices, the targeted businesses eventually dispensed with their more overtly antigay policies. In a society that was generally becoming more skeptical of differential treatment in the workplace based on personal traits, the LGBTQ corporate activism made clear to the targeted companies that they had more to lose from negative publicity arising from those practices than they had to gain from retaining them. It would become more challenging, and it would take more time and effort, to persuade corporations without overt antigay practices that they, too, should adopt internal practices and support public policies that promoted LGBTQ equality.

It would not be until the late 1990s that LGBTQ activists began achieving more systematic reforms across several different corporate sectors that included not only the adoption of sexual orientation and gender identity antidiscrimination policies, but also the implementation of domestic partnership benefit policies. And it would not be until the 2000s that a significant number of large corporations began to openly support LGBTQ equality in government policy.

Even if the political and social impact of the LGBTQ corporate activism of the 1970s was, at the time, relatively limited, it established crucial precedents by proving that the LGBTQ movement could influence corporate conduct in ways that accounted for the rights, interests, and aspirations of queer people. By the end of the 1970s, the more significant gains from LGBTQ rights activism targeting corporations were still to come. But the seeds for those gains were planted in the generally successful activism of that decade aimed at companies such as Pacific Bell, the big television networks, and Coors.

The AIDS crisis of the 1980s brought a new set of challenges for LGBTQ people in the United States. The epidemic inflicted much suffering and pain on LGBTQ communities, among others; not only were there unrelenting illnesses and growing deaths to cope with, but the disease also led to the further social stigmatization of racial minority groups, immigrant populations, and queer people. At the same time, however, the AIDS crisis spurred a great deal of energetic and effective political activism by impacted communities. As had happened during the previous decade, the actions of corporations proved to be a crucial focal point of LGBTQ rights activism during the 1980s.

CHAPTER 3

AIDS Corporate Activism in the 1980s

T HE FIRST INDICATION that something was amiss came in 1980 after a few gay men in San Francisco started complaining to doctors about swollen glands. Although it was clear that these men's immune systems had shifted into overdrive, no one knew precisely why. A few months later, gay men in New York and California started developing unusual diseases such as Kaposi's sarcoma, a skin cancer that until then had afflicted mainly older men of Mediterranean descent, and Pneumocystis carinii, a rare form of pneumonia. The Centers for Disease Control and Prevention (CDC) issued its first bulletin on the AIDS epidemic in June 1981, reporting on a small cluster of pneumocystis cases in Los Angeles. A month later, the *New York Times* published a brief but ominous article titled "Rare Cancer Seen in 41 Homosexuals."[1]

At first, public health officials were unsure what was causing so many gay men to become sick. The transmission of some organism, perhaps through sex, was only one of several possible explanations in the epidemic's early days. Other speculated explanations included the use of certain recreational drugs or the frequenting of specific venues such as bars. It was not until halfway through 1982 that the CDC uncovered evidence linking together forty gay men with AIDS in a network of sexual relationships in ten different cities, strongly suggesting that the disease was caused by a single infectious agent transmitted sexually and perhaps in other ways as well.

The LGBTQ community quickly mobilized to communicate what little was known about the disease and how it was transmitted, and to begin to care for the hundreds of gay men who were becoming sick every month. The community also began mobilizing politically to try to address the discrimination against people with AIDS that was already pervasive in a society that, even before the epidemic, was deeply suspicious of gay men and their sexuality.

The vilification of gay men intensified in 1983 when it was discovered that the disease could also be transmitted through blood, meaning that anyone who needed a blood transfusion was potentially at risk of developing AIDS. Even though heterosexuals also started developing the disease, the media kept the spotlight almost exclusively on gay men and their sexual practices.

The AIDS epidemic fomented and exposed the raw prejudices of those who thought that individuals who engaged in same-sex sexual conduct were perverse and morally depraved. To make matters worse, the epidemic's early years coincided with the strengthening of the Christian Evangelical political movement, whose leaders frequently and shamelessly claimed that HIV was God's punishment for those who engaged in "immoral sexual conduct." As the Reverend Jerry Falwell, the head of the Moral Majority, starkly put it in 1983 when speaking about the AIDS epidemic, "When you violate moral, health, and hygiene laws, you reap the whirlwind. You cannot shake your fist in God's face and get away with it." For his part, Republican US senator Jesse Helms of North Carolina declared that "Americans who don't want to risk being killed by AIDS have a clear choice and a safe bet available: reject sodomy and practice morality."[2]

For many years after the appearance of AIDS, far too many officials at all levels of government responded with general indifference to the devastation that the virus was wreaking in the lives of marginalized individuals—including gay men, intravenous drug users, and racial minorities—an indifference prominently manifested in a pervasive and stubborn unwillingness to commit the necessary financial resources to study and treat the disease. The courts did not help matters by upholding the closing of gay establishments and allowing hospitals to fire gay health-care employees suspected of being infected, rulings that institutionalized discrimination without advancing public health objectives.[3]

By April 1984, when the government announced that its scientists had discovered that AIDS was caused by a specific virus, later named HIV (human immunodeficiency virus), there were more than four thousand reported AIDS cases in the United States. A year later, when a test was finally developed to detect the presence of the virus in human blood, the number of reported cases nationwide had doubled. By the end of 1985, there had been more than twelve thousand AIDS-related deaths in the United States, turning the disease into the leading cause of death among twenty-five- to forty-four-year-olds in the country. According to CDC estimates at the time, between half a million and a million Americans were infected with HIV. In 1986, about the same number of people died of AIDS as had died in the previous five years combined, laying bare the frighteningly exponential growth of the disease. By 1988, AIDS was being diagnosed in the United States at a daily rate of almost fifty new cases (with an accumulated total of more than sixty thousand, more than had died fighting the Vietnam War), while more than twenty-five Americans were dying of AIDS every day.

During these years, discrimination against those who were HIV-positive, or were suspected of being so, occurred in a broad range of settings, from housing to education to health care to the workplace. An ACLU survey of legal and advocacy organizations across the country conducted in 1989 found that the respondents had received approximately thirteen thousand complaints of HIV-related discrimination during the previous six years. Employment discrimination was the most frequent type of discrimination reported, accounting for 37 percent of all the complaints. The pervasive discrimination against people with AIDS became another reason for LGBTQ individuals to fear disclosing their sexual orientation at work, to say nothing of revealing that they or their partners might be HIV-positive.[4]

By the middle of the 1980s, it was medically well understood that the virus was transmitted only through the exchange of bodily fluids and not through casual contact. Nonetheless, fears of workplace transmission fueled much of the discrimination against HIV-positive individuals. The irrational fear of contraction, coupled with homophobia, racism, and disdain for needle-injecting drug users, proved to be a toxic combination that led to widespread employment discrimination. As the ACLU report put it, "Our results strongly suggest that in the workplace, reason is often overwhelmed by AIDS paranoia. In the public mind, myths about casual transmission of HIV have not been sufficiently dispelled, highlighting the acute need for massive HIV public education."[5]

Big companies were particularly affected by AIDS because their employment of large numbers of workers significantly increased the chances of their facing HIV issues in the workplace. United Airlines in 1983 placed several male flight attendants diagnosed with AIDS (or suspected of having the disease) on medical leave without bothering to conduct evaluations to determine whether the employees could perform the job's functions. In 1985, panic spread among employees at a General Motors plant in Mississippi after they learned that one of their coworkers had been diagnosed with AIDS. Many employees refused to use equipment and bathrooms touched by the HIV-positive man and some threatened to stay away from work altogether if the company permitted him to return to the plant. That same year about thirty New England Bell Telephone Company workers walked out of their jobs in Boston after the company allowed an employee diagnosed with AIDS to return to work.[6]

At the time, most corporate executives did not believe it was either appropriate or necessary to develop specific policies to address AIDS issues in the workplace. Indeed, by the fall of 1987, only 5 percent of employers in the United States had developed an AIDS policy. Many corporate leaders and managers believed that AIDS was a personal rather than a workplace issue. They also feared raising issues of sex and sexuality, and other taboo topics such as intra-venous drug use, at work. Furthermore, some companies viewed AIDS primarily through the prism of costs. For example, some corporations eschewed AIDS educational programs for their employees because of the purported costs, while others, ostensibly concerned about health-care expenses, responded to the epidemic by denying or significantly limiting health insurance coverage for AIDS-related conditions. This made corporate animus toward people with AIDS crystal clear, given that the same companies did not attempt to limit coverage for other life-threatening illnesses, such as cancer and heart disease, with greater associated medical costs.[7]

Despite the fact that most large corporations initially responded to AIDS by denying that a problem existed and that some made matters worse by instituting discriminatory policies, a handful of companies became social pioneers of sorts by responding differently and positively to the disease. Starting in the mid-1980s, a few companies began implementing sensible and humane AIDS policies, including developing AIDS educational programs that informed employees about HIV and its modes of transmission, tailoring employer-provided health insurance to the needs of HIV-positive employees, and accommodating employees diagnosed with AIDS so that they could keep working as long as they could while they managed their illnesses. Interestingly, the relatively small number of corporations that instituted helpful AIDS workplace policies during the first years of the epidemic did so largely on their own, without being prodded by AIDS activists or forced by government mandates.

Much of the AIDS activism aimed at corporations during the 1980s sought to pressure pharmaceutical companies to develop medical cures for AIDS and to make the treatments available to affected individuals at affordable prices. AIDS activists also mobilized to protest and agitate against the actions of other large corporations, including those that supported politicians who opposed funding for effective AIDS education and prevention programs, as well as companies that discriminated against HIV-positive employees and customers.

Early AIDS Corporate Workplace Policies

Many large companies were first confronted with AIDS when some of their employees began expressing fears about being "exposed" to HIV-positive individuals in the workplace. This is what occurred at the Pacific Bell Telephone Company. In 1984 alone, a Pacific Bell employee refused to collect coins from payphones in San Francisco's predominantly gay Castro neighborhood; a telephone crew in Los Angeles refused to install phones at the Los Angeles AIDS Foundation while another crew in San Francisco demanded head-to-toe protective gear before servicing phones in a San Francisco hospital's AIDS ward; and a telephone lineman refused to use a company truck, previously driven by a man suspected of having died of AIDS, until it was sterilized. Incidents like these were creating managerial and administrative headaches for California's largest provider of telephone services, with a workforce of about ninety thousand employees. For the company, it soon became clear that it made little sense to continue to deal with incidents like these on an ad-hoc basis. As a result, Pacific Bell's medical, legal, and human resources staffs worked together to develop and implement policies that sought to address a disease that, by 1984, was the second leading cause of death (after cancer) among its active employees.[8]

After internal deliberations, the company decided to treat its employees with AIDS in the same ways it treated employees with other life-threatening diseases. This meant, in the first instance and most obviously, not making it more difficult for HIV-positive employees to continue working for the company after they were diagnosed with AIDS. As Pacific Bell's executive director of human resources policy and services succinctly put it, "People with AIDS are sick. We don't fire sick people." The growing incidence of AIDS among its employees also led Pacific Bell to recalibrate its health insurance coverage by offering to pay for alternatives to hospitalization (such as hospice and in-home care) that were particularly important to individuals with AIDS. In addition, the company strengthened its health insurance's capacity for individual health-care case management and extended coverage to pay for mail-order drugs, with the aim of assisting HIV-positive employees.[9]

Furthermore, given the growing instances of workplace disruption caused by some of its employees' irrational fears that they would contract HIV on the job, the company concluded it needed to take steps to educate its workers about the virus. On July 22, 1985 (the same day the actor Rock Hudson garnered an immense amount of media attention by publicly revealing that he had AIDS), members of Pacific Bell's medical and educational staffs published an article in *Update*, the firm's newspaper, explaining the facts about HIV and how the virus was transmitted. Employees' demand for the article was so high that the company had to order several additional reprints. The company's foundation in 1986 produced a video, called *An Epidemic of Fear*, which emphasized the known medical facts about the disease and its modes of transmission while working to dispel the myths that fueled panic, fear, and discrimination. The company encouraged all supervisors to show the video to their employees as part of educational sessions on AIDS.[10]

Pacific Bell was not alone among large corporations in proactively and positively responding to the AIDS epidemic; another company that did so was Bank of America. AIDS issues first arose at the bank in 1983 when a male employee at its San Francisco headquarters was hospitalized with HIV-related complications for several weeks. After his health improved, the employee told his supervisor that he had AIDS and that his doctor had approved his return to work. The well-meaning supervisor decided to tell other employees in the office about the man's condition, hoping that they would support him in his return. Instead, the disclosure engendered office panic and turmoil, with several of the man's coworkers complaining forcefully to managers that their health was now at risk. The father of a pregnant employee went so far as to warn the bank that he would file a complaint with the Occupational Safety and Health Administration (OSHA) if the company allowed the employee with AIDS to return to work.[11]

Bank of America officials persuaded the disgruntled and fearful employees to take a short paid leave while it studied the matter. Seeking guidance, the company's human resources department contacted the CDC, the local health department, and private medical specialists. The advice that came back was consistent and clear: allow the HIV-positive employee to return to work since the scientific evidence showed that the virus was not transmitted via casual contact. The bank followed that advice, permitting its recently ill employee to return to the office while requiring the objecting employees to return to work. (The OSHA complaint was never filed.)[12]

Following this incident, Bank of America executives decided it was essential to adopt a formal company-wide AIDS policy; after all, it was only a matter of time before similarly disruptive occurrences would arise among its huge workforce of more than fifty thousand employees. For the executives, dealing with AIDS issues in the workplace on an ad-hoc basis made little sense. After considerable internal deliberations, company officials concluded that there was no business or medical justification for treating AIDS differently from other life-threatening diseases. At the same time, the company used AIDS as a catalyst to clarify the company's policies regarding all employees with life-threatening illnesses, including cancer and heart disease. A company task force issued a statement in 1985 titled *Assisting Employees with Life Threatening Illnesses* that, among other things, called on managers (1) to reasonably accommodate employees with such illnesses in ways that were consistent with their units' business needs; (2) "to be sensitive to the fact that continued employment for an employee with a life-threatening illness may sometimes be therapeutically important in the remission or recovery process, or may help to prolong the employee's life"; and (3) not to give "special consideration . . . beyond normal transfer requests for employees who feel threatened by a co-worker's life-threatening illness."[13]

The bank's decision to treat AIDS in the same way it dealt with other life-threatening diseases among its employees had the effect of normalizing the illness by making it clear that there was nothing dangerous or problematic about the presence of individuals with

AIDS in its workplaces. At the same time, AIDS presented company managers and supervisors with unique challenges that made it different from other life-threatening diseases. It was exceedingly unlikely, for example, that workers would demand that a coemployee with cancer or heart disease be kept away from the workplace. It was also highly unlikely that workers would ask for transfers simply because someone in the office had been diagnosed with cancer or had suffered a heart attack. It was the appearance of AIDS in its workplaces that led Bank of America to emphasize explicitly in its policies that sick employees benefited from being allowed to remain on the job for as long as possible and that it was inappropriate to grant transfer requests for some employees based on the life-threatening diseases of other employees.

A few other large companies, including AT&T, Chevron, Citibank, Motorola, and Westinghouse, adopted policies in the 1980s that sought to treat AIDS in the workplace no differently from other life-threatening diseases. In addition, some major firms implemented AIDS workplace educational programs. For example, General Motors, in response to a threatened walkout by some employees at its Mississippi manufacturing plant after a worker was diagnosed with AIDS, invested in a $2 million HIV education campaign for its workforce. IBM mailed copies of a CDC brochure on AIDS to all 240,000 of its domestic employees in 1987, with an accompanying letter in which the company's medical director explained that "IBMers affected by AIDS will be encouraged to work as long as they are able, and their privacy will be respected." In addition, several big companies, led by Levi Strauss and Pacific Bell, helped form the National Leadership Coalition on AIDS, an organization consisting of corporations, trade and professional associations, unions, educational institutions, and religious and racial minority groups that sought to mobilize the private and not-for-profit sectors in the fight against AIDS.[14]

It is important to make two points about the sensible and humane ways in which some large corporations responded to AIDS during the epidemic's early years. First, the companies that did so represented a small minority of corporations in the United States. The vast majority of American businesses in the 1980s, both large and small, failed to adopt specific AIDS programs or policies. This meant that HIV-positive employees at those firms were left to navigate the work-related challenges created by their medical conditions without their employers' support. Like many other important social institutions, both public and private, a majority of large corporations in the epidemic's early years chose to ignore AIDS, while refusing to challenge the many prejudices and misunderstandings about the disease that existed both inside and outside their enterprises. By failing to act, the corporations irresponsibly contributed to the fear, discrimination, and suffering that accompanied the disease.[15]

Second, the companies that proactively and positively responded to AIDS in the epidemic's early years did so largely on their own without outside pressure from either AIDS activists or clear legal mandates. At the time, the AIDS movement was primarily focused on demanding greater public- and private-sector research in medical treatments while pressing for greater government spending on housing, health care, and counseling services for HIV-positive individuals. In addition, the AIDS movement, primarily through the work of local AIDS organizations, was focused on making available to affected communities the types of crucial services and education that government agencies were generally unwilling or unable to provide.

It was, of course, not the case that the internal policies of large American corporations were unimportant to the AIDS community. Many HIV-positive individuals worked for such companies. It was just that the early AIDS movement, given its limited resources and influence, had to prioritize its objectives. When the movement, toward the end of the 1980s, began to grow and become more powerful and assertive, it did focus more intently on the actions and omissions of corporations as they affected people with AIDS. But that activism primarily focused on the pharmaceutical industry's development and pricing of AIDS medications and on corporate funding of legislators who supported laws that harmed people with AIDS while opposing regulations that benefited them.

It also bears noting that companies that responded sensibly and humanely to AIDS during the epidemic's early years did so in the absence of meaningful pressure from LGBTQ employees. By the end of the 1980s, for example, only eight Fortune 500 companies had LGBTQ employee groups, which meant that the vast majority of sexual minority employees at large corporations lacked internal vehicles through which to attempt to influence company policies.[16] By the time LGBTQ employees at big companies began creating such groups in significant numbers in the 1990s, many large corporations had already followed the lead of pioneering firms such as Pacific Bell and Bank of America by instituting policies aimed at supporting their HIV-positive employees and educating their workforces about AIDS.

Also by the 1990s, Congress had enacted the Americans with Disabilities Act (ADA), a broad federal antidiscrimination statute that, among other things, prohibited employers from discriminating on the basis of disability, including AIDS. The ADA (1) mandated that covered employers reasonably accommodate employees with AIDS and (2) prohibited them from responding in prejudiced and irrational ways to the presence of HIV-positive individuals in their workplaces, even if urged to do so by some of their employees and customers. But neither of those legal requirements were in place in the 1980s when a few corporations began adopting sensible and humane AIDS policies. Although the federal Rehabilitation Act of 1973 prohibited disability discrimination by the federal government acting as an employer and by entities that received federal funding, it was not clear, during the epidemic's early years, whether that statute—or state disability antidiscrimination laws—applied to a communicable disease such as AIDS. As a result, it cannot be said that the companies that adopted proactive and positive AIDS policies during the 1980s did so because they were legally required to do so.

Given the lack of internal and external pressure on companies in the mid-1980s to take appropriate and helpful steps in responding to AIDS, the question becomes why some corporations, as two authors put it in 1988, "have so far provided most of the demonstrated leadership for sensible approaches to the AIDS epidemic."[17] As a general matter, commentators since then have not acknowledged that—much less explained why—these pioneering companies were among the very first important institutions in American society to respond positively to the AIDS crisis—before most government agencies, religious organizations, labor unions, and educational institutions.

At least three reasons help explain the pioneering AIDS policies adopted by some companies in the mid-1980s. One reason was that the LGBTQ rights activism aimed at corporations during the 1970s had urged America's largest companies to recognize that their workforces included sexual minorities. The activism had also made a powerful case for the proposition that such minorities deserved equal workplace opportunities. Although the visibility of lesbians, gay men, and bisexuals in corporate America was still quite low, given the threats to career advancement that usually accompanied coming out of the closet, sexual minorities in the corporate sphere were no longer *entirely invisible*, as they had been before the mid-1970s. The LGBTQ rights activism aimed at corporations that preceded the AIDS epidemic helped at least some corporate executives to understand that LGBTQ people were not some strange others; instead, sexual minorities, whether in or out of the closet, were part and parcel of their enterprises. If the AIDS epidemic was affecting LGBTQ America, then by definition it was also affecting corporate America.

A second reason for the pioneering policies adopted by some companies was that the presence of AIDS in the workplace raised issues of productivity and efficiency. One such issue was how best to retain productive employees with AIDS who had been contributing to the corporations' bottom lines. The rate of retention of such employees was linked to several factors, including the benefits available through employer-provided health insurance and the willingness of employers to accommodate employees with AIDS as they coped with their physical impairments and medical treatments. In addition, as the workplace incidents noted above illustrate, the lack of clear and protective AIDS employment policies encouraged significant workplace disruptions, given that coworkers frequently responded to the mere presence of HIV-positive individuals in the workplace with prejudice and fear. It was important, in such charged and volatile work environments, for companies to take an active role in educating their employees about the facts of HIV transmission while making it clear that changes in work assignments and duties would be based on medically sound reasons rather than on speculation and fear. In short, considerations of workplace productivity and efficiency favored the crafting of sensible and humane corporate AIDS policies.

Finally, some corporations adopted proactive and positive AIDS policies because it was, quite simply, the right thing to do. The AIDS epidemic was imposing a huge physical, emotional, and financial toll on affected individuals. It was as morally wrong for companies to stop caring about their employees once they were diagnosed with AIDS as it would have been for them to do so after employees became ill with cancer, multiple sclerosis, or any other ailment. To embrace this basic moral position was to view employees with AIDS as equal human beings, who were entitled to the same protections and benefits available to other ill employees. This position was crystallized by the already-noted comment of a Pacific Bell executive who explained the issue succinctly: "People with AIDS are sick. We don't fire sick people." The medical director of United Airlines made a similar point in 1988 after the company, under considerable pressure from the flight attendants' union, ended its unofficial policy of placing employees with AIDS on medical leave regardless of their ability to continue working: "We have a philosophy about the welfare of our employees: People with AIDS or any other life-threatening disease are treated with respect, dignity and compassion. They can continue to work as long as they are physically able to."[18]

Some corporations explicitly disagreed with conservative leaders and activists who blamed individuals with AIDS for their illnesses. As the San Francisco Chamber of Commerce put it in a 1987 report on AIDS in the workplace, "There is an alarming tendency to label people as belonging to AIDS 'risk groups.' This is not only misleading, it is dangerous. AIDS is not confined to any single community. It is not caused by life-style or sexual orientation. It is caused by a virus—a virus that can be transmitted to anyone who engages in high-risk activity." The medical director at Westinghouse expressed a similarly tolerant corporate perspective in a 1986 letter to company officials when he explained that "Westinghouse views AIDS as an illness, not as a crime or punishment. We encourage compassion for the victims, and the provision of accurate and appropriate information to all employees as an antidote to underground fears and unreasoning exaggerations."[19]

In short, the handful of large companies that first adopted sensible and humane AIDS policies during the epidemic's early years, policies that almost every large corporation had in place about a decade later, had good reasons for doing so. Those policies reflected the reality that the companies' workforces included LGBTQ people in general and HIV-positive individuals in particular who were productive contributors to corporate missions. The policies also reflected the unfortunate reality that corporate workplaces were by no means immune to the rampant prejudice and irrational fears engendered by the epidemic. The implementation of sensible and humane corporate AIDS policies made a great deal of managerial sense; it was also the appropriate moral response to the human pain and suffering caused by the growing epidemic.

AIDS Activists and Pharmaceutical Companies

Public advocacy by the AIDS community was relatively muted and restrained during the epidemic's first few years. Typical of that advocacy were candlelight marches organized by AIDS activists in Chicago, Houston, New York, and San Francisco in 1983. Participants in the New York march, for example, walked somberly from Greenwich Village to the federal building in lower Manhattan with the objective of mourning the dead, raising public awareness, and demanding more federal funds for the medical treatment of people living with AIDS.[20]

But as the epidemic's death toll mounted, and as members of the AIDS community grew increasingly angry and frustrated at the nation's failure to respond to the epidemic with the urgency that the health crisis demanded, AIDS activism became progressively louder and more confrontational. In early 1987, the AIDS activist Larry Kramer—a cofounder of the Gay Men's Health Crisis in New York City who was later ousted from the AIDS advocacy and service organization because he was viewed as too confrontational—gave a rousing speech at the New York City Lesbian and Gay Community Center demanding that the AIDS community respond to the deadly combination of intolerance and indifference engendered by the epidemic through coordinated protests, picketing, and acts of civil disobedience. Two nights after Kramer's angry and stirring speech, 350 people came together for the first meeting of what became the AIDS Coalition to Unleash Power, or ACT UP. The organization quickly attracted new members and the public's attention because of its willingness to advocate aggressively and confrontationally on behalf of people with AIDS. ACT UP publicly pressured, cajoled, and embarrassed those in positions of power—including government officials, corporate executives, media representatives, and religious leaders—to take the epidemic with the seriousness that its growing death toll demanded. The new group's slogan SILENCE = DEATH brilliantly captured the stakes for queer people and other affected communities of remaining passive in the face of the deadly epidemic.

ACT UP's principal objective was to hasten finding a cure for AIDS. Much of the energy and sometimes anger of ACT UP members was fueled by the fact that, as of early 1987, there were still no medical treatments for the disease. ACT UP activists placed much of the blame on the Food and Drug Administration's (FDA) cumbersome and time-consuming drug-approval process. As ACT UP saw it, FDA regulations were unnecessarily and cruelly delaying bringing AIDS medications to market—while regulators demanded that researchers continue to study, test, and prove the efficacy of potential treatments, people with AIDS were dying by the thousands. As a result, ACT UP strenuously and repeatedly demanded that the FDA streamline its regulatory processes in order to expedite the approval of AIDS drugs. The group also insisted that the government allow pharmaceutical companies to make promising medications available to people who were dying of AIDS *before* it gave final approval to the treatments.

But it was not just the government that was the problem. AIDS activists grew increasingly frustrated by the pharmaceutical companies' general lack of interest in developing treatments for the disease. As one AIDS historian puts it, "Drug companies responded slowly to a disease not viewed as an emergency or a large source of profit."[21] As a result, ACT UP soon began to apply public pressure on drug companies to speed up their development of new medicines.

To encourage companies to get more involved, researchers at the federal government's National Cancer Institute (NCI) in 1984 contacted pharmaceutical companies pleading for compounds that might be effective in treating AIDS. The NCI offered to test the substances in return for a commitment by the companies to develop and market the drugs that seemed promising. Following this outreach to the private sector, about fifty companies and laboratories sent government researchers dozens of experimental compounds. One of those companies was Burroughs Wellcome, which sent the government AZT (azidothymidine), among other potential medicines.[22]

The compound that made up AZT was first synthesized in the 1960s by government-funded researchers studying potential cancer medications. When early testing suggested that AZT did not kill cancerous cells, research on the compound ended. In 1984, a Burroughs Wellcome scientist began working with the compound as a possible antiviral agent. After the researcher's preliminary findings showed that it was possible AZT might be effective in fighting HIV, the company sent the compound to the NCI for additional testing.[23]

Government researchers conducted test-tube studies of all the compounds they received and concluded that AZT was the most effective in slowing the reproduction of HIV. In the summer of 1985, the NCI tested AZT in a study of nineteen individuals who were dying of AIDS. After several weeks on the medication, the immune system of fifteen participants improved, while almost all of them gained weight. When the study's results were published in 1986, it spread a jolt of enthusiasm and hope throughout the AIDS community: here, for the first time, was a medical treatment that offered tens of thousands of HIV-positive individuals, who were living under an apparent death sentence, the possibility of survival.

Additional and more comprehensive testing of AZT in 1986 seemed to confirm that the drug boosted the immune systems of a significant proportion of people with AIDS, leading the FDA to approve the use of the drug as the first medical treatment for AIDS in early 1987. By that time, Burroughs Wellcome had announced that it would sell AZT for the staggering annual price of $10,000 (or about $23,000 today), rendering it, at the time, one of the most expensive prescription drugs ever sold in the United States. The high price made the drug unobtainable for the many people with AIDS who lacked health insurance (some of whom had lost the insurance as a result of losing their jobs) or whose health insurers refused to pay for AIDS-related costs above minimal amounts.

Five days after the FDA's announcement, ACT UP held its first demonstration by organizing a sit-in on Wall Street. The protest attracted more than six hundred participants and led to the arrests of nineteen demonstrators for blocking traffic, making it, by far, the largest manifestation of civil disobedience by AIDS activists up to that point. A flyer distributed during the demonstration demanded the quick approval of promising AIDS drugs, a coordinated response to the epidemic by the federal government, better and more effective public education about the disease, and an end to discrimination against people with AIDS. The protestors also aimed their ire at pharmaceutical companies for the slow pace of AIDS medicine development and, as the pricing of AZT seemed to show, for caring more about profits than about the lives of people with AIDS. The three leading television networks covered the demonstration in their news shows, as did newspapers across the country.[24]

The fact that a greater number of experimental AIDS drugs were available at more affordable prices in countries with less cumbersome drug-approval processes (such as Canada and France) only deepened the suspicion of many AIDS activists in the United States that public officials and pharmaceutical companies were not sufficiently committed to the finding of a cure. Taking matters into their own hands, AIDS activists by 1987 had created underground distribution systems for illegally imported medications in more than forty American cities. Activists also operated underground laboratories that produced unapproved substances and then illegally distributed them to individuals with AIDS who believed they had little to lose by ingesting highly experimental compounds.[25]

In the meantime, AIDS activists repeatedly called on Burroughs Wellcome to lower the price of AZT. In San Francisco, hundreds of protestors, aiming to bring attention to AZT's high price, gathered in the city's Castro neighborhood to kick off a thirty-mile, two-day march to the company's offices south of the city. Once they reached the offices, some ACT UP members proceeded to trespass onto company property, leading to the arrests of about twenty protestors. Activists and other members of the AIDS community also inundated Congress with calls and letters complaining about Burroughs Wellcome's AZT pricing policy. This led liberal congressman Henry Waxman from California, the chair of the House of Representatives' Subcommittee on Health and the Environment, to hold a hearing to scrutinize the company's actions. Several legislators at the hearing strongly criticized Burroughs Wellcome's president for the company's pricing of AZT.[26]

By the end of 1987, Burroughs Wellcome responded to the public pressure by reducing the price of AZT to $8,000 a year. Although the company's AZT-related costs did not seem to come close to justifying even the reduced price, Burroughs Wellcome argued that it needed to charge a high price for AZT to defray costs incurred as a result of expensive research and testing of compounds that never made it to market. The company also contended that it had to make its profits relatively quickly, given the likelihood that competitors would soon begin selling other AIDS medications.[27]

AIDS activists were not mollified by either the reduction in price or the company's efforts to defend its pricing policy. Activists were also angered when the federal government announced that it would permit Burroughs Wellcome to seek an exclusive patent for AZT. AIDS activists complained that it made no sense to allow the company to keep all of AZT's profits, given that the compound had been first synthesized by government-funded cancer researchers in the 1960s. In addition, the federal government had conducted or paid for much of the clinical testing of AZT to determine its effectiveness in fighting HIV. AIDS activists therefore demanded that the government require Burroughs Wellcome either to share the patent with other researchers who had worked on AZT or to reduce the medicine's price in return for receiving the exclusive patent. In the end, the government granted the company an exclusive patent without conditions or limitations, a decision that further infuriated AIDS activists. In an example of how history repeats itself, AIDS activists thirty years later similarly complained that the government was allowing a pharmaceutical company to hold an exclusive patent and charge a list price of more than $20,000 for a medication (with the brand name of Truvada) that was developed and tested mostly with taxpayer and private-charity money, and that has been shown to be effective in preventing the transmission of HIV.[28]

In the fall of 1988, hundreds of loud and angry ACT UP demonstrators from across the country converged on the FDA's headquarters in suburban Washington demanding that the agency speed up its processes for approving AIDS medications. The protestors' banners and placards displayed slogans such as "AIDS doesn't discriminate. The government does" and "The government has blood on its hands. One AIDS death every half an hour." Some protestors lay down on the street and held cardboard tombstones with epitaphs accusing the FDA of responsibility for AIDS deaths. The ten-hour protest received nationwide media coverage and led to the arrest of 176 activists. A few days later, the FDA announced new regulations intended to expedite the drug approval process.[29]

AIDS activists' anger at Burroughs Wellcome came to a boiling point in early 1989 when a small group of ACT UP members, wearing suits and ties, entered the company's headquarters in North Carolina, talked their way past security guards, made their way upstairs, and then sealed themselves inside an office by using power tools to bolt steel plates to the frame door. After word spread that AIDS activists had holed themselves up inside the building, members of the national and local media descended on the scene. The ACT UP activists had planned to hang a banner from the building that read "Burroughs Wellcome's AZT: Pay or Die," but that plan failed when they were unable to smash through the sealed office window. Sheriff's officers had to use sledgehammers to enter the barricaded office, after which they quickly arrested the trespassers. Media outlets across the country covered both the incident and ACT UP's demand that the company reduce the price of AZT by 25 percent, while subsidizing the medication's cost for individuals with AIDS who lacked the insurance or money necessary to pay for the drug.[30]

The pressure on Burroughs Wellcome continued to mount after the release, in the summer of 1989, of preliminary research findings showing that AZT might help not only those who had been diagnosed with AIDS, but also asymptomatic HIV-positive individuals; crucially, the findings suggested that taking the medication delayed the development of AIDS-related illnesses. There were significantly more asymptomatic HIV-positive individuals than there were individuals diagnosed with AIDS. If the preliminary findings proved to be correct, it would mean that the market for AZT would grow exponentially. Within a month of the preliminary findings' release, the stock value of Burroughs Wellcome's parent company increased 43 percent. By the end of 1989, the company had sold $225 million worth of AZT. And by 1991, the cumulative sale of the drug in the United States and abroad exceeded $1 billion.[31]

The *New York Times* published a scathing editorial in the summer of 1989, titled "AZT's Inhuman Cost," berating Burroughs Wellcome for its intransigent position on the drug's price. At around the same time, a national alliance of AIDS organizations issued a statement critical of the company and urged it to lower the price of AZT. By this time, protestors were picketing in front of the company's headquarters in North Carolina on a weekly basis. In addition, activists went into drugstores in different parts of the country to place "AIDS Profiteer" stickers on over-the-counter drugs, such as Actifed and Sudafed, manufactured by Burroughs Wellcome.[32]

In the fall of 1989, several ACT UP members used fake Bear Stearns identification cards to enter the New York Stock Exchange and chain themselves to a VIP platform overlooking the trading floor. When the bell rang to announce the start of the trading day, the activists unfurled a large banner that read, "Sell Wellcome." The protestors then used piercingly loud marine foghorns to drown out the traders and halt oral trading for a few minutes. They also tossed to the traders below fake one hundred dollar bills imprinted with the words "Fuck your profiteering. We die while you play business." About an hour after the police arrested the ACT UP trespassers and carted them off to jail, some fifteen hundred additional protestors congregated outside the Exchange for a loud and energetic demonstration. A leaflet distributed by ACT UP accused Burroughs Wellcome of "medical apartheid" for pricing its drug so high that it effectively rendered it out of reach for almost everyone in Africa and for many people of color, women, and children in the United States. The leaflet demanded that the company give AZT for free to all those who wished to use it: "With a million and a half Americans infected with HIV and millions more infected worldwide, ANYTHING ELSE WOULD BE GENOCIDE." The day's audacious protest action was covered by media outlets all over the country and abroad.[33]

Four days after the Wall Street zap action, Burroughs Wellcome announced it was lowering the price of AZT to $6,500 a year. The company also agreed, in negotiations with Peter Staley, an ACT UP member who a few months earlier had occupied an office at its corporate headquarters, to make a contribution of $1 million to the American Foundation for AIDS Research (amfAR) for community-based drug trials. (These were drug trials run by community-based physicians and AIDS groups rather than by university medical research centers that dominate the nation's prescription drug testing.) In making the donation, a company spokesperson stated, "We as an organization have come to realize that the goals of ACT UP—most notably, the discovery of treatments for HIV disease—are not all that different than ours." In the years that followed, Burroughs Wellcome provided more than four hundred grants to AIDS organizations for treatment-related education, with a total donated amount of $3 million.[34]

Following Burroughs Wellcome's controversial handling of AZT, government officials and AIDS activists used a different approach with ddI (didanosine), the second antiviral drug approved by the FDA (in 1991) for the treatment of AIDS. This time around, scientists at the National Cancer Institute, after putting their names on the patents for ddI, reached an agreement with Bristol-Myers Squibb, one of the nation's largest pharmaceutical companies, whereby the firm agreed to a "reasonable price clause" in return for receiving a license to test and develop ddI. Government officials and activists also persuaded the company to distribute ddI for free to patients who either did not qualify for the formal trials or whose health was not improving while taking AZT, a decision hailed by Larry Kramer for putting "compassion before greed." In total, about twenty-five thousand people received the medication under a new FDA "expanded access" policy, instituted as a result of pressure from AIDS activists. The new policy allowed drug companies to distribute medicines to individuals with terminal illnesses, as long as the medicine was free, before the compounds were officially approved. Bristol-Myers Squibb's decision to make the AIDS medicine available before the government deemed it to be safe and effective exposed the firm to potential legal liability; the fact that the company was willing to take such a risk showed the considerable influence of AIDS activists. When ddI reached the market in 1991, Bristol-Meyers Squibb priced it at $1,745 a year, less than one-fifth of what Burroughs Wellcome had originally charged for AZT. After the FDA approved the drug, the company provided the medicine for free to individuals who could not afford it.[35]

A different, more adversarial relationship developed between AIDS activists and Hoffman-La Roche, another large pharmaceutical company. That company developed a drug called ddC (dideoxycytidine), which was similar in composition to AZT. But unlike Bristol-Meyers Squibb, Hoffman-La Roche refused to make the drug available under the auspices of the FDA's "expanded access" policy before the government agency approved the medicine for the treatment of AIDS. This decision led ACT UP members to barge into a Hoffman-La Roche management meeting in the summer of 1991, startling company officials who were handed leaflets demanding free access to ddC. The zap action led to nine months of tense negotiations between the company and ACT UP. In the end, Hoffman-La Roche agreed to implement an expanded access program for its drug. However, AIDS activists complained that the company had put in place unnecessarily restrictive criteria for who could participate in the program and, as a result, called for a boycott of Hoffman-La Roche products. ACT UP members also wrote to several dozen doctors in large cities informing them about substitutes for Hoffman-La Roche non-AIDS medications that were manufactured by other companies and asking them to prescribe those drugs instead. In early 1993, members of ACT UP's New York chapter led a large demonstration in front of Hoffman-La Roche's headquarters in New Jersey, leading to several arrests.[36]

Activists also targeted the pharmaceutical company Abbott Laboratories for its unwillingness to make its medicine clarithromycin, used to treat an opportunistic lung infection that was killing scores of people with AIDS, available on a compassionate-use basis prior to the completion of ongoing drug trials and FDA approval of the medicine. At the time, Abbott was making millions of dollars in profits each year from tests that detected HIV antibodies in blood. In the spring of 1991, members of ACT UP's San Francisco chapter occupied Abbott's offices in that city. The following year, after the company refused to test a drug that activists believed might prevent HIV transmission from pregnant women to their unborn babies, ACT UP activists invaded the Pacific Stock Exchange in San Francisco chanting, "Save babies, sell Abbott."[37]

As zap actions and other forms of protests aimed at pharmaceutical companies proliferated in the early 1990s, a rift developed within the AIDS community on questions related to medical research. While many activists wanted to continue pressuring pharmaceutical companies from the outside, others now sought to join forces with the companies to ensure that the most promising drugs were tested first. Many of these latter activists had become self-educated experts in the pharmacology of AIDS, an expertise they believed could help drug companies steer the most promising medicines to market. This group of activists, many of whom were ex–ACT UP members who had formed a new organization called Treatment Action Group (TAG), came to believe that civil disobedience and zap actions targeting drug companies were producing diminishing returns for the AIDS movement. It seemed that the media and the general public were paying less attention to the protest actions, reducing their effectiveness in pressuring the companies. In addition, the increase in public and private funding for AIDS research that began in the early 1990s was starting to bear fruit as there now seemed to be promising new treatments on the horizon. People living with AIDS, TAG members argued, would be better served by creating partnerships between activists who had gained significant expertise on the science of HIV and medical researchers working for pharmaceutical companies. From TAG's perspective, people with AIDS had more to gain if activists shifted to an insider strategy that sought to work jointly with companies' researchers than from continuing to angrily agitate from the outside.

TAG in 1993 went so far as to ask the FDA to *slow down* the AIDS drug approval process to ensure that medicines approved for sale were actually beneficial to individuals with the disease. TAG's position on the speed with which AIDS medications should be approved was assailed by much of the rest of the AIDS activist community, a majority of whom continued to believe strongly that the government's drug-approval process was contributing to the deaths of people with AIDS.[38]

As these debates were raging within the AIDS community, some pharmaceutical companies were working to make their interactions with AIDS activists less confrontational and more productive for both sides. One of those corporations was Merck, the New Jersey–based pharmaceutical company that, along with other drug firms, eventually developed a new line of medications, known as protease inhibitors, which became quite effective in treating AIDS (more on the inhibitors below). Merck asked the Hyacinth AIDS Foundation, New Jersey's leading AIDS services organization, to conduct training for its scientists and public affairs employees on how best to interact with the AIDS activist community. In addition, to make the human side of the AIDS epidemic more palpable for its workers, the company published several articles in its employee magazine and newsletters about the challenges, fears, and hopes of people living with AIDS. The firm also invited AIDS activists to tour its research facilities and meet with its top researchers as a way of trying to persuade them that the company was doing everything it could to find effective medical treatments for AIDS as quickly as possible and to get them approved by the FDA.

Over a six-year period, Merck representatives held more than one hundred meetings with AIDS activists, some of whom were participating as patients in the company's drug trials, to listen to activists' concerns and to explain the company's positions to them. Although these meetings, especially in the early years, were often heated and confrontational, most of the participants, on both sides, believed they were constructive and helpful. As a result of these ongoing meetings, Merck made changes to its testing protocols as suggested by AIDS activists. And when Merck brought Crixivan, its protease inhibitor, to market in 1996, activists persuaded the company to price it at around $4,400 a year, almost $1,500 less than similar medications developed by its competitors.[39]

The AIDS community was devastated by news in 1993 that a large European study concluded that AZT did not, in fact, slow the progression to AIDS in asymptomatic HIV-positive individuals.[40] Fortunately, at about the same time, several pharmaceutical companies began developing and testing protease inhibitors, an entirely new class of AIDS drugs that became a game changer in the treatment of AIDS. Approved by the FDA in 1995, the wide use of protease inhibitors, developed primarily by Abbott Laboratories, Hoffman-La Roche, and Merck, led to a rapid decline in the number of AIDS deaths in a short period of time. The use of the inhibitors, in different combinations according to different patients' needs and responses, changed the disease from a fatal one to a largely manageable one, at least for those who had access to the new medications. Although the development of effective medications took years longer than most AIDS activists believed had been necessary, at the cost of tens of thousands of lives, pharmaceutical companies—with considerable assistance from increasingly available federal research money—did eventually develop new medications that, for most people with access to them, made the disease a manageable one.

The AIDS medical activism of the late 1980s and early 1990s had several profound and long-lasting effects. First, it changed the FDA's approach to the regulation of medicines from one that almost exclusively focused on protecting the public from hazardous compounds to one that balanced that objective against the need to approve potentially lifesaving treatments as expeditiously as possible. Second, AIDS activists empowered patients and their doctors to participate in the process of determining which treatments were brought to market and approved by the government in ways that had never occurred before in American history. As law professor Lewis Grossman notes, "The AIDS activists' successful advocacy regarding drug access permanently shifted decision-making power previously exercised by the FDA to individual patients and their physicians." The effects of that shift are still being felt today as treatment advocacy groups and patients with other diseases, from breast cancer to diabetes, now regularly play active roles in determining the best courses of treatment.[41]

Third, AIDS medical activism forced the pharmaceutical industry, one of the country's most important corporate sectors, to account for the lives, perspectives, and demands for equal treatment and respect of sexual minorities. The AIDS activism of the late 1980s and early 1990s repeatedly brought together—sometimes in angry disputes, other times in strained negotiations, and yet other times in constructive dialogue—two groups of people who previously had few occasions to speak to and learn from each other: representatives of some of the country's leading corporations and LGBTQ individuals.

As a result of ongoing pressure applied by AIDS activists, executives at the country's leading pharmaceutical companies had no choice but to invite members of the LGBTQ community to the table. For many of these executives, their interactions with AIDS activists was the first time they were exposed to large numbers of noncloseted queer people and was therefore the first time they could learn about the lives, challenges, and aspirations of sexual minorities. These ongoing encounters were important in combating stereotypes of and prejudice against LGBTQ people inside corporate walls. As with the LGBTQ rights corporate activism of the 1970s, the AIDS medical activism of the late 1980s and early 1990s created opportunities for engagement and dialogue between representatives of corporate America and members of the LGBTQ community. Not only did those interactions help in the development of effective AIDS medications, but they also planted seeds of LGBTQ equality on important corporate soil. By the mid-1990s, large pharmaceutical companies such as Wellcome Burroughs and Merck had added sexual orientation to their nondiscrimination policies. And, after the turn of the century, the pharmaceutical industry as a whole became a strong supporter of marriage equality and of the enactment of laws prohibiting discrimination on the basis of sexual orientation and gender identity.

AIDS Activism Targeting Other Corporations

It was not only the dearth of new medications coming out of the laboratories of America's leading pharmaceutical companies that angered activists during the epidemic's early years; AIDS activists were also frustrated by corporations that donated large amounts of money to elected officials who opposed meaningful funding for AIDS research, treatment, and prevention programs. Not surprisingly, many of the same politicians who opposed AIDS funding were committed opponents of LGBTQ rights.

No politician in the country better fit that double bill than Jesse Helms, the Republican US senator from North Carolina. In 1987, Helms outrageously called for the quarantining of people with AIDS. That same year, he proposed, and Congress approved, an amendment to an appropriations bill that prohibited the CDC from funding AIDS programs that "promote, encourage or condone homosexual activities." The amendment's passage meant that federal money could not be used for educational HIV-prevention campaigns that honestly and directly addressed the sexuality of gay men. Senator Helms, while defending his proposal, made clear his animus toward LGBTQ people, at one point condemning them by saying, "We have to call a spade a spade and a perverted human being a pervert."[42]

In 1988, Senator Helms succeeded in amending the first comprehensive federal law aimed at AIDS education, prevention, and research in order to prohibit the use of federal money for the provision of "educational, informational or risk-reduction materials or activities [that] promote or encourage, directly or indirectly, homosexual activity." The senator claimed that "there is not one single case of AIDS in this country that cannot be traced in origin to sodomy."[43]

Senator Helms's demonization of queer people, when coupled with his opposition to AIDS research and educational programs aimed at preventing the transmission of HIV among gay men, led AIDS activists to repeatedly denounce him, picket some of his public appearances, and, in 1991, hang a giant condom over his house. (The AIDS activist who organized the condom caper was Peter Staley, the same activist who, two years earlier, had led the occupation of Burroughs Wellcome's headquarters in North Carolina.)[44] Helms's shamefully homophobic positions on AIDS and LGBTQ people also led activists to denounce corporations that gave money to the Republican senator.

In particular, AIDS activists focused their ire on Philip Morris, the country's largest cigarette company, which for years had been one of Helms's leading corporate supporters—not only had the company's political action committee repeatedly donated generously to Helms's reelection campaigns, but the cigarette maker had also agreed to pay $200,000 to build the Jesse Helms Citizenship Center in Monroe, North Carolina. Philip Morris's significant and ongoing financial support for one of the leading homophobic and AIDS-phobic right-wing politicians in the country led ACT UP's Washington, DC, chapter in 1990 to call for a boycott of the company's products. In doing so, the group demanded that the corporation stop giving money to Helms, renounce its past support of the senator, and agree to meet with activists to discuss the steps that the company could take to assist the AIDS and LGBTQ communities.

The boycott called on the public to refrain not only from buying Philip Morris's cigarettes, but also from purchasing the company's Miller Beer products. National LGBTQ organizations, such as the Human Rights Campaign (HRC) and the National Gay and Lesbian Task Force (NGLTF), quickly endorsed the boycott. Six months after it began, the boycott had spread to thirty cities and three hundred bars and restaurants nationwide. In conjunction with the boycott, ACT UP members in several large cities plastered posters in public places of a jowly and foolish-looking Senator Helms, wearing a ten-gallon hat, identifying him as "the real Marlboro Man." Activists received considerable media attention when they dumped Miller Beer into the streets outside gay bars that had stopped selling the brand after also removing Philip Morris cigarettes from their vending machines. By then, there was some evidence that the boycott was having a negative impact on Philip Morris, especially in the distribution of its Miller Beer products, which had been a leading seller in gay bars.[45]

As had happened with the boycott of Coors more than a decade earlier, there were disagreements within LGBTQ communities about the boycott's appropriateness. Boycott opponents pointed out that Philip Morris had donated money to some pro–LGBTQ rights candidates for elected office and had given $500,000 to amfAR. In response, boycott proponents argued that these donations were not enough to counteract the harm to sexual minorities caused by the company's extensive financial support of Helms. As one ACT UP boycott leader put it, Philip Morris's funding decisions evinced a dangerous form of "corporate schizophrenia" analogous to simultaneously donating money to the NAACP and the KKK.[46]

In the fall of 1990, Philip Morris sponsored a multistate tour of an original copy of the Bill of Rights to celebrate the upcoming two hundredth anniversary of that document. The tour sponsorship was a way for the company, which was finding itself constantly fighting efforts by public health officials and activists to institute new anti-smoking regulations, to associate itself with values of constitutionally protected freedoms and rights. As the company saw it, those values supported the right of individuals to choose to smoke cigarettes. For their part, ACT UP activists took advantage of the publicity surrounding the Bill of Rights tour by holding demonstrations at several of the tour stops, including in Baltimore, Burlington (Vermont), and Seattle. Activists at these demonstrations accused Philip Morris of rank hypocrisy: on the one hand, the company claimed to be a strong supporter of the Bill of Rights; on the other hand, the cigarette maker was a leading financial contributor to Helms, an extreme right-wing politician whose policy proposals and public statements repeatedly sought to limit the civil rights and liberties of sexual minorities and of people with AIDS.[47]

Although Philip Morris officials initially refused to meet with boycott organizers, they relented after the boycott picked up steam and as the company continued to be the subject of negative media stories as a result of the AIDS activism. After a series of meetings between company representatives and those of ACT UP and the HRC, a compromise was reached between the two sides. Although the company refused to end its financial support of Senator Helms, it did commit to double its donations to AIDS programs and organizations from $1.3 to $2.6 million over the course of four years. In return, the AIDS activists agreed to end the boycott.[48]

Philip Morris's willingness to substantially increase its AIDS funding following the boycott quickly turned the company into a corporate leader in AIDS donations. As the 1990s progressed, a growing number of large firms followed the cigarette maker's lead (and that of other corporations such as Levi Strauss, which by the end of 1993 had given $5.7 million to AIDS organizations) by donating increasing amounts of money to AIDS programs and groups. Philip Morris in 1992 also became the first tobacco company to advertise in a gay magazine. In addition, representatives of Miller Beer testified before the California legislature that same year, and the Illinois legislature in 1993, in support of the adoption of sexual orientation antidiscrimination laws. As had happened with companies targeted by LGBTQ rights activists in the 1970s, Philip Morris, in a relatively short period of time, changed from undermining LGBTQ equality to taking proactive steps to promote that equality.[49]

AIDS activists also targeted American Airlines following two incidents that took place in 1993. The first episode occurred after some participants in that year's LGBTQ rights march on Washington took an American Airlines flight headed to California with a stop in Texas. The flight attendants quickly became aware that the plane was full of LGBTQ people, some of whom appeared to have AIDS-related symptoms. During the flight's first leg, the attendants asked the pilot to request that the pillows and blankets on board be replaced at the Dallas-Fort Worth airport before the flight continued to California. The pilot then sent a message to the ground crew asking for "a complete change of all pillows [and] blankets due to gay activists on board."[50] An outraged company employee (presumably LGBTQ) leaked the request to the Associated Press, leading newspapers across the country to publish articles about the episode. The incident viscerally illustrated how, more than a decade into the AIDS epidemic, there were still individuals, including employees of some of the nation's largest corporations, who viewed queer people as sources of contagion and danger.

A few months later, Timothy Holless, a frail passenger with AIDS who was attempting to self-administer medication intravenously while on board an American Airlines plane in Chicago waiting to take off, was asked by a member of the flight crew to cover the

Kaposi's sarcoma lesions on his face and stop administering the medicine or leave the aircraft. When Holless refused to do either, the flight crew called the police. Four police officers quickly entered the aircraft and proceeded to forcibly remove Holless, who weighed no more than 120 pounds, from the plane. Another passenger later told reporters that "the cops dragged him off the plane, leaving his cane and glasses. They dragged him face down on his belly. He was screaming 'Chicago police abuse, Chicago police abuse' and screaming in pain."[51]

After these two highly disturbing incidents, LGBTQ rights and AIDS activists vigorously criticized American Airlines for not having policies in place that would have prevented its employees from treating customers in homophobic and AIDS-phobic ways. The activists demanded that the airline take immediate and concrete steps to make sure that episodes like these were not repeated. In doing so, activists took advantage of the extensive and negative publicity in the media that resulted from the incidents. For his part, Holless sued the airline with the assistance of the Lambda Legal Defense and Education Fund.

American Airlines responded to the activism and the lawsuit by taking several steps to address bias against LGBTQ people and individuals with AIDS by its workforce. The company began by having its CEO issue a formal apology to LGBTQ customers and the broader LGBTQ community, which forthrightly acknowledged that the firm's employees had acted inappropriately on both occasions. The company also quickly settled the Holless lawsuit—two days before he died of complications from AIDS—and agreed to revamp its employee training program with guidance from the National Association of People with AIDS and the National Leadership Coalition on AIDS. In addition, the company for the first time offered discounted fares to customers traveling to LGBTQ events such as Gay Games IV and the Stonewall 25 commemoration.[52]

At around this time, American added sexual orientation to its nondiscrimination policy, becoming one of the first major airlines to do so, and encouraged its sexual minority employees to form

GLEAM, a company-wide LGBTQ employee resource group. By the end of the 1990s, the airline had become a strong corporate supporter of LGBTQ equality, as shown by its extensive advertising in gay publications, provision of domestic partnership benefits, donation of large amounts of money to AIDS causes and LGBTQ community groups, and public calls for the adoption of sexual orientation antidiscrimination laws.[53]

The suffering, prejudice, and discrimination unleashed by the AIDS epidemic left affected communities with little choice but to engage in forceful and sometimes disruptive political and social activism, as illustrated by the assertive activism aimed at the pharmaceutical industry, Philip Morris, and American Airlines. For many LGBTQ people, the epidemic, quite simply, made remaining in the closet politically and morally untenable. Indeed, it is fair to say that the AIDS crisis played a crucial role in further awakening queer people politically. As a result of the epidemic, large numbers of gay and bisexual men, among others, found themselves literally fighting for their lives. This stark reality left many LGBTQ people with little choice but to forcefully criticize, cajole, and embarrass government officials and corporate leaders to respond to the health crisis with the seriousness that its mounting death toll demanded. The epidemic, and the problematic ways—ranging from indifference to homophobia—in which many Americans responded to it, encouraged scores of queer people across the country to work collectively through organizing, mobilizing, and protesting in order to fight for their lives and for those of their friends and loved ones. As one historian of the epidemic puts it, "AIDS brought the gay community *as a community* out of the closet."[54]

AIDS activism had many other important social and political consequences, including empowering groups of individuals with other life-threatening conditions to advocate on behalf of more effective medical treatments and more expeditious governmental approval of them. The AIDS epidemic also served as a prelude to and an instigator of the push for greater legal protections for sexual minorities in general and for marriage equality in particular. The epidemic exposed the many hardships suffered by queer people due to their legal status as second-class citizens. The fact that a wide array of entities, from state agencies to private employers to hospitals to insurance companies to places of public accommodation, were not legally obligated to afford rights, benefits, goods, and services to LGBTQ people only served to magnify the torment and suffering faced by sexual minority individuals as they tried, as best they could, to cope with the consequences of a devastating illness that was affecting them in disproportionate numbers. Among other repercussions, the epidemic helped place the lack of legal protections for queer people in general, and marital discrimination and the need for marriage equality in particular, at the top of the LGBTQ movement's priorities.[55]

Another consequence of AIDS activism was that it forced large sectors of corporate America to recognize for the first time that LGBTQ people constituted important and valued segments of their workforces and of the public they served. A handful of corporations responded early to the AIDS epidemic by instituting, largely on their own without outside pressure, sensible and humane workplace policies aimed at protecting employees with AIDS from discrimination while permitting them to work for as long as their health permitted. And when other corporations failed to respond adequately to the AIDS epidemic, AIDS activists, starting in the late 1980s, engaged in generally effective public campaigns to pressure them to do the right thing.

One reason why the first decade of the AIDS epidemic had such profound political and social consequences was that it helped humanize LGBTQ people. It might have been relatively easy, before the advent of HIV, for most Americans, including many corporate executives, who did not know much about sexual minorities to accept without questioning prevailing prejudices about LGBTQ people, their sexuality, and their relationships. One of the most invidious stereotypes about sexual minorities had been that they cared about sex and sexual gratification above all else. Despite the best efforts of some right-wing leaders, such as Senator Helms and Reverend

Falwell, to use the epidemic as an excuse to further demonize the sexuality of queer people, the response to AIDS by the LGBTQ community showed the extent to which sexual minorities were willing to care for, protect, and fight for their loved ones. Ironically, it took the human suffering and devastation wrought by the disease to help prove to those willing to look that the relationships of love and care of LGBTQ people were not different in any fundamental way from the relationships of heterosexuals.

During the first decade of the AIDS epidemic, several large corporations recognized and responded in positive and helpful ways to the human suffering caused by the disease and its impact on the LGBTQ community. A growing number of corporations, around the start of the epidemic's second decade, responded to the continued human suffering caused by AIDS and the lack of legal recognition of same-sex relationships by taking the further (and, for its time, groundbreaking) step of adopting domestic partnership policies. Those policies made available to employees in same-sex relationships the same health insurance and other benefits that employers had for decades offered to their married heterosexual employees as a matter of course.

CHAPTER 4

Corporate Domestic Partnership Benefits in the 1990s

T HE LGBTQ MOVEMENT'S PUSH for domestic partnership benefits (DPBs) started in the same way that the campaign for the enactment of sexual orientation laws had commenced a decade earlier: with the actions of a handful of local governments. LGBTQ activists in the 1980s persuaded some of the liberal municipalities that had adopted ordinances prohibiting sexual orientation discrimination in the 1970s to formally recognize same-sex relationships and to grant gay and lesbian couples some of the benefits that the municipalities made available to married heterosexual couples. As local governments, municipalities did not have the authority to enact measures permitting same-sex couples to marry; but in many states they did have the power to provide their employees in same-sex relationships with benefits not available to them under state law.

In 1985, Berkeley, California, became the first municipality to provide DPBs to its employees, including health insurance—by far the most valuable and important employer-provided benefit—for their unmarried partners. A handful of other local governments, including West Hollywood, California, and Madison, Wisconsin, did the same in the years that followed. Although not all the municipalities that enacted measures initially provided health insurance benefits, they did make other benefits available to their employees in nonmarital intimate relationships (both heterosexual and same sex), including the opportunity to take leaves if their partners or their partners' legal children became sick or died. The ordinances also sometimes permitted all residents, and not just municipal employees, to register their relationships with government clerks and to later dissolve them if necessary; some of these relationship-recognition provisions afforded unmarried couples limited benefits, such as the right to visit partners in city hospitals and jails.[1]

Although LGBTQ rights supporters hailed the new measures, the reality was that the total number of LGBTQ employees who worked for the handful of relatively small municipalities that had adopted the ordinances was not large. (The first big city to provide health insurance to its employees' domestic partners was Seattle in 1990.) There was another, significantly bigger group of LGBTQ employees who had similar needs for domestic partnership benefits: those who worked for America's large corporations.

By the end of the 1980s, only two small companies (the Village Voice and Ben & Jerry's Homemade Ice Cream, which then had only about three hundred employees) offered DPBs. In sharp contrast, dozens of Fortune 500 companies by 2000 offered such benefits (including some of the biggest and most prominent corporations, such as Boeing, Citigroup, and IBM). The adoption of DPBs by a growing number of large firms was one of the LGBTQ movement's most important accomplishments of the 1990s—it resulted in thousands of queer individuals becoming eligible, for the first time, to receive benefits that public- and private-sector employers had long made available to their married heterosexual employees as a matter of course. Employee benefits, in particular health insurance, were (and remain today) crucial components of employee compensation in the United States. In 1989, benefits accounted for nearly 30 percent of the total cost of such compensation.[2] In the absence of DPBs, the domestic partners of LGBTQ employees who did not have access to other forms of subsidized health insurance had to make a difficult choice not faced by spouses of heterosexual married employees: either pay for expensive insurance in the individual insurance market or assume the financial and health risks of not having any health coverage at all.

The adoption of DPBs by a growing number of large corporations not only provided significant financial and health benefits to LGBTQ employees and their same-sex partners; it also had considerable positive political and social consequences for the LGBTQ movement. The implementation of DPBs policies by large corporations constituted the most important form of recognition of LGBTQ relationships and families prior to the recognition by states of same-sex marriages (and roughly equivalent forms of government recognition such as civil unions). The fact that large segments of corporate America, by the end of the 1990s, had embraced the idea that meaningful equality for queer people required some form of recognition of same-sex relationships made it easier for the LGBTQ movement, after the turn of the century, to persuade other segments of society of the legal and moral imperative of marriage equality.

Why Corporate Domestic Partnership Benefits?

In the early 1970s, some pioneering LGBTQ activists filed a handful of lawsuits contending that same-sex couples had a constitutional right to marry.[3] After the courts quickly rejected those claims, it seemed that the marriage equality objective, and the accompanying access to the thousands of rights and benefits that the government provides through the institution of marriage, would be unobtainable for sexual minorities anytime soon. Although marriage seemed out of reach, the LGBTQ movement, as early as the mid-1970s, did have sufficient political strength to persuade a few liberal local governments to add sexual orientation to their antidiscrimination ordinances and, in the 1980s, to convince some of those same municipalities to offer DPBs to their employees. Although DPBs were generally limited to *employer*-provided benefits, and therefore did not come close to matching the society-wide rights and benefits that accompany marriage, the provision of DPBs was nonetheless an important first step toward the formal recognition of same-sex relationships and the making available to sexual minorities at least some of the benefits provided to married heterosexuals.

The success in gaining DPBs from some local governments helped pave the way for private-sector DPBs. Once activists persuaded some municipalities to adopt DPBs, there was reason to believe they could convince at least some large companies to do the same. And when corporate executives raised concerns about the benefits' possible high costs, activists were able to allay those fears by showing that the municipalities that were already providing DPBs to their employees were not incurring significant financial burdens.

By the end of the 1980s, no American company of any significant size had made DPBs available to their employees. But by then, several dozen large corporations had added sexual orientation to their nondiscrimination policies. In adopting such policies, these firms publicly committed themselves to promoting equal opportunities for sexual minorities. The existence of such policies sent an important message to supervisors and coemployees about how the firm expected them to treat LGBTQ employees. And the policies allowed prospective LGBTQ employees to choose companies that had publicly committed themselves not to discriminate against sexual minorities. This was the case even though the antidiscrimination policies almost always applied only to current employees and not to applicants.

However, there were two important limitations to corporate antidiscrimination policies. First, a company's adoption of a nondiscrimination policy, unlike a legislature's enactment of an antidiscrimination law, did not usually grant employees the legal right to sue for a violation of that policy. Second, companies interpreted their nondiscrimination policies to apply to personnel decisions and not to the allocation of employer-provided benefits. This meant that when a company adopted a nondiscrimination policy, it agreed in principle that a refusal to retain or promote employees on the basis of sexual orientation constituted impermissible discrimination. But it did not mean that the company acknowledged that its failure to provide benefits to its LGBTQ employees' same-sex partners and nonbiological or nonadopted children, benefits it made available to the opposite-sex spouses and legal dependents of its heterosexual employees, also constituted wrongful discrimination.

The limits of corporate antidiscrimination policies were reflected in a lawsuit filed by a lesbian woman by the name of Sandra Rovira against AT&T in 1990. Rovira shared a home with her partner, Marjorie Forlini, for twelve years. Forlini worked for the telephone company for eight years before she died of cancer in 1988. During most of the time the lesbian couple lived together, they jointly raised two children that Rovira had from a prior opposite-sex marriage. After Forlini died, AT&T denied Rovira and the two children financial death benefits, including a full year's salary, that it made available to the spouses and legal dependents of its deceased employees.

The company took the position that Rovira was not entitled to the benefits because she had not been Forlini's legal spouse. A company spokesperson explained, "We recognize that this is someone who is hurting, but this was not a legally protected marriage." The spokesperson added, "If we have a benefit for spouses and you don't have a spouse, that doesn't mean we've discriminated on the basis of marital status. If you're single, you're not being discriminated against, you just don't have anybody who's eligible for that benefit." It is clear from this reasoning that the company believed Forlini, for all intents and purposes, was a *single person* at the time she died even though (1) she had been in a committed relationship for twelve years and (2) the law denied her the opportunity to marry the person of her choice. Furthermore, despite the fact that Forlini had helped raise the children in her home for more than a decade, AT&T denied them the death benefits because Forlini had not been their biological or adoptive parent.[4]

Forlini and the children, with the assistance of the Lambda Legal Defense and Education Fund, sued the phone company in federal court, contending, among other things, that denying the financial benefits constituted sexual orientation discrimination in violation of AT&T's nondiscrimination policy. But the company argued successfully in court that the policy did not confer enforceable contractual rights on either their employees or on "third parties" such as Rovira and her children. To support its claim, the company pointed to a disclaimer in its employment manual, which contained the antidiscrimination policy, that it was "not a contract of employment but a set of guidelines for the implementation of personnel policies. It should not be interpreted to create any expressed [*sic*] or implied contractual rights between AT&T and any employee." The company also successfully argued in court that its nondiscrimination policy was limited to personnel decisions (such as firing or promoting employees) and had no application to employment benefits.[5]

The legal defeat in *Rovira v. AT&T* showed LGBTQ activists that a company's mere adoption of a sexual orientation nondiscrimination policy guaranteed sexual minorities neither equal opportunities in the workplace nor equal access to employer-provided benefits. It also demonstrated to activists that it was essential to push for DPBs as a distinct issue when demanding that companies treat their LGBTQ employees fairly and equally. In the years to come, LGBTQ activists repeatedly sought to persuade corporate leaders that unequal access to employee benefits was in fact *a form of discrimination* against their LGBTQ employees.

The AIDS epidemic also highlighted the urgent nature of DPBs issues for the LGBTQ rights movement. The epidemic laid bare the almost complete lack of legal protections and benefits afforded by both the public and the private sectors to sexual minorities and HIV-positive individuals. Many government agencies, private employers, insurance companies, hospitals, landlords, and others responded to the epidemic with irrational fear of and prejudice toward those who were infected (or suspected of being so). Scores of HIV-positive individuals lost their jobs because of discrimination or because they were simply too ill to work. And the loss of jobs usually meant the loss of health insurance.

For LGBTQ employees who had HIV-positive partners and who were able to keep their jobs, the absence of DPBs meant that they could not add their partners to their employer-provided insurance, or take time off to care for their partners if they became sick, or even take bereavement leaves if their partners died. As sociologist Nicole Raeburn notes, AIDS "added tragic salience to the issue of equitable benefits. Without bereavement leave, for example, many gay men who had just lost their partners to the disease were forced to stay at work and 'grieve in the bathroom.'"[6] By the time a significant number of large corporations finally began offering DPBs, hundreds of thousands of Americans had died of AIDS. To be specific, by the end of 2000, 774,467 persons in the United States had been reported with AIDS, of whom 448,060 had died.[7]

The adoption of DPBs by large corporations constituted the most important formal recognition of same-sex relationships and families in American society through the 1990s. When a company offered DPBs, it sent a clear message that the firm took issues of LGBTQ equality seriously. At the same time, the adoption of corporate DPBs had crucial practical consequences: for at least some queer people and their loved ones, having access to DPBs represented the difference between having access to health care or not, being able to care for a sick partner or not, and in the case of a loved one's death, being able to take time off from work to grieve and to make funeral arrangements or not. Of course, even in the absence of AIDS, corporate DPBs would have been important to LGBTQ people. What the health epidemic did was to make the need for the benefits even starker and more pressing.

Another reason why the LGBTQ movement in the 1990s prioritized DPBs was a strategic one: outside of a few liberal municipalities and a handful of progressive states, it was difficult for sexual minorities to persuade elected officials to pay attention to their issues. In contrast, LGBTQ activists could attain significant gains in the corporate sphere by persuading a relatively small number of board members and executives at any given company that the adoption of DPBs was both the right thing to do and in their companies' best interests. As an organizing manual published by the National Gay and Lesbian Task Force explained,

> in many regards, the workplace is the leading edge of change for the GLBT community. Company CEOs and executives can often wield even more power than state and local officials in creating significant changes that affect their employees' lives.

They can enact new policies with the approval of a few board members rather than thousands or even millions of voters. Moreover, the policies they create have a profound influence on us, since we spend a large part of our lives at work. Through the enactment of DP benefits, employers send the message that all employees, including GLBT workers, are valued and accepted as equal, which paves the way for more employees to come out of the closet and fully contribute to their work and their community. DP benefits are not the final step in the GLBT quest for equality, but they are integral to its achievement.[8]

LGBTQ activists during the 1990s repeatedly made the case that DPBs promoted values of equality and fairness while allowing companies to hire and retain the most qualified employees. The latter argument was consistent with promoting the bottom-line interests of corporations: the ability to attract and retain the most qualified employees helped companies compete and maximize profits.

Arguments based on egalitarian values tied in nicely with the growing embrace by many large American corporations of equality principles, as seen, for example, in the corporate defense of affirmative action programs, in the face of conservative critiques in the 1980s and 1990s.[9] While many conservatives claimed that affirmative action programs promoted "special rights" for minorities and discriminated against whites, the corporate defense of affirmative action showed that large American companies were committed to a strong rhetoric of equal opportunity and, in at least some instances, to relatively robust policies aimed at attaining it. As sociologist Raeburn explains in writing about this period, "Whereas in the political arena the cause of diversity is subject to attack, in the corporate world it is more likely to be celebrated."[10]

It also bears noting that even when the LGBTQ rights movement made gains in the public sphere, those victories were subject to significant conservative backlash, as manifested, for example, in ballot measures and lawsuits aimed at reversing those gains. In fact, the movement had been coping with political backlash ever since the mid-1970s when LGBTQ rights opponents, in places like Dade County, Florida, and Eugene, Washington, ran ugly campaigns hoping to persuade voters to overturn ordinances prohibiting discrimination on the basis of sexual orientation. Some opponents went so far as to outrageously claim that LGBTQ activists were pushing for antidiscrimination laws to make it easier for gay men to "recruit" boys in order to sexually molest them. LGBTQ rights opponents in 1992 pushed to persuade voters in Colorado and Oregon—unsuccessfully in the latter, but successfully in the former—to amend their state constitutions to prohibit the government from legally protecting sexual minorities from discrimination.[11]

The conservative backlash was not limited to the enactment of antidiscrimination laws. There was also considerable political backlash against the decision by some municipalities to recognize same-sex relationships through domestic partnership ordinances. Conservative activists in San Francisco in 1989 and in Austin, Texas, in 1994 persuaded voters to overturn domestic partnership ordinances. (A second referendum in each city eventually reinstated the benefits.) Conservative groups also recruited taxpayers in several jurisdictions to sue their local governments, claiming that the localities lacked authority under state law to enact domestic partnership ordinances. Although such lawsuits failed in Colorado, Georgia, and Illinois, they succeeded in Massachusetts, Minnesota, and Virginia.[12]

The 1990s also saw intense conservative backlash against the idea that the government should recognize same-sex relationships as marital. After the Hawai'i Supreme Court in 1993 questioned the constitutionality of the state's same-sex marriage ban, Congress enacted the Defense of Marriage Act (DOMA), prohibiting the federal government from recognizing (then nonexisting) marriages by same-sex couples. Around the same time, voters in more than twenty states approved ballot referenda making it clear that a legal marriage could only exist between one man and one woman.

In contrast to the backlash to LGBTQ rights gains in the public sphere, conservatives paid relatively little attention to the issue of corporate DPBs. As an ideological matter, conservatives were generally less troubled when private entities, including for-profit corporations, voluntarily chose to provide protections and benefits to sexual minorities than when taxpayer-funded government entities did the same.[13] And, as a practical matter, there was little that conservative activists could do, short of organizing successful boycotts, to force corporate executives to reverse LGBTQ-friendly policies.

The Southern Baptist Convention (SBC) in 1996 voted to censure the Walt Disney Company for extending DPBs to its LGBTQ employees. (The SBC also criticized the company for allowing LGBTQ groups to organize an annual "gay day," attended by thousands of LGBTQ people, at its recreation parks in Florida and California.) The following year, the SBC tried to ratchet up the pressure on Disney by calling for a boycott of its theme parks, stores, movies, books, and television shows. But neither the censure nor the boycott had any significant impact on the large entertainment corporation or its policies. As Disney explained, its adoption of DPBs did nothing more than bring "health benefits in line with [its] corporate policy against discrimination." The company added that while it regretted "that people are offended by a decision to provide health care to our employees," it had no intention of changing its "new health program." Although the boycott remained in place for years, it did not affect the policies of either Disney or any of the dozens of other large companies that eventually adopted DPBs.[14]

A similar public pressure campaign organized by conservative activists failed to influence Apple, another early corporate adopter of DPBs. At around the time the technology company began offering DPBs in 1993, it agreed to build an $80 million, seven-hundred-employee facility in Williamson County, Texas, a suburban area near Austin. But after the elected members of the county commission learned of Apple's new benefits, a majority of them criticized the company for "encouraging homosexuality." As one commissioner put it, "I personally don't approve of health benefits policies which encourage same-sex marriages." Another commissioner claimed, rather preposterously, that Texas's sodomy law prevented the company from offering DPBs to LGBTQ employees. Members of the public who opposed the Apple plant attended commission hearings wearing tags pinned to their shirts that read, "Just Say, No! An Apple today will take family values away."[15]

The commission voted to deny Apple the almost $1 million in tax abatements that it had previously approved as a means to persuade the company to build the facility in the county. In doing so, the Texas county became the first public entity that sought to penalize a private company for adopting a pro-LGBTQ rights policy. Apple responded by informing county officials, in no uncertain terms, that its DPBs policy was nonnegotiable and that the company would build its facility, and create hundreds of jobs, elsewhere rather than rescind its new DPBs. The commission reversed itself less than a week later by approving the tax incentives once again, albeit while also passing a resolution denouncing the company for its gay-friendly policy.[16]

In short, there were several reasons why corporate DPBs became a priority for the LGBTQ rights movement during the 1990s, including the fact that the full protection afforded by marriage equality seemed unlikely to be achieved anytime soon, the limitations that inhered in the mere adoption by companies of sexual orientation antidiscrimination policies, the onset of the AIDS epidemic, and the relative insulation of corporate DPBs policies from effective conservative backlash.

Lotus Goes First

The Lotus Development Corporation, a software company based in Cambridge, Massachusetts, became a leading technology company in the 1980s after developing a popular spreadsheet program that operated on IBM computers. The company, which had about three thousand employees in the early 1990s, prided itself in its progressive values. It refused, for example, to sell its products in South Africa during that country's apartheid regime and it helped finance *Eyes on the Prize*, a popular PBS documentary on the civil rights movement. The company also prided itself in hiring and promoting employees of all racial, cultural, and other backgrounds. In fact, the company had included sexual orientation in its nondiscrimination policy from the moment of its founding in 1981.

Nonetheless, during the first decade of its existence, Lotus, like almost all companies in the United States at the time, did not offer DPBs to its employees. In practical terms, this meant that the firm, despite its professed egalitarian values, was compensating sexual minority employees less than married heterosexual employees for the same amount of work. Three lesbian employees in 1989 formed the Lotus Extended Benefits Group with the objective of persuading the company to adopt DPBs. For the three women, their internal lobbying for DPBs was an extension of their activism on behalf of the LGBTQ community outside the workplace. As one of them later told the *New York Times* about the push to get Lotus to offer DPBs: "I know it sounds funny in the corporate context, but this is grassroots organizing."[17]

After researching the issue, the three employees submitted a proposal to company executives for extending benefits to unmarried employees with domestic partners. The proposal reasoned that the issue of DPBs was one of simple fairness: since benefits constituted as much as a third of an employee's total compensation, the company was denying sexual minority employees with partners the same level of compensation it provided to its married heterosexual employees. As a result, this was a straightforward fairness issue of "equal pay for equal work." If Lotus was truly committed to the values of equal opportunity and diversity in the workplace, then making DPBs available to its employees was a necessity. In addition, the proposal emphasized that offering DPBs would help the company recruit and retain the most qualified employees, regardless of their sexual orientation or marital status.[18]

The company's principal concern in response was the potential cost of the proposed benefits. Health-care costs were increasing dramatically across the country, and Lotus executives initially worried that providing DPBs would impose a significant financial burden on the firm. But when company executives, with the assistance of the Lotus Extended Benefits Group, looked into what other entities that offered DPBs—at the time, mostly municipalities—were paying in additional health-care expenses, they quickly determined that the costs would likely be reasonable and manageable. Indeed, there was no evidence that health benefits for domestic partners were costing employers any more than health benefits for spouses.

One reason that DPBs were not unduly expensive was that relatively few employees had been signing up for them. Studies in the 1990s found that between approximately 1 and 3 percent of employees enrolled in DPBs programs.[19] There were several reasons for the relatively low rates of participation. First, some life partners of LGBTQ employees already had access to health insurance through their own employers. Second, many LGBTQ employees reasonably feared that they would put their jobs at risk if they came out at work. There was no guarantee, after all, that supervisors and fellow employees, even in progressive companies that had adopted DPBs, would react positively to having open LGBTQ people in their workplaces. In the absence of legal protections against discrimination, many LGBTQ employees, even in organizations that offered DPBs, remained in the closet. Finally, enrolling in a DPBs program came with significant negative tax consequences for employees (more on that point follows).

On the issue of adding to corporate costs, some conservative opponents of DPBs raised the specter of HIV to contend that employers that offered the benefits, along with their outside insurers, would soon be overwhelmed with catastrophic AIDS-related claims. However, growing empirical evidence from existing DPBs programs demonstrated that such fears were unfounded. This was not surprising given that AIDS-related medical expenses were almost always lower, for example, than medical costs associated with maternity care and giving birth in a hospital, as well as with the long-term treatment of coronary disease and cancer. It revealed much about the prejudice of those who opposed DPBs based on purported AIDS-related medical costs that they never suggested that employer-provided health insurance policies cease paying for medical services associated with giving birth or having heart disease or cancer due to their costs. The reliance on the supposedly high HIV-related expenses to justify the denial of DPBs to same-sex couples—many of whom were lesbians, who as a group had a relatively low AIDS incidence rate—was a clear case of invidious prejudice against sexual minorities masquerading as financial prudency.

Pushed on by the three lesbian employees, Lotus in 1991 agreed to offer DPBs to its LGBTQ workers, making it the first publicly traded company in the United States to do so. Lotus's announcement of its new policy received an immense amount of national attention. The lesbian employees who pushed for the benefits appeared on several television network news shows. The story was also covered by national and international newspapers, as well as corporate and human resources publications. That a large company was willing, in the name of fairness and equality, to provide benefits to the domestic partners of its LGBTQ employees was big news. As a *Wall Street Journal* commentator noted almost twenty-five years later, the fact that a company like Lotus was willing to take "a stance in support of LGBTQ advocacy [in 1991] was as notable as when a company opposes it today."[20]

It is important to note that the DPBs program proposed by the three lesbian employees at Lotus was not limited to same-sex couples; instead, the proposal, if adopted, would have permitted employees to extend benefits to any "significant person" in their lives. This would have benefited not only those in same-sex relationships, but also cohabiting heterosexual employees, as well as employees who shared a home and had a close and ongoing nonintimate relationship with another person who was not a spouse. However, the company viewed the question of whether to offer DPBs as a fairness issue that affected LGBTQ individuals in distinct ways. Lotus executives reasoned that their heterosexual employees with unmarried partners could render themselves eligible for the benefits in question by marrying. In contrast, LGBTQ employees lacked the legal ability to marry the person of their choice. As the company's vice president for human resources told the press, Lotus was providing same-sex couples with "a parallel process to getting married." The company did not believe it needed to create such a process for heterosexual employees who chose not to marry their opposite-sex partners.[21]

Most large corporations that, in the years to come, followed Lotus's lead in adopting DPBs also limited participation to employees in same-sex relationships. This was in contrast to early municipal (Berkeley and West Hollywood, for example) and private sector (the Village Voice and Ben & Jerry's Homemade Ice Cream, for example) adopters of DPBs—those employers had generally made the benefits available to all unmarried employees regardless of their sexual orientation.

Bell Atlantic in 1996 denied DPBs to a heterosexual male employee who lived with his female partner. The employee sued the phone company in federal court alleging a violation of Title VII's prohibition against sex discrimination. The plaintiff argued that if he were a female employee with a female domestic partner, the two would have been eligible to receive the health, dental, vision, bereavement, life insurance, and adoption reimbursement benefits the company made available to LGBTQ employees and their domestic partners. Therefore, the only reason the company denied him the benefits, the plaintiff claimed, was because he was a man. A similar argument had recently been accepted by the Hawai'i Supreme Court in questioning the constitutionality of same-sex marriage bans; that court took the position that when the state, for example, allows a man to marry a woman but not another man, it classifies individuals on the basis of gender. But the federal court in the Bell Atlantic case rejected the sex discrimination claim—it reasoned that the plaintiff was, in fact, not similarly situated to a female employee with a female domestic partner because he was legally able to marry his partner. The court concluded that since the plaintiff was able to gain the employment benefits in question by marrying his female partner, he was not in the same position as lesbian employees who were legally barred from marrying their domestic partners. As a result, the court held that the employer had not discriminated on the basis of gender.[22]

It bears noting that Lotus's DPBs policy, like those of the vast majority of employers that offered the benefits in the years to come, required more of same-sex couples than of married heterosexual ones. To qualify for benefits, married heterosexuals did not have to live with their spouses, comingle their finances, or even, in most instances, provide a copy of their marriage licenses. In contrast, to qualify for DPBs, Lotus employees had to sign affidavits asserting that they were in exclusive and permanent relationships with their partners and that they shared a home and finances. The reason why most DPBs policies required more of potential beneficiaries than employers required of married heterosexual employees before dispensing the benefits in question was because of a concern that employees might try to add roommates or friends as domestic partner beneficiaries. However, there was no factual support for the proposition that those signing up for DPBs were more likely than married couples to commit fraud to gain employee benefits. As the NGLTF put it in 1999, "To date, there have been no reports of fraud involving DP registration."[23]

Another aspect of DPBs made them less attractive than the benefits employers provided to married heterosexual employees. The Internal Revenue Service determined in 1990 that employees had to pay income taxes on the value of the DPBs. In contrast, heterosexual employees who added their spouses to their employer-provided health insurance did not have to pay income taxes on the value of that insurance. The IRS's determination led LGBTQ employee groups, when lobbying employers to adopt DPBs, to request that the companies make their sexual minority employees whole by providing them with additional income to cover the higher taxes paid by LGBTQ people. The groups argued that this was the only way to assure parity between LGBTQ employees with same-sex partners and married heterosexual employees. Although some companies agreed to do so, most employers in the 1990s, including Lotus, refused. The negative tax consequences that came with taking advantage of DPBs was significant enough that it led some LGBTQ employees, including one of Lotus's lesbian workers who pushed for the benefits, to decide not to enroll in the program.[24]

Despite the limitations of DPBs, practically no other forms of recognition of same-sex relationships and families were available at the time in the United States. Only a handful of liberal municipalities scattered across the country allowed same-sex couples to register their relationships with their local governments, and doing so provided them with a very limited menu of rights, such as the ability to visit partners in city hospitals and jails. There had also been a handful of courts that recognized the ability of LGBTQ individuals, in particular circumstances, to be named legal guardians of their incapacitated partners or to take over the leases of rent-regulated apartments after the deaths of their same-sex partners.[25] Although those judicial victories were important because they made some legal protections available to same-sex couples, they required LGBTQ petitioners, in many instances, to engage in protracted and expensive lawsuits with the objective of persuading courts that their relationships and families were functionally equivalent to the types of heterosexual relationships and families that were automatically recognized and protected by law. In contrast, it was possible for LGBTQ employees to sign up for DPBs relatively quickly and easily.

Although Lotus received mostly positive responses from customers, competitors, and employees after it began offering DPBs, not everyone associated with the company was pleased with the new policy. One customer angrily informed the firm that he would suggest to clients that they not invest in a company that "hires queers." In addition, some of the corporation's straight employees worried that, as a Lotus product developer told the *Wall Street Journal*, "unless the world follows Lotus, it will almost certainly, over time, make Lotus increasingly gay."[26]

It turned out that most big companies *did* eventually follow Lotus down the DPBs road. Indeed, what seemed like revolutionary corporate policy in the early 1990s became mainstream corporate fare in the 2000s. But that outcome would first require additional pioneering companies to take the path-breaking step of offering DPBs to their employees. During the 1990s, one crucial difference between corporations that decided to offer the new benefits and those that did not was that the former almost invariably had active LGBTQ employee groups. It is clear that in the absence of internal grassroots activism by these LGBTQ organizations, not as many corporations would have adopted DPBs as early as they did.

LGBTQ Corporate Employee Groups

In the 1970s, employees at some corporations started organizing groups formed around shared racial, ethnic, gender, and sexual orientation identities. One pioneering organization of this kind was the Black Caucus created in 1972 at Xerox Corporation. The caucus was formed by African American employees who wanted to promote the interests and prospects of the small number of black employees in what was then an almost entirely white company.

The first LGBTQ employee group was formed at Hewlett Packard in 1978. A handful of other LGBTQ employee organizations were founded inside other companies in the 1980s, most of them in the technology sector, including at Apple, AT&T, and the Digital Equipment Corporation. In reporting on the challenges, including overt discrimination, faced by many LGBTQ employees in the private sector, a 1991 article in *Fortune* began by noting that "homosexuality, once a career-destroying secret, is coming out of the closet in corporate America. Anxious and alienated, but unwilling to remain so, gay men and lesbians are rapidly forming employee groups."[27]

By the end of the 1990s, LGBTQ employees at more than eighty large companies had created such groups. In addition, LGBTQ employee groups from different companies in the late 1990s began organizing annual conferences called Out and Equal, which brought together corporate executives, LGBTQ rights advocates, and others to discuss how best to promote LGBTQ equality in America's corporate workplaces. The conferences eventually became large affairs, cosponsored by many large companies and attended by thousands of individuals.[28]

Those who founded early LGBTQ employee groups did not generally think of them as advocacy organizations intended to pressure their respective corporations to adopt LGBTQ-friendly policies. Instead, the founders initially thought of the organizations mostly as vehicles for creating supportive work environments, advancing the careers of sexual minorities, and providing opportunities for socializing. But it did not take long for many of the groups to take on advocacy roles within corporations, particularly regarding the issue of DPBs.

In the two years following Lotus's adoption of DPBs, ten other Fortune 1000 companies did the same. (Levi-Strauss was the first Fortune 500 company to offer DPBs, making them available to its twenty-three-thousand employees in 1992.) According to sociologist Nicole Raeburn, all ten of those corporations "changed their policies in response to pressure from gay employee networks." An additional eighty-three Fortune 1000 companies had adopted DPBs by the end of the 1990s; over two-thirds of them "faced pressure from mobilized groups of gay and lesbian employees."[29]

The crucial involvement by LGBTQ employee groups with the issue of corporate DPBs is another example of how queer activism at the end of the twentieth century was not aimed solely at reforming government policy. Instead, as had happened in preceding decades, and would continue to occur in subsequent years, LGBTQ activism in the 1990s included an important private sphere component. As Raeburn points out, the work of the LGBTQ employee groups served "as powerful reminders that the state is not the only contested terrain." Instead, "these 'institutional activists' demonstrate that committed individuals 'do' politics not simply on the streets or in voting booths but also in the cubicles, offices, and boardrooms of companies across the country."[30]

At first, LGBTQ employee activists pushing for DPBs emphasized issues of fairness and equal opportunity. But activists soon began supplementing those arguments with more bottom-line ones that underscored the importance of increasing employee productivity, enhancing recruitment, and expanding markets. All these bottom-line arguments were linked to the challenges and opportunities that corporations faced in competing in an increasingly egalitarian era, one in which a growing number of employees and customers expected companies to promote equal opportunities in their workplaces. As a 1995 report accompanying a survey conducted by the NGTLF on the degree of "gay-friendliness" inside America's leading companies stated, there was no more important indicator of a company's willingness to "offer a conducive environment for gay employees generally" than its willingness to adopt DPBs. Similarly, adopting DPBs was one of the most effective ways for corporations to signal to LGBTQ consumers that the firms welcomed their business. Indeed, by the 1990s, the growing visibility of LGBTQ communities was making clear to many corporations, especially those whose goods or services were bought by the general public, that sexual minorities constituted an important segment of their consumer base.[31]

It is important to note that LGBTQ employee groups, like other identity-based employee organizations, did not function in adversarial ways rendering them analogous to unions. The groups, for example, did not threaten job actions or stoppages unless their companies adopted specific policies. Instead, the organizations sought policy changes in informal and nonconfrontational ways largely outside public view. As one study of LGBTQ employee groups puts it, their members "wear dual hats as organizational members *and* activists [and, as a result,] often behave as 'tempered radicals' by using their knowledge of the firm and relationships with coworkers to advocate for their interests, but without strongly violating the norms and rules of the organization."[32]

LGBTQ employee groups during the 1990s engaged in DPBs activism by, for example, organizing informational sessions with company executives, encouraging human resources personnel to reach out to companies that had already adopted DPBs to learn from their experiences, and gathering data—oftentimes provided by LGBTQ rights groups like the National Center for Lesbian Rights, the NGLTF, and the Human Rights Campaign—to address company concerns about costs in general and the expense of AIDS health insurance claims in particular.

The informal, but effective, ways in which LGBTQ employee groups worked to advance LGBTQ equality during the 1990s can be gleaned from a study of the work and tactics of such groups in the Minneapolis area. At one large company, described as one of the oldest in the Twin Cities (the study did not use actual company names), two employees (a gay man and a lesbian woman) started an LGBTQ employee group in 1993. The company agreed to name the woman as the group's contact person in an email to its ten thousand employees. The group's first official act was to make a formal request of the company for DPBs. The senior vice president for human resources responded with a curt letter explaining that the company had no interest in providing such benefits. After receiving the letter, the lesbian employee asked for a lunch meeting with the vice president and he agreed. At that lunch, the employee explained in personal and human terms the need that she and her partner had for DPBs. The vice president left the lunch persuaded, and soon convinced the company's chief executive officer of the need to offer DPBs to the firm's LGBTQ employees. The two of them then held several meetings with other high executives and members of the board of directors at which they presented compelling arguments in favor of the benefits. After several months of internal deliberations, the company began offering the benefits.[33]

Following a similar pattern, the LGBTQ group at an industrial company headquartered in Minneapolis issued invitations to company executives to attend informational sessions sponsored by the group. Executives at first refused, but the vice president for human resources later accepted an invitation to attend a talk, sponsored by the employee group, given by Karen Thompson. In 1983, Sharon Kowalski, Thompson's lesbian partner of four years, was left paralyzed and cognitively impaired by a terrible car accident. Kowalski's parents, who did not learn of the women's intimate relationship until after the accident, prohibited Thompson from visiting her partner or taking her out of the nursing home in which they had placed their daughter. This led to an eight-year legal and emotional battle between Thompson and Kowalski's parents, an ordeal that ended only after a Minnesota appellate court ordered that Thompson be named as her partner's legal guardian.[34]

The executive vice president who attended Thompson's talk later recounted that it constituted a breakthrough moment for her as she tried to imagine what it would be like to take care of her husband, should he become seriously ill or injured, without any legal rights. The executive eventually persuaded the company's chief executive officer of the need to adopt a DPBs program. She also created a working group of human resources representatives from other large companies in the Twin Cities whose mission became to quietly promote inclusive policies, such as DPBs, within corporations in the area.[35]

These types of internal efforts spearheaded by LGBTQ employee groups went a long way in humanizing issues related to equal opportunities and benefits for sexual minorities inside large corporations. The internal lobbying did not center on abstract claims to equality rights on behalf of "outsiders"; instead, the lobbying implicated corporate policies that affected the lives, relationships, and children of members of "corporate families." By the 1990s, many board members and executives at large American companies were cognizant of the importance of fairness, diversity, and equal opportunity in the workplace. What LGBTQ employee groups accomplished, through their informal and behind-the-scenes efforts, was to persuade a growing number of those same board members and executives that their companies' commitment to fairness, diversity, and equal opportunity was crucially incomplete if it did not account for the lives, relationships, and children of the firms' lesbian, gay, and bisexual employees.

In short, internal advocacy on behalf of DPBs by LGBTQ employee groups led to countless meetings and conversations within corporate walls about whether there were, in fact, any meaningful differences between the committed relationships and families of the firms' LGBTQ employees and those of their heterosexual employees. As had happened early on during the AIDS epidemic with issues related to the presence of HIV-positive employees in corporate workplaces, top executives at some of the large companies that first adopted DPBs became convinced that providing such benefits to their LGBTQ employees was the right thing to do. And, as had happened with AIDS, large numbers of big businesses, in a matter of only a few years, followed the lead of a few pioneering companies. While in the early 1990s, a corporation's adoption of DPBs seemed like a socially radical step, those same benefits became mainstream corporate fare relatively quickly.

The Cutting Edge Becomes Mainstream

Although sexual minority employees in a growing number of large companies succeeded in forming LGBTQ employee groups, a considerable number of big businesses still did not have such groups. By the turn of the century, however, the activism of LGBTQ employee groups was no longer as much of a catalyst behind the corporate adoption of DPBs policies. This was because, by then, many executives at companies that lacked LGBTQ employee groups had come to see the adoption of DPBs not as a niche concern important only to LGBTQ activists, but as (1) a question of basic fairness and equal treatment and (2) a necessary means to attract and retain qualified employees and loyal customers. In this changing normative and marketplace environment, the existence of an active LGBTQ employee group was no longer essential to persuade companies to adopt DPBs. As one study of DPBs puts it, "The diffusion of domestic partner benefits fits the pattern of a practice that spread initially among a small group of likely targets of activism but that eventually spread to the mainstream."[36]

The fact that some of the biggest and most prominent companies in several important economic sectors took the lead in adopting DPBs encouraged other companies to follow suit. As Raeburn notes, "In highly competitive environments and in industries in which career tracks entail movement from one firm to another, once an industry leader grants DPBs, many others follow suit in order to compete for the best talent in the field."[37] The intrinsically competitive nature of the corporate marketplace, in turn, helped explain why it was more likely that corporations would adopt DPBs than governmental or educational entities. As an NGLTF report explained,

> It is no surprise that there are more companies which offer DP benefits than municipalities or universities. Corporate change is a quick process relatively speaking. Within each industry, companies are competing for customers' dollars and market share. Moreover, companies compete for talented employees and strive to keep the employees they have happy. Within this climate, strategic trends beneficial to a company's productivity and bottom line catch on quickly. As one company enacts a DP policy which attracts employees and improves efficiency, other companies within the industry are likely to do the same.[38]

National LGBTQ rights groups like the NGLTF were effective in helping keep the pressure on corporations regarding equal benefits. In 1999, the NGLTF's Policy Institute published a 140-page document titled *Domestic Partnership Organizing Manual for Employee Benefits*. In the manual's introduction, the institute's director, Urvashi Vaid, noted that a recent survey had found "that one in ten employers offered domestic partnership benefits. This manual is designed to persuade the other 90%." The manual advised employees interested in lobbying internally for DPBs how to (1) reach out to employee organizations and human resources personnel at companies in the same industry or region that had already adopted DPBs, (2) develop specific DPBs policy proposals and implementing mechanisms, and (3) determine which company executives were best situated to help make DPBs a reality. The manual also included sample DPBs policies and proposals, lists of employers that had adopted DPBs categorized by sectors and industries, and contact information for groups across the country involved in the issue.[39]

The Human Rights Campaign, another leading national LGBTQ organization, formed a workplace project called HRCWorkNet that served as a source of information for both employers and employees on laws and policies involving sexual orientation and gender identity in the workplace, including those related to DPBs. HRC in 2002 issued the *Corporate Equality Index* (published annually to this day), which rated large companies on a scale of zero to one hundred using several factors, including whether they had a nondiscrimination policy that covered sexual orientation and gender identity, offered DPBs, incorporated sexual orientation and gender identity issues in diversity training, and engaged in respectful advertising to LGBTQ communities or donated money to LGBTQ or AIDS organizations. At a press conference announcing the *Index*'s publication and highlighting how far many companies had come on LGBTQ issues in a relatively short period of time, Elizabeth Birch, HRC's executive director and Apple's former general counsel, stated that "the truth is, it's corporate America that has been the unlikely hero in the movement for equality for gay and lesbian Americans."[40]

Media outlets reported extensively on the *Index*'s publication, a fact that helped put pressure on companies that ranked low in the *Index*. For example, after newspapers identified Lockheed Martin—a large manufacturer of airplanes and military equipment that earned hundreds of millions of dollars from contracts with the US military—as one of only three companies that received a zero rating in the 2002 *Corporate Equality Index*, the firm announced that it was amending its nondiscrimination policy to include sexual orientation and would soon begin offering DPBs.[41]

Within a week of the publication of the first *Index*, more than thirty corporations contacted HRC inquiring how to obtain a rating or improve the one they had received. And companies with high *Index* ratings began citing that fact in advertisements and public forums, while LGBTQ employee groups relied on the *Index* to push for changes in company policies in ways that would improve their employers' rankings. The number of companies that received a one-hundred rating jumped from seven in 2002 to twenty-one in 2003, while the number that received a zero dropped from three to none. By the end of the decade, 260 companies achieved the top *Index* rating of 100; collectively, those businesses employed more than nine million individuals in the United States. Also by the end of the decade, more than half of the Fortune 500 companies were offering DPBs to their employees.[42]

The embrace by large corporations of DPBs may seem anomalous given that the benefits implicated a highly contested issue of social policy: whether and how to recognize same-sex relationships and families headed by LGBTQ individuals. As a general matter, corporations avoid taking sides on divisive social policy issues for several reasons, including a sense that those issues do not implicate corporate concerns and not wanting to offend one side or the other on highly charged "culture wars" disputes.

For corporate leaders, the embrace of LGBTQ rights in general and DPBs in particular did risk alienating social and religious conservatives. But that was a risk a growing number of corporate leaders were willing to take because DPBs implicated firms in their roles as employers. Questions surrounding DPBs did not raise abstract questions of equality and justice; instead, they raised questions about how a particular firm should allocate its resources in ways that were fair to employees and promoted the long-term interests of the corporation. As business professor Timothy Werner notes, disputes over employer-provided benefits "require firms to adjudicate a moral issue while engaging in a decision more akin to redistributive policymaking, as they seek to balance the demands of a portion of their employees and potential impacts on other stakeholders, especially their shareholders and customers."[43]

Furthermore, given the issues at stake, it was impossible for corporations to remain neutral on the question of LGBTQ relationship recognition in the same way, for example, that they could remain neutral on other controversial social issues such as abortion, gun control, and school prayer. This was because, once the claim to equal treatment was made by LGBTQ activists, *the continued failure to recognize* the same-sex relationships of their employees was reasonably perceived by many as taking sides with LGBTQ equality opponents. Indeed, after LGBTQ activists began to repeatedly demand DPBs, a particular company's refusal to provide them was, at a minimum, an implicit statement that the firm did not consider the same-sex relationships and families of its LGBTQ employees to be as valuable and worthy of recognition as those of its heterosexual employees. At the same time, when a corporation extended benefits to its employees in same-sex relationships, the firm, at the very least, sent an implicit message that it saw no important differences between those relationships and heterosexual marriages.

This point was not lost on LGBTQ rights opponents. As a representative of the conservative advocacy group Family Research Council put it in 1998, "Offering domestic-partner benefits isn't a neutral position for companies; it represents a radical social change. The [benefits] imply that a homosexual relationship is valid enough to merit subsidy and societal support. Once you get to that point, it's hard to deny the case for homosexual marriage itself."[44] The difficulty in staking out a neutral position on issues related to employment benefits and sexual orientation, as was possible with other divisive social policy issues, was an additional reason why so many corporations proved willing, in a relatively short period of time, to adopt internal policies that recognized the relationships and families of their LGBTQ employees.

It is important to emphasize how far ahead of the curve corporate America was in the 1990s on the question of legal recognition of same-sex relationships when compared, for example, to state governments. By 1998, at a time when dozens of large companies offered DPBs to their employees, no state in the country did the same. In fact, that same year California governor Pete Wilson vetoed a modest domestic partnership bill that would have created a statewide domestic partnership registry and offered registered couples only a handful of rights, such as the ability to visit sick partners in hospitals. Two years later, 60 percent of California voters approved a ballot measure making it explicit that only marriages between a man and a woman were legally valid in California. While even the country's most liberal states were refusing to recognize the committed relationships of same-sex couples, significant segments of corporate America were doing precisely that.

It also bears noting that the adoption of DPBs by large corporations was almost entirely a voluntary decision not affected by legal mandates. Most states did not have laws that prohibited discrimination on the basis of sexual orientation and gender identity. And in jurisdictions that did have such laws, courts had generally ruled that they did not require employers to provide DPBs to their employees.[45]

One exception to the absence of legal mandates was a San Francisco ordinance enacted in 1996 requiring companies that contracted with the city to offer DPBs to all their employees nationwide.[46] Several corporations, including Bank of America, Chevron, and Pacific Gas and Electric, responded to the new ordinance by adopting company-wide DPBs. But an airlines trade group filed a federal lawsuit contending that the city did not have the legal authority to require airlines, which are regulated by the federal government, to offer the benefits. This led the Human Rights Campaign to call for a national boycott of United Airlines, which had a large presence at the San Francisco airport. Some LGBTQ activists responded by publicly destroying their United frequent flyer cards and by picketing in front of airline offices. In the summer of 1999, as the litigation was still making its way through the courts, United Airlines announced that it would voluntarily offer DPBs to its unmarried employees. Shortly after that, American Airlines declared that it would also offer the benefits. The country's other major airlines, as well as the Boeing Corporation, quickly followed suit.[47]

A few months later, the three leading American automobile manufacturers (General Motors, Ford, and Chrysler), under pressure not just from LGBTQ groups, but also from the United Auto Workers union, announced that they, too, would offer DPBs.[48] This development was particularly significant because it showed the extent to which DPBs were now embraced not only by technology and entertainment companies, among others, headquartered on the coasts, but also by manufacturing firms with headquarters and workers in the country's midsection. The question of benefits equality as a crucial component of equal opportunity in the workplace was no longer a niche issue limited to a handful of progressive companies. DPBs instead had become a mainstream, and increasingly noncontroversial, corporate policy.

In short, with the prodding of LGBTQ activists, most large corporations chose to adopt DPBs not because of legal mandates and the threat of lawsuits, but because (1) it was the right thing to do, (2) it helped with recruitment and retention of employees, and (3) DPBs, as a 2004 article in the *Journal of Homosexuality* explained, became "part of the corporate cultural diversity milieu." By the turn of the century, a growing segment of the American public did not view a company as fully committed to promoting equality and diversity unless it offered DPBs to its LGBTQ employees.[49]

One fascinating aspect of corporate DPBs policies was that they were simultaneously transgressive and normalizing. The policies were transgressive because, when they were first put into place in the early 1990s, they represented, by far, the most comprehensive and widely available mechanisms in American society for recognizing same-sex relationships and families headed by LGBTQ individuals. To put it simply, few other important institutions in the United States were willing to accept the basic normative premise that same-sex relationships and families were as deserving of respect and support as heterosexual marriages and so-called traditional families. But at the same time, the policies were normalizing because large corporations in the United States are generally understood to be firmly embedded in the political and cultural mainstream of society. Even if the justifications for and implications of DPBs policies were transgressive for their times, the entities adopting the policies were anything but radical institutions.

Under the prevailing atmosphere of growing corporate support for LGBTQ equality, it was those businesses that refused to adjust their policies to account for the existence of queer people that now found themselves outside the corporate mainstream on sexual orientation issues. One of those firms was Exxon Mobil, a socially conservative company that, by refusing to include sexual orientation in its nondiscrimination policy or to offer DPBs while actively working for years to defeat shareholder resolutions calling on it to do so, earned the *only* negative ranking ever given by the HRC's *Corporate Equality Index*.[50]

Another such outlier company was the Cracker Barrel Corporation. In the early 1990s, Cracker Barrel operated about one hundred restaurants and gift shops, most of them along interstate highways in the south, and employed more than ten thousand workers. In 1991, the company's vice president for human resources distributed a memo to restaurant managers reminding them that the company "was founded upon a concept of traditional American values," and that it was therefore "inconsistent with our concept and values . . . and those of our customer base to continue to employ individuals . . . whose sexual preferences fail to demonstrate normal heterosexual values which have been the foundation of families in our society." Following company orders, store managers conducted brief interviews with their employees to determine whether they were in violation of the company's sexual orientation policy. The firm then proceeded to fire at least sixteen employees because of their same-sex sexual orientation.[51]

The company's explicit adoption of an antigay employment policy, and the firings that followed, was covered extensively by the media and was met with calls by LGBTQ groups and activists to boycott and picket the restaurants. A few weeks later, Cracker Barrel attempted to quiet the furor by announcing that it would from now on focus only on employing individuals who were committed to providing good service to its customers. This ambiguous proclamation failed to satisfy LGBTQ activists, in part because the company did not rehire the fired LGBTQ employees. For the next few months, activists repeatedly criticized the company, while holding dozens of protests outside and inside the chain's restaurants, some of which resulted in arrests. Some of the company's shareholders also tried to force the firm to adopt and abide by more explicitly inclusive hiring and retention policies. After more than a decade of pressure by activists and shareholders, the company in 2002 finally relented by amending its nondiscrimination policy to include sexual orientation.[52]

Although it was seemingly short-lived, Cracker Barrel's adoption of an explicit policy of discrimination against LGBTQ individuals rendered it a corporate outlier. The strong trend among large corporations was precisely in the opposite direction: By the end of the 1990s, the vast majority of large companies in the United States had policies prohibiting sexual orientation discrimination, and many offered DPBs. Years of experience proved to corporate executives and board members that such policies helped companies attain diversity objectives, hire and retain qualified employees, bolster morale, and attract business from members of LGBTQ communities. As a result, when LGBTQ rights issues reached a level of national prominence in the 2000s that they had never enjoyed before, corporations began to more frequently and vigorously promote LGBTQ equality not only within their walls, but in the public sphere as well.

The adoption by many corporations of nondiscrimination policies and their recognition of same-sex relationships through DPBs programs made those firms better and fairer places to work while contributing to their bottom lines. There was every reason to think, many corporate leaders came to believe, that the nation as a whole (and not just its largest private employers) would benefit from the adoption of policies prohibiting discrimination on the basis of sexual orientation and gender identity while offering same-sex couples the opportunity to marry.

CHAPTER 5

Corporate LGBTQ Advocacy
in the Public Sphere

QUEER ACTIVISTS CONTINUED to pressure corporations to embrace LGBTQ rights positions well into the new century. A prominent example of that activism was the targeting of the Chick-fil-A restaurant company after its CEO stated in 2012 that "we are inviting God's judgment on our nation when we shake our fist at Him and say, 'We know better than you as to what constitutes a marriage.'" The executive added that his company supported traditional marriage and was "very much supportive of the . . . biblical definition of the family unit." LGBTQ rights activists strongly criticized the CEO's comments. They also held protests in front of company restaurants and called for a boycott. After only a few days, the company issued a statement asserting that "going forward, our intent is to leave the policy debate over same-sex marriage to the government and political arena."[1]

Unlike Chick-fil-A's new announced position of neutrality, many large companies increasingly refused to remain silent on government policies that affected the lives and rights of queer people. Indeed, the queering of corporate America took a new direction at around the turn of the century. Up until then, corporations had been almost exclusively the *targets* of LGBTQ rights activism as activists sought to influence their internal policies and practices; now, those same companies also increasingly became the *sources* of political activism on behalf of LGBTQ equality in the public sphere. As a general matter, the more corporations became internally committed to LGBTQ equality, the more they were willing to engage in external political advocacy on behalf of LGBTQ rights.

That external activism was manifested in the ways in which some large companies—at first only a few, but later many—pushed for laws at the federal, state, and local levels that protected individuals from discrimination on the basis of sexual orientation and gender identity. And, as the new century progressed, a growing number of companies started to advocate publicly on behalf of marriage equality.

Many corporations became public advocates for LGBTQ equality because doing so made a great deal of financial and business sense. But two additional (and related) factors also help explain corporate political advocacy on behalf of LGBTQ antidiscrimination laws and of marriage equality: First, the decades-long LGBTQ activism aimed at corporate practices helped turn several large firms from subjects of LGBTQ rights activism to sources of that activism; second, many high-level corporate executives became convinced that leaving public- and private-sector discrimination against queer people unaddressed, and the relationships and families of LGBTQ individuals unrecognized, was fundamentally inconsistent with their firms' professed values of diversity, inclusion, and equality. In short, the corporations that engaged in political advocacy on behalf of LGBTQ rights did so for several reasons, including seeking financial rewards, responding to pressure by activists, and because they believed their corporate values demanded it.

It is important to note that corporate support for antidiscrimination laws and marriage equality were not the only ways in which corporations promoted LGBTQ visibility and causes in the public sphere. For example, at a time when the place of same-sex relationships and families in society continued to be the subject of much debate and controversy, some large companies began to include LGBTQ individuals and same-sex couples in their advertising and marketing campaigns and, in the process, attracted media attention, praise from LGBTQ activists, and criticism from social and religious conservatives. In addition, large companies cosponsored and helped pay for gay pride parades in cities such as Detroit, Salt Lake City, and St. Petersburg. Furthermore, big companies donated increasingly large amounts of money to LGBTQ community organizations and AIDS groups.[2]

It is also important to keep in mind that many factors contributed to the decision by particular states to enact LGBTQ antidiscrimination laws or embrace marriage equality. It is difficult to establish conclusively that any one factor had a causal effect in changing particular public policies affecting queer people in particular jurisdictions. Nonetheless, it is reasonable to believe that corporate political activism on behalf of LGBTQ rights was one of several factors that helped persuade growing segments of the American population that LGBTQ people, too, were entitled to basic civil rights and legal protections.[3]

The struggle over LGBTQ rights has been ultimately a struggle over conflicting moral values and positions.[4] For most of the twentieth century, government, educational, religious, and corporate leaders, along with large segments of the American public, viewed queer people as either mentally disturbed or morally compromised (or both). These understandings were reflected in laws and practices that saw countless LGBTQ people denied civil service and private sector jobs; harassed and assaulted by police officers on the streets and in bars, while in many instances left unprotected by the same police forces from the physical and verbal assaults of others; kicked out of the military for doing nothing more than acknowledging having a same-sex sexual orientation; denied custody of or visitation with their biological children while being denied the opportunity to adopt children; denied entry into the United States (for noncitizens), and, of course, denied the ability to marry the individuals of their choice. As late as 1986, the US Supreme Court rejected the notion that the Constitution granted LGBTQ people a fundamental right to choose how and with whom to be sexually intimate, claiming that the idea was "at best facetious." The Court reasoned (if that is the correct word) that moral disapproval of sexual minorities was a constitutionally sufficient justification to criminalize consensual sexual conduct between two adults of the same gender.[5]

Although the LGBTQ rights movement at the end of the twentieth century succeeded in mitigating some of the most harmful injuries caused by anti-LGBTQ laws, practices, and prejudice, the reality was that, by the turn of the century, it was still legal to discriminate against LGBTQ people under federal law and under the laws of the vast majority of states. It was also still constitutional in all fifty states to deny same-sex couples the opportunity to marry. And it was not until well into the twenty-first century that a majority of Americans began telling pollsters that they supported marriage equality for LGBTQ people.

In this challenging political and moral environment for LGBTQ equality, public corporate advocacy on behalf of LGBTQ rights eventually helped the movement achieve some of its most important objectives. The fact that a growing number of large corporations had internally adopted the same types of nondiscrimination and relationship-recognition policies that the LGBTQ movement, with the assistance of several of those same companies, was now demanding of the government made those demands seem less threatening and destabilizing.

Many social and religious conservatives had for decades claimed that affording basic equality rights to queer people rewarded immorality, promoted promiscuity, spread HIV, destabilized families, harmed children, and threatened the institution of marriage (thus the apparent need for laws such as the *Defense* of Marriage Act). The LGBTQ movement, of course, had reasoned answers to each and every one of those absurd claims. But for many Americans at the time, the claims were not so outlandish. The fact that a growing number of large corporations were willing initially to embrace LGBTQ equality measures internally, and later to advocate externally on behalf of public policies that promoted LGBTQ rights, went a long way toward normalizing and mainstreaming LGBTQ equality claims. After all, how radical or destabilizing could equal treatment of queer people and relationships actually be if such treatment had been publicly embraced by blue chip corporations such as Apple, General Mills, Google, IBM, Microsoft, and Procter & Gamble? The bottom line is that corporate advocacy on behalf of public policies aimed at promoting LGBTQ equality has been one of several important factors that both reflects and accounts for changes in how our society views LGBTQ people, their relationships, and their families.

Antidiscrimination Laws

Although many large companies would eventually publicly support the enactment of laws prohibiting employment discrimination on the basis of sexual orientation, it would take years of litigation and activism to reach that result. For example, after gay former employees sued AT&T and Western Union in 1990 under San Francisco's sexual orientation antidiscrimination ordinance, the companies argued, ultimately unsuccessfully, that the ordinance violated the state constitution. At around the same time, a former employee of the Shell oil company sued his former employer of twenty years after he was summarily fired when his supervisors learned he was gay. The plaintiff, who had been previously promoted by the company nine times, claimed that the energy firm had violated his rights under California law to privacy and to engage in political activity. A state judge, after a two-week trial, agreed and awarded the gay man $5.3 million. As the judge noted, "This case presents the relatively new issue of how far a corporation may go in demanding that its managerial staff, in their respective private lives, deport and conduct themselves in a manner acceptable to and meeting the corporation's concept of propriety."[6]

In 1991, as the California legislature was considering amending its civil rights law to prohibit discrimination on the basis of sexual orientation, the California Chamber of Commerce and the California Manufacturing Association remained neutral on the bill, while the Merchants and Manufacturing Association, a statewide

organization representing 4,100 medium- and large-size corporations, opposed the bill, claiming it would lead to too many lawsuits.
Republican governor Pete Wilson eventually relied on that argument
to veto the bill following its approval by the legislature.[7]

The LGBTQ community in California, already battered by the
devastating effects of the AIDS epidemic, responded angrily to Governor Wilson's veto of the gay rights law. In the days that followed,
activists led protest marches in Los Angeles and San Francisco,
engaged in acts of civil disobedience, and repeatedly disrupted the
governor's speeches. The veto galvanized LGBTQ groups to recom-
mit themselves to persuade the legislature to pass a similar measure
the following year while simultaneously daring the governor to veto
the bill again.[8]

The legislature once again took up the issue of a gay rights
employment law in 1992. Several large corporations in the state,
including Bank of America and Pacific Bell, supported the legislation. This time around, the California Chamber of Commerce and
the California Manufacturers Association, while ostensibly remaining neutral on the measure, in fact worked closely behind the scenes
with the bill's leading supporter in the state assembly in drafting the
new provision that was, once again, approved by the legislature.
Governor Wilson, hoping to avoid the criticism from LGBTQ activists and the ensuing political furor engendered by his earlier veto,
signed the bill into law. By doing so, California became the sixth
state to enact a statute prohibiting employment discrimination on
the basis of sexual orientation.[9]

One large corporation, Microsoft, was also involved in the eventual passage of an LGBTQ antidiscrimination law in Washington
State. The computer giant was an early supporter of LGBTQ rights
positions. In 1992, it publicly opposed constitutional amendments
in Colorado and Oregon aimed at denying LGBTQ people antidiscrimination protections under the law. A year later, LGBTQ workers
at the company formed one of the first LGBTQ corporate employee
groups in the country, naming it the Gay and Lesbian Employees at
Microsoft (GLEAM). The company shortly thereafter implemented

a DPBs program for its LGBTQ employees. In addition, the technology firm supported several bills introduced in the Washington state legislature in the 1990s and early 2000s aimed at prohibiting discrimination on the basis of both sexual orientation and gender identity in housing, insurance, and employment.

In 2004, Microsoft's manager of government affairs wrote a public letter to Democratic state representative Ed Murray, the principal sponsor of the antidiscrimination bill, strongly supporting the measure. After noting that the company had its own sexual orientation antidiscrimination policy, the executive added that "unfortunately, not all Americans experience this basic protection in their employment. It remains legal in 38 states to fire someone because of their sexual orientation. This is not only bad for business, it is bad for America. House Bill 1809 would simply and fairly extend to Washingtonians the fundamental right to be judged on one's own merits. And it does so without any undue burden on our business environment. . . . The principles it fosters are consistent with our corporate principles in treating all employees with fairness and respect."[10]

Given the company's strong endorsement of the civil rights law, Microsoft in 2005 surprised many people when it abruptly decided to withhold its support from that year's bill following two meetings between company officials and Ken Hutcherson, a Seattle-based Evangelical minister. At the time, Hutcherson was threatening to call for a national boycott of the company if it continued to support LGBTQ rights causes. In criticizing the company, the minister claimed he did not care about its internal business practices, including its nondiscrimination policy protecting sexual minorities. But he contended that it was a different matter altogether when the computer giant sought to influence public policy. As the minister put it, "What I was upset about was when they tried to step outside their four walls and make their policy my policy. That gave me the right to step out of my world into theirs."[11]

Unlike Microsoft, other big companies with a large presence in Washington State, such as Boeing, Coors, Hewlett Packard, and Nike, continued to support the antidiscrimination measure. But in the end, although the 2005 bill was approved by the state House of Representatives, it failed to pass the Senate by one vote. Given that Microsoft's change of position from supporting the bill to one of neutrality did not become public until the day of the Senate vote, it was unlikely that the firm's shift was responsible for the bill's defeat. Nonetheless, LGBTQ activists were furious at the company, accusing it of caving in to pressure from Evangelical Christians, a claim that the firm denied. The Los Angeles Gay and Lesbian Center asked Microsoft to return the corporate vision award it had given the company four years earlier. For its part, the Human Rights Campaign wrote a public letter to the company asking that it clearly state its support for sexual orientation antidiscrimination laws at the federal and state levels. Many Microsoft employees also expressed displeasure with the company's decision. The firm's seven-hundred-person LGBTQ employee group, GLEAM, wrote a public letter to CEO Steve Ballmer expressing shock and disappointment at Microsoft's decision to withhold support for the LGBTQ rights measure, explaining that it "shook our trust in executive management, and has left us feeling abandoned, depressed, and embarrassed for Microsoft."[12]

Ballmer initially responded to the uproar by writing an email to employees explaining that even though he and Bill Gates, Microsoft's founder and chairman, personally supported gay rights legislation, the company itself "shouldn't be picking sides on social-policy issues." But in the face of continuous and strong criticism from LGBTQ rights groups and his own employees, Ballmer changed course two weeks later, sending employees another email stating that diversity in the workplace was an important business issue and that it was, after all, appropriate to make it part of the company's legislative agenda. Ballmer added, "I'm proud of Microsoft's commitment to non-discrimination in our internal policies and benefits, but our policies can't cover the range of housing, education, financial and similar services that our people and their partners and families need. Therefore, it's appropriate for the company to support legislation that will promote and protect diversity in the workplace." Ballmer finished his email by explaining that the company would continue to abide by its policy not to "take a position on most other public policy issues, either in the US or internationally." But, in the company's view, diversity issues were different because they were closely linked to how a corporation such as Microsoft operated its business.[13]

Shortly after the start of the following year's (2006) legislative session, a group of Washington State's biggest companies, including Boeing, Hewlett Packard, Microsoft, and Nike, at the behest of Equal Rights Washington—the largest LGBTQ rights group in the state—wrote a letter to state Republican and Democratic legislative leaders supporting the antidiscrimination bill. Much of the letter contained exactly the same language as Ballmer's email to Microsoft employees. Representative Murray, the longtime sponsor of the bill, welcomed the letter, saying that it "feeds the argument that business is for this and Republicans should support it." For their part, some Evangelical ministers argued that Microsoft was paying lip service to LGBTQ rights, but doing little in practice to promote them. A company spokesperson disagreed, noting, "We're actively lobbying for the bill. We're down [at the state house] every day."[14]

At around the same time that the state's biggest private employers sent their joint letter to legislative leaders, Republican state senator Bill Finkbeiner, whose district included Microsoft's headquarters in Redmond, announced that he had changed his mind and would now vote in favor of the civil rights bill. Two weeks later, the legislature passed the law and the governor signed it shortly thereafter, ending a more than twenty-year quest to codify protection from discrimination for LGBTQ people into state law. After the law passed, the executive director of Equal Rights Washington praised companies like Microsoft and Boeing for standing "up against the antigay extremists."[15]

Large companies provided similar support for the enactment of state antidiscrimination laws in, for example, Illinois in 1995 and in Iowa in 2007. Big companies also got involved in gay rights battles at the local level, though it frequently took both time and prodding by LGBTQ activists before they did so. In 1993, for example, after conservative activists placed a measure before voters in Cincinnati to amend the city charter to prohibit the municipality from protecting sexual minorities from discrimination, large corporations, including Cincinnati-based Procter & Gamble (P&G), stayed on the political sidelines by refusing to either support or oppose the initiative. Shortly after 65 percent of city voters approved the ballot measure, LGBTQ employees at P&G formed an employee group called GABLE (Gay, Ally, Bisexual, and Lesbian Employees), with the aim of making the company a more welcoming place for sexual minorities. At first, P&G resisted pressure from the group to make the company more LGBTQ friendly. For instance, it was several years before P&G allowed GABLE to use the firm's email network. And in 1998, the children of LGBTQ employees were not allowed to attend a company-sponsored "family event" at a local amusement park.[16]

However, the company gradually began agreeing to GABLE's demands. For example, at the group's urging, the firm pulled its ads from a right-wing radio show hosted by a homophobic commentator, placed ads on NBC's gay-themed *Will & Grace* television show, and, in 2002, began offering DPBs to its employees. Shortly thereafter, the company agreed to support an effort to repeal Cincinnati's antigay charter amendment approved by voters almost a decade earlier; it donated $40,000 to a local LGBTQ rights group called Citizens to Restore Fairness, created for the specific purpose of repealing the measure. (Other large companies, including GE Aircraft Engines, Hewlett Packard, and Kroger, also donated money to the LGBTQ rights group.) Procter & Gamble's CEO gave a speech at a meeting of a civil rights organization in which he stated that the amendment "is neither inclusive nor just, and it has severely harmed the economic vitality of our city."[17]

In 2004, Cincinnati voters repealed the city charter amendment by a margin of 54 to 46 percent. Although it is impossible to quantify exactly what effect corporate support had on the successful repeal, it is reasonable to conclude that it was one of several factors that contributed to an important political victory for the LGBTQ rights movement at the local level.

Large companies were also early supporters of a congressional

LGBTQ equality bill, known as the Employment Nondiscrimination Act (ENDA), first introduced in 1994. The early versions of ENDA sought to prohibit sexual orientation discrimination; starting in 2007, the bill also included a prohibition on employment discrimination on the basis of gender identity. Corporate support for ENDA grew increasingly stronger and more visible during the two decades that the measure was before Congress. Although the bill was introduced in every Congress for twenty years, it never became law.

Gerry Studds, an openly gay Democratic congressman from Massachusetts, introduced the first ENDA bill in Congress in June 1994. A month later, the Senate Committee on Labor and Human Resources, under the leadership of Massachusetts senator Ted Kennedy, held the first congressional hearings on ENDA. Shortly before the hearings, the CEOs of AT&T, Honeywell, and Xerox, as well as Microsoft's senior vice president for law and corporate affairs, wrote separate letters to Senator Kennedy in support of the legislation. The executives emphasized the high value their companies placed on the full diversity of their employees and how that diversity promoted their corporations' financial interests. As AT&T's CEO put it, his firm supported diversity and nondiscrimination policies because "we realize that our company's ultimate goal—delighted customers—begins internally with delighted associates. Our company's only sustainable competitive advantage is our people."[18]

It is important to keep in mind that when ENDA was first introduced in Congress, only nine states had laws prohibiting discrimination on the basis of sexual orientation and only one (Minnesota) prohibited discrimination against transgender individuals. Although when Americans at around that time were asked in polls whether they supported equal opportunities for gay men and lesbians in employment, a majority responded affirmatively, the polls also revealed that 44 percent of respondents believed that same-sex relationships "should not be legal," that 57 percent agreed with the proposition that "homosexuality should not be considered an acceptable alternative lifestyle," and 68 percent opposed the recognition of same-sex marriages.[19] In other words, the polls made clear that large segments of the American population opposed crucial LGBTQ rights positions. Despite that opposition, leading executives of several large American companies were willing to publicly proclaim their firms' support for LGBTQ equality as early as the mid-1990s.

By 2000, nineteen additional large corporations, including Eastman Kodak, General Mills, and Merrill Lynch, had come out in favor of ENDA. Four years later, the number of Fortune 500 companies that had publicly expressed support for ENDA grew to forty-nine, and now included British Petroleum, IBM, JP Morgan Chase, Nike, and Yahoo!. And in 2002, when Senator Kennedy's Health, Education, Labor, and Pensions Committee held another set of hearings on ENDA, representatives from two large companies—Eastman Kodak (with seventy thousand employees) and FleetBoston Financial Corporation (at the time, the largest bank in New England, with forty-five thousand employees)—shared with senators their enthusiastic support for the proposed legislation. The president and CEO of FleetBoston told the committee,

> This legislation is an opportunity to further advance the work we have already begun. FleetBoston stands with thousands of companies across America that have already successfully addressed discrimination based on sexual orientation in the workplace. ENDA will guarantee that this progress continues and accelerates. In the wake of the attacks on our country on September 11, we believe that we must be galvanized to a stronger collective purpose. The lack of workplace protections based on sexual orientation leaves a gaping hole in America's commitment to equal opportunity and is an invitation to the perpetuation of stereotype and prejudice.[20]

When company executives testify before Congress, their objective is usually to defeat, lessen, or weaken federal regulation of their businesses. It is highly unusual for company representatives to lobby Congress in favor of *greater* federal oversight of their enterprises. But that was precisely what many large businesses were requesting when they pushed for ENDA, a point recognized by East-man Kodak's director of human resources in his testimony before the Senate committee in 2002. The executive acknowledged that it was "unusual for a company to support legislation that invites further Federal regulation of our business." But, he explained, Eastman Kodak "believes that protection against discrimination because of one's sexual orientation is a basic civil right. This issue is so fundamental to core principles of fairness that we believe the value of Federal leadership outweighs concerns we might otherwise have about Federal intervention with our business."[21]

In subsequent years, other large company executives testified before congressional committees considering ENDA, including one from General Mills in 2007 and another from Nike in 2009. By then, the bill had been amended to also include a prohibition on discrimination on the basis of gender identity. The last time an ENDA bill came up for a vote was in 2013, when the Senate, at that time controlled by Democrats, approved the measure on a bipartisan vote of 64–32.[22]

However, many in the Republican majority in the House of Representatives, led by Speaker John Boehner of Ohio, remained opposed to the bill. According to the Speaker's spokesperson, the proposed law would "increase frivolous litigation and cost America jobs," a frequently raised objection by Republicans to the legislation. The Business Coalition for Workplace Fairness, a business group organized by the Human Rights Campaign composed of 125 large companies—including Bristol-Myers Squibb, Chevron, Coca-Cola, Dow Chemical, Google, Hilton, Procter & Gamble, Verizon, and Whirlpool—attempted to counter those claims by running television ads in the Washington, DC, area emphasizing businesses' support for the bill. As a representative of Marriott, a company that lobbied in favor of ENDA, explained, "If the concern is the business community's response, we want to show that we are comfortable and that this is consistent with our internal policies already in place." One LGBTQ activist working on behalf of ENDA stated, "Business has been and will continue to be an essential ally in passing ENDA."[23]

Corporate backing of ENDA angered many social and religious conservatives. Some of these conservatives had for years joined forces with corporate America in pushing for smaller government while emphasizing the need for less, not more, state regulation of private enterprise. Corporate support for LGBTQ equality strained the ideological alliance between traditional conservatives and large corporations. Indeed, many traditional conservatives were incredulous in the face of the increasingly visible corporate support for ENDA. As a representative of the right-wing Family Research Council explained, "For business to actively lobby for this bill is something that I don't understand. They have the power to write their own non-discrimination policy. Why do they want to force other companies to adopt this policy as well?"[24] Conservative groups also began claiming that LGBTQ rights measures such as ENDA constituted threats to religious liberty. And, by extension, when large corporations began publicly supporting such measures, social and religious conservatives started complaining that the firms were undermining religious freedom.

The politics surrounding the antidiscrimination bill required Republicans in the House of Representatives to choose between the wishes of some of the nation's biggest and most important companies, on the one hand, and those of social and religious conservatives, on the other; most chose the latter option. After it became clear that a majority of his caucus would not vote to support ENDA, Speaker Boehner refused to allow the measure to come up for a vote, killing any prospect of its passage during the 2013–2014 Congress. Shortly thereafter, large corporations shifted their support from ENDA to the Equality Act, a much more expansive federal bill that would prohibit discrimination not only in employment, but also in housing and in the provision of goods and services by places of public accommodation. Dozens of corporations, including Airbnb, Amazon, CVS Health, Facebook, IBM, Kellogg's, Mastercard, Monsanto, Oracle, Pepsi, Target, and Twitter, formed the Business Coalition for the Equality Act to work in conjunction with the Human Rights Campaign to push for the enactment of the legislation.

Although there is still no federal law that explicitly prohibits employment discrimination on the basis of sexual orientation and gender identity, marriage equality became a national reality in 2015 after the Supreme Court held that same-sex couples have a constitutional right to marry. Large corporations played a crucial role in helping the LGBTQ rights movement achieve what had become, in many ways, its most important objective.

Same-Sex Marriage

In 2006, *Fortune* magazine published an article titled "Queer Inc.: How Corporate America Fell in Love with Gays and Lesbians." The article explained that the previous spring, the Fortune 500 listing had reached a milestone: more than half of its companies offered DPBs, up from twenty-eight such companies only a decade earlier. The article noted that along with health benefits, the large firms provided LGBTQ employees with bereavement leaves, adoption assistance, paid leaves after having children, and relocation assistance for same-sex partners if the employees were transferred. As the article explained, "Put another way, gay marriage—an idea that has been banned by all but one of 27 states that have voted on it—has become a fact of life inside many big companies."[25]

A crucial motivating factor for large companies in adopting DPBs was a bottom-line one: a growing number of companies realized that DPBs were necessary in order to be optimally positioned to hire and retain the most qualified employees. But many companies also came to see the adoption of DPBs as the right thing to do. A spokesperson for IBM, explaining why the company implemented DPBs in 1995, put it this way: "We realized it was unfair to have an employee working for our company who couldn't get benefits for a loved one."[26]

In 2004, Massachusetts became the first state to allow same-sex couples to marry, after being required to do so by its highest court. By that time, several large companies in the state had already been treating committed same-sex relationships in the same way they treated married different-sex ones. As a spokesperson for Gillette explained that summer, "We had already been treating gay partners as spousal equivalents."[27]

In the years that followed, the supreme courts of California, Connecticut, and Iowa also required their states to recognize same-sex marriages. But with this progress in the marriage equality front came considerable backlash and crucial defeats: by the end of the 2000s, almost thirty states (including California in 2008) had amended their constitutions to ban same-sex marriages; there was little interest in Congress in repealing the Defense of Marriage Act; and there were many conservatives—including President George W. Bush—calling for a federal constitutional amendment prohibiting same-sex couples from marrying. Indeed, absent intervention by the US Supreme Court, which most legal experts did not expect anytime soon, it seemed that nationwide marriage equality was many years away. Given the politics of and backlash against same-sex marriage, when coupled with Congress's year-after-year failure to enact a federal law explicitly prohibiting discrimination on the basis of sexual orientation and gender identity, it was difficult to disagree with Joe Solmonese, president of the Human Rights Campaign, when he stated in 2006 that "corporate America is far ahead of America generally when it comes to the question of equality for GLBT people."[28]

Although same-sex marriage remained a highly controversial and divisive social policy issue, top executives at many large companies had already been persuaded of the essential equivalence between committed different-sex and same-sex relationships. It was therefore a natural progression for these executives to begin participating in public debates over same-sex marriage. Even though companies traditionally steer away from controversial social issues, the question of equal access to rights and benefits for same-sex couples was, at least in part, an employment and workplace issue, rendering corporate executives both qualified to comment on the subject and interested in participating in the relevant public policy debates.

One way in which business representatives participated in public debates over marriage equality was by opposing efforts by social and religious conservatives to amend state constitutions to ban same-sex marriages. In 2006, for example, several prominent Massachusetts business executives, including leaders of the Boston Chamber of Commerce, joined a group of liberal civic leaders in opposing a proposed constitutional amendment banning same-sex marriages that was strongly supported by Republican governor (and future GOP presidential nominee) Mitt Romney. Two years later, the giant utility Pacific Gas and Electric donated $250,000 to opponents of Proposition 8, the measure that aimed to overturn the California Supreme Court's ruling requiring the state to allow same-sex couples to marry.[29]

For its part, Apple donated $100,000 to the anti–Proposition 8 campaign. Although some business commentators noted that it was risky for a company that primarily sold goods to consumers to take a stand on a controversial social issue such as same-sex marriage because it might lead some customers to choose not to buy their products, Apple argued that it had an obligation to take sides on what it viewed as an issue of fairness and justice. As the company explained, "We strongly believe that a person's fundamental rights—including the right to marry—should not be affected by their sexual orientation." The company, after noting that it had been one of the first firms to offer DPBs to its employees, added that it viewed same-sex marriage as a civil rights issue and not just a political one.[30]

In 2009, five large companies in Washington State, including Boeing, Microsoft, and Nike, along with the Seattle Chamber of Commerce, came out against a voter referendum that sought, ultimately unsuccessfully, to overturn a state statute providing registered domestic partners the same rights and benefits that state and local laws made available to married different-sex couples. Three years later, Amazon, Microsoft, Nike, and Starbucks joined other large companies headquartered in Washington State in support of proposed legislation recognizing same-sex marriages. In advocating for the recognition of such marriages, Microsoft pointed out that companies in Washington were at a competitive disadvantage in trying to attract the most qualified employees when compared to companies based in states that had recognized marriage equality. In the end, more than one hundred companies, big and small, across the state came out in support of the same-sex marriage bill before it was approved by the state legislature.[31]

According to the principal sponsor of the same-sex marriage legislation in the Washington Senate, corporate support for the bill from high-profile businesses such as Microsoft and Nike was crucial to its passage because "it's how we got moderate Republicans and conservative Democrats to vote for this." Several months later, after right-wing groups submitted more than 230,000 signatures in favor of holding a statewide referendum to overturn the legislation, Microsoft's Bill Gates and Steve Ballmer each donated $100,000 of their own money to the successful antireferendum campaign, while Amazon founder Jeff Bezos donated the astounding amount of $2.5 million to help keep same-sex marriage legal in the state of Washington.[32]

Several large corporations and their executives also endorsed and supported same-sex marriage in Minnesota. Three months before state residents went to the polls in 2012 to vote on a constitutional amendment that would have prohibited same-sex couples from marrying, General Mills' CEO announced at a gathering of several hundred of the company's LGBTQ employees that the corporation opposed the ballot measure. The CEO's comments led the chairman of Minnesota for Marriage, the conservative advocacy group pushing for the constitutional amendment, to tell the media that "it's ironic and regrettable that a corporation that makes billions marketing cereal to parents of children would take the position that marriage should be redefined." For his part, a spokesperson for the National Organization for Marriage complained, "Marriage is a cultural issue, not a business issue. We simply ask [corporations] to remain neutral." Although some of the state's biggest employers, including Cargill and Target, remained neutral on the amendment, others, such as Thomson Reuters and the medical device maker St. Jude Medical, came out against it.[33]

It is important to point out that large corporations did not push for same-sex marriage only in so-called blue states like Washington and Minnesota. They did the same in some conservative states. For example, in 2013 a group of businesses and advocacy organizations in Indiana formed the Freedom Indiana Coalition to oppose a state constitutional amendment seeking to ban same-sex marriages. The coalition brought together liberal organizations such as the ACLU of Indiana and Indiana Equality Action (an LGBTQ rights group) with more than thirty businesses in the state, both big and small, including two of the state's largest private employers: the pharmaceutical company Eli Lilly and the engine manufacturer Cummins. Those two companies alone donated $100,000 to the coalition. Eli Lilly's director of corporate responsibility explained that the amendment would make it more difficult for businesses in the competitive life sciences industry to recruit "the very best and brightest" employees from around the world. He added that "it was important for us to lead [on this issue]. If we didn't do it, who would?"[34]

The Indianapolis Chamber of Commerce also came out against the constitutional amendment, noting that the state already had a well-documented problem retaining its college-educated population and that many young people saw the amendment as intrinsically discriminatory. This led the executive director of the conservative American Family Association of Indiana to complain that "the myth that public policy support for traditional marriage is somehow bad for business is a red herring and a scare tactic. The future of marriage belongs in the hands of Hoosier voters, not the boardroom of the Indianapolis Chamber of Commerce." The extent to which corporate concerns became a part of the debate over same-sex marriage in the state was captured succinctly by an article in *Bloomberg* that began as follows: "Indiana's debate about same-sex marriage [used to be] all about morals. Now it's about business."[35]

Although the marriage amendment was strongly supported by then governor (and future vice president) Mike Pence, and Republicans enjoyed large majorities in both chambers of the legislature, that body decided against placing the amendment before voters. The state's largest newspaper accurately portrayed the legislature's decision as a win for big business and a loss for social and religious conservatives in the state.[36]

Throughout this period, LGBTQ groups continued to encourage large corporations to take ever-increasing public steps in support of marriage equality. This was true not only of national LGBTQ organizations such as the Human Rights Campaign and the National Gay and Lesbian Task Force, but also of groups that (1) worked only on marriage equality issues (such as Freedom to Marry), (2) focused on the actions and policies of private employers (such as Out & Equal Workplace Advocates), and (3) operated at the state level (such as Indiana Equality Action). This multiplicity of groups worked in numerous ways to keep the pressure on corporate America, including by holding private meetings with leading executives, helping to coordinate companies' actions through the formation of coalitions and the issuance of joint corporate statements, and publicly praising companies for speaking out on behalf of marriage equality.

Corporate support for same-sex marriage helped change the nature of the public debate across the country. Proponents of LGBTQ rights had long insisted that the question was one of basic equality. In contrast, conservative opponents argued that the issue was one of traditional values and the need to protect and promote families headed by married men and women. For their part, corporations emphasized primarily business and hiring concerns, though, as we have seen, they frequently supplemented those arguments with ones based on considerations of basic fairness and the importance of diversity, inclusion, and equal treatment. Clearly, the corporate arguments dovetailed nicely with those of marriage equality activists while standing in direct opposition to those raised by social and religious conservatives. By the time the US Supreme Court decided to weigh in on constitutional issues related to same-sex marriage, a natural political alliance had developed on the issue between LGBTQ rights activists and some of the nation's biggest and most influential corporations.

In 2012, Goldman Sachs CEO Lloyd Blankfein, who had written

to New York legislators the previous year urging them to pass a marriage equality law, became the Human Rights Campaign's first national corporate spokesperson for same-sex marriage. The following year, HRC helped form a group called the Business Coalition for DOMA Repeal, consisting of about a dozen companies, including Aetna, Bristol-Myers Squibb, eBay, and Marriott. A few months later, more than two hundred companies—including Alcoa, Amazon, Citigroup, Google, Johnson & Johnson, Morgan Stanley, and Pfizer—signed an amicus brief urging the Supreme Court to strike down the Defense of Marriage Act in *United States v. Windsor*. (DOMA prohibited the federal government from recognizing same-sex marriages that were valid under state law.) As the attorney who filed the brief explained, "I really wanted to do a brief that would demonstrate that marriage equality was now a mainstream American issue. And I thought, what better way to do that than to demonstrate that corporate America now embraces equality."[37]

The brief emphasized the extent to which DOMA required employers to treat their employees differently depending on whether they were married to someone of the same or opposite sex. The differential treatment imposed significant financial costs and administrative burdens on employers because it required them, in states that allowed same-sex couples to marry, to have separate accounting systems for the distribution of benefits regulated by federal law and the imputation of income associated with those benefits for tax purposes. The brief strenuously objected to the ways in which DOMA conscripted companies into discriminating against their own employees for no reason other than that they had same-sex spouses. As the brief explained, "In the modern workplace, the employer becomes the face of DOMA's discriminatory treatment, and is placed in the role of intrusive inquisitor, imputer of taxable income, and withholder of benefits. The employer is thus forced by DOMA to participate in the injury of its own workforce morale."[38]

Two years after the Supreme Court struck down DOMA as unconstitutional in *Windsor*, an even larger group of corporations— nearly four hundred, both big and small—joined an amicus brief asking the Court to also strike down state laws prohibiting same-sex couples from marrying. Among the corporations that joined the brief in *Obergefell v. Hodges*, but had not done so in *Windsor*, were American Express, Barclays, Dow Chemical, General Electric, MillerCoors, PepsiCo, and TD Bank. It bears noting that although conservative organizations, religious groups, academics, and elected officials filed dozens of amicus briefs *on behalf* of DOMA's constitutionality in *Windsor* and of the constitutionality of state laws prohibiting same-sex marriage in *Obergefell*, the number of for-profit corporations that joined an anti-LGBTQ rights amicus brief in either case was precisely zero.

The corporations' brief in *Obergefell* highlighted a study conducted by a consulting company, in partnership with the advocacy organizations Freedom to Marry and Out & Equal Workplace Advocates, that estimated marriage inequality cost the private sector $1.4 billion in 2014. This enormous financial price tag was the result of administrative expenses and the costs some companies voluntarily assumed in order to mitigate the financial inequality same-sex marriage bans imposed on their LGBTQ employees.[39] At the same time, the brief argued that LGBTQ equality was good for business by relying on a study of about three hundred firms that had adopted DPBs between 1990 and 2006. The study found "an approximate ten percent average stock price increase over the sample period—a performance better than ninety-five percent of all U.S. professional mutual funds—as well as significant improvement in operating performance relative to companies that did not adopt such policies."[40]

The *Obergefell* amicus brief elaborated on other ways in which the signatory corporations benefited from internal policies aimed at promoting diversity and inclusion of all kinds, including those involving sexual orientation and gender identity, gains that were undermined and threatened by laws that discriminated against some of the companies' employees. In explaining the harms created by anti-LGBTQ laws, the brief emphasized how same-sex marriage bans impeded the ability of corporations to hire and retain the most qualified employees. As the companies explained to the Court,

"States that refuse to allow or recognize same-sex marriages require businesses that regularly deal with state marital benefits (like amici) to single out colleagues with same-sex partners or registered domestic partnerships for separate and unequal treatment, as compared to employees with different-sex partners. These state mandates upset our business philosophy and prevent employers like amici from reaching their full economic potential by discouraging highly-qualified employees from living and working in all of the jurisdictions where we do, or want to do, business."[41]

Corporate support for equality in the US Supreme Court same-sex marriage cases was the logical culmination of almost two decades of corporate public advocacy on behalf of LGBTQ rights. Gary Gates, a scholar at UCLA's Williams Institute, put it this way in 2013: "Corporate America has largely led the way, well ahead of public agencies and often public opinion, on LGBT supportive policies. Antidiscrimination policies and recognition of same-sex couples is much more pervasive in the Fortune 500 than in U.S. federal policy and the laws of most states. So it should not be surprising that these companies have taken stances supportive of marriage equality. Many have had LGBT supportive policies for a decade or more."[42] The director of a workplace equality program at HRC made a similar point when she noted in 2014 that "what's changed even in the last five years is that business has gone from implementing policies aimed at their own employees to turning around and weighing in forcefully on public policy beyond the four walls of their business. They've become legislative and social change agents."[43]

The nationwide recognition of marriage equality brought public policy into line with the internal practices of most large companies in the United States. The recognition allowed those companies to achieve what they had been seeking to do for some time, that is, to have the ability to offer their LGBTQ employees the same opportunities and benefits they offered their heterosexual employees. Among many other consequences, *Obergefell* meant that private employers in the United States no longer had to be complicit in state-mandated discrimination against sexual minorities.

Profits, Values, and Activism

There can be little doubt that economic and competitive concerns were crucial motivating factors leading some corporations to engage in political advocacy on behalf of LGBTQ equality. A growing number of American companies came to view the provision of equal opportunities and benefits for LGBTQ individuals as necessary to maximize competitiveness and optimize the hiring and retention of qualified employees. In addition, for companies that made their goods and services available directly to the general public, LGBTQ-friendly policies had the potential for market rewards as consumers who cared about equality began basing purchasing decisions, in part, on a corporation's willingness to support LGBTQ rights. The more that queer equality principles became accepted by growing segments of customers who purchased their goods and services, the more corporations had to gain and the less to lose when they publicly embraced LGBTQ rights positions.

However, it would be too simplistic to conclude that bottom-line economic concerns *fully* explain why a growing number of American companies, starting around the turn of the century, began to advocate publicly on behalf of the government adopting LGBTQ-friendly policies. Two other related factors contributed to corporate political advocacy on behalf of LGBTQ rights. First, the companies did not approach these controversial public policy issues as blank slates; instead, companies themselves had been the subject of LGBTQ rights activism for decades. That activism helped turn the companies from subjects of activism to sources of activism. Second, due in part to that activism, the companies in question came to view both the lack of laws protecting LGBTQ people against discrimination and the continued resistance to same-sex marriages as fundamentally inconsistent with their corporate values grounded in notions of diversity, inclusion, and equality.

During the last three decades of the twentieth century, LGBTQ activists targeted large corporations on several different fronts. During the 1970s, activists focused their sights on highly visible corporations that had explicit anti-LGBTQ policies and practices. That activism (1) brought greater public attention to the existence of and discrimination against sexual minorities and (2) led several large firms to change their policies and practices in LGBTQ-friendly ways.

During the 1980s and into the 1990s, AIDS activists pressured, cajoled, and embarrassed pharmaceutical companies into finding new and more effective medical treatments for AIDS-related conditions. Activists also strongly criticized corporations that helped fund right-wing politicians who promoted anti-AIDS and anti-LGBTQ rights agendas, while pressuring companies to change policies that discriminated against HIV-positive employees and customers. As they forcefully advocated for the humane treatment of people with AIDS, activists laid bare the harmful consequences of government laws and corporate policies that were constructed around the assumption that LGBTQ people, their relationships, and their families were unworthy of consideration and respect.

In addition, during the 1990s and into the 2000s, LGBTQ employee groups inside many large corporations quietly but effectively pressured their employers to recognize and address the unequal treatment that resulted from the firms denying LGBTQ workers the ability to gain crucial and valuable work-related benefits that the companies, as a matter of course, provided to their heterosexual employees. The concerns behind the push for DPBs were twofold: first, that the failure to recognize the relationships of LGBTQ people was a form of wrongful and unjust discrimination because it denied them important benefits available to others; and second, that offering DPBs was an effective and inexpensive way for companies to hire and retain the types of qualified employees who were essential for maintaining competitiveness and profitability.

It is important to point out that the political and policy debates involving LGBTQ antidiscrimination laws and marriage bans that occurred with growing frequency and intensity starting around the turn of the century implicated precisely the same issues—fairness, discrimination, and relationship recognition—that LGBTQ activists had been raising with corporations for several decades.

In other words, LGBTQ activists for years had been encouraging and pushing companies to grapple with how the interests of their LGBTQ employees and customers fit with their corporate missions. It is therefore not particularly surprising that companies *that had already decided* that issues of LGBTQ equality were important to their objectives as firms became increasingly willing to advocate on behalf of LGBTQ equality in the public sphere.

Of course, corporations routinely promote public policies they believe enhance their competitiveness and ultimately their profitability. But the arguments made by corporations on behalf of LGBTQ-friendly public policies were not only grounded in financial and business concerns. Instead, an important aspect of public corporate advocacy on behalf of antidiscrimination laws protecting LGBTQ people and in favor of marriage equality centered around considerations of values, in particular those associated with equality, inclusion, and fairness. The firms that were the most visible in their advocacy on behalf of LGBTQ rights issues in the public sphere were those that believed most strongly that the government's policies at issue—the absence of legal protections for LGBTQ individuals and the existence of same-sex marriage bans—were fundamentally inconsistent with their corporate values.

We have already seen examples of corporate executives who publicly complained about the troubling disconnect between public policies that negatively impacted queer people and corporate values in support of LGBTQ equality. There was, for example, the congressional testimony of the Eastman Kodak executive who told senators in 2002 that it was precisely because the question of whether LGBTQ individuals were entitled to antidiscrimination protection raised such fundamental issues of basic civil rights and of core principles of fairness that the company was taking the unusual step of *asking for additional government regulation.* As we also saw, Apple partially framed its opposition to California's Proposition 8 on the ground that the right to marry the person of one's choice was an issue of civil and fundamental rights. There were other instances of companies framing the issues at stake as implicating not only their business interests, but also values such as equality and fairness that were important to them as organizations.

For example, Google explained its opposition to Proposition 8 as follows: "While we respect the strongly-held beliefs that people have on both sides of this argument, we see this fundamentally as an issue of equality. We hope that California voters will vote no on Proposition 8—we should not eliminate anyone's fundamental rights, whatever their sexuality, to marry the person they love." After framing the issue in this value-laden way, the company then proceeded to explain its political advocacy against the ballot measure:

> As an Internet company, Google is an active participant in policy debates surrounding information access, technology and energy. Because our company has a great diversity of people and opinions—Democrats and Republicans, conservatives and liberals, all religions and no religion, straight and gay—we do not generally take a position on issues outside of our field, especially not social issues. So when Proposition 8 appeared on the California ballot, it was an unlikely question for Google to take an official company position on. However, while there are many objections to [Proposition 8]—further government encroachment on personal lives, ambiguously written text—it is the chilling and discriminatory effect of the proposition on many of our employees that brings Google to publicly oppose [it].[44]

A similar point was made in the amicus brief filed with the Supreme Court by a large number of corporations in *United States v. Windsor*. As the brief explained, the injury caused by the Defense of Marriage Act "runs far deeper than mere litigation risk; deeper even than the morale of the work force. For many employers, DOMA does violence to the morale of the institution itself. Like other persons, legal and natural, [the signatories] are motivated by core principles." The brief also emphasized the disconnect between what the federal statute required of companies and the firms' organizational values: "Our principles are not platitudes. Our mission statements are not simply plaques in the lobby. Statements of principle are our agenda for success: born of experience, tested in laboratory, factory, and office, attuned to competition. Our principles reflect, in the truest sense, our business judgment. By force of law, DOMA rescinds that judgment and directs that we renounce these principles or, worse yet, betray them." An even larger number of companies made a similar point, albeit more succinctly, in the corporate amicus brief in *Obergefell:* "The denial of marriage rights to same-sex couples . . . goes against our core values and principles."[45]

In making the case that corporate support for same-sex marriage was not motivated exclusively by economic and business considerations, two academic commentators note that part of what was at issue for some companies in the marriage equality debates were questions of organizational *integrity*, defined "in terms of the consistency between what a company thinks (fundamental values), what it says (communication of values), and what it does (concrete, value-driven behavior)." For these corporations, there came a point when their strong internal commitment to LGBTQ equality no longer permitted them to remain silent on public policy debates related to the place of LGBTQ people, their families, and their relationships in the broader society. To maintain organizational integrity, it became necessary for these companies to take sides on a controversial issue of social policy affecting sexual minorities and transgender individuals. As the authors explain,

> Standing for one's foundational values . . . literally means *to take a stand* for those values, especially when they are threatened. This holds not only toward the inside, but also toward the outside of the company, which brings the "public" aspect of corporate political advocacy into play. A company of integrity, that is, a company that vows to stand for certain foundational values on the inside cannot express indifference when those values are systematically violated in its immediate surroundings, especially so, if the threat to such values in the immediate environment of the company threatens the viability of those very values also within the organization.[46]

True integrity can be assessed by the extent to which entities and individuals speak and act in ways that are consistent with their values. To be consistent with their internal principles, that is, to express and conduct themselves with organizational integrity, some corporations, on the issue of marriage equality, found it necessary to do something that most companies are loath to do: take sides in political debates over controversial social policy issues. Other factors, such as market forces and LGBTQ rights activism aimed at corporations, had encouraged many large companies to adopt measures that promoted LGBTQ equality within corporate walls. But no matter how much companies internally embraced LGBTQ-friendly policies and practices, the reality was that their LGBTQ employees remained vulnerable to discrimination and to the denial of crucial rights and benefits outside those walls. Even if a corporation, for example, provided health insurance to the same-sex partners of its employees, that did not mean those employees or their partners would be protected from discrimination in the provision of medical services or that they would be able to make health-care decisions for each other if one became ill or otherwise incapacitated. For some companies, the disconnect between equal internal benefits and unequal external rights for their LGBTQ employees did not sufficiently raise questions of organizational integrity to justify political advocacy on a contested social issue. But for other companies, doing what they could internally regarding LGBTQ issues to optimize the hiring and retaining of the most qualified employees *was not enough* because for those firms the matters at stake were not just ones of business necessities and financial interests, but also concerned fundamental values of equality and fairness. The LGBTQ issues that implicated those values were not just internal to the companies; instead, the issues spilled over to the setting of public policy.

In making these points, my intent is not to challenge the view that corporations act only in ways that they believe best serve their financial interests. If large corporations had determined that publicly promoting LGBTQ rights would threaten their business interests and profits, they would not have engaged in political activism on behalf of LGBTQ causes. Indeed, it is worth nothing that many of the same corporations that have taken such strong stands on LGBTQ rights issues in the United States have done close to nothing in challenging or criticizing harmful government policies toward sexual minorities and transgender individuals in some of the other countries where they conduct business. Many of those policies, which can include incarceration and government-sponsored violence, are obviously much worse than any of the anti-LGBTQ rights proposals considered recently in conservative jurisdictions in the United States. But to challenge those nation's policies would threaten the ability of multinational corporations to continue to conduct business in those countries. While recent corporate public advocacy on behalf of LGBTQ rights has not imperiled basic corporate interests in places like Arkansas and North Carolina, it might in countries ranging from Uganda to Russia to Saudi Arabia to China. Clearly, then, there are significant limits to how far American corporations are willing to go in advocating for LGBTQ equality.

One way of thinking about all this is to understand the profit motive as a necessary but not sufficient factor in explaining why so many large corporations in the United States have increasingly engaged in public and forceful advocacy on behalf of LGBTQ equality. The decision by many corporations to promote LGBTQ rights has been, as an initial and crucial matter, a business decision based on what corporate executives believe is in the best interests of their firms. But those business judgments have not been *the sole* motivating factor; instead, for at least some corporate leaders, values of diversity, inclusion, and equality have also justified political activism on behalf of LGBTQ rights.

Given that values related to equality and fairness have served as a motivating factor in leading some corporations to politically advocate on behalf of the enactment of LGBTQ antidiscrimination laws and marriage equality, it is fair to ask why those same companies have not also advocated for public policies aimed at reducing or mitigating other forms of social and economic inequality, including ones associated with race and income. There are at least two related reasons for the discrepancy between corporate political activism on

LGBTQ rights and the lack of corporate advocacy on other social issues that also raise questions of equality and fairness. First, the contested LGBTQ rights issues explored in this chapter were directly linked to either the absence of laws (in the case of employment discrimination) or the existence of laws that discriminate on their face (in the case of marriage bans). In both instances, the threat to equality and inclusion in the public sphere could be fixed relatively easily by either enacting or repealing particular laws. In contrast, successfully addressing many other forms of social and economic inequalities requires more complicated policy reforms. For example, it is clear that neither the adoption of the Civil Rights Act of 1964 nor the success in defending at least some forms of affirmative action in the courts— a defense that large corporations have supported—has been enough to address the country's deeply embedded and institutional causes of economic and racial inequality. The apparent absence of "quick fixes" to the structural and society-wide causes of economic and racial inequality have made those topics less appealing subjects of corporate political advocacy.

Second, many forms of pervasive and troubling inequalities in the United States directly raise questions of distributive justice and the corresponding need to consider more robust forms of wealth redistribution, primarily through greater governmental regulation of economic actors and the imposition of higher taxes. And of course, for-profit corporations have traditionally viewed higher levels of government regulation and taxation as being inconsistent with their best interests. In contrast, the recognition by the government of same-sex marriage was never framed or understood as a question that implicated wealth redistribution as such. Furthermore, while legally prohibiting corporate employers from discriminating on the basis of sexual orientation and gender identity constitutes an additional form of government regulation of their enterprises, big companies have by now become largely used to and comfortable with the legal imposition of nondiscrimination obligations.

All this helps explain why it was that for some companies, at least, business considerations were not the sole motivating factor for engaging in public policy advocacy on behalf of LGBTQ rights. It also helps explain why some corporations chose to engage in that advocacy while remaining on the sidelines of other important and pressing social issues, some of which also raised fundamental questions of equality and fairness.

Large corporations in the United States have played crucial roles in expanding legal antidiscrimination protections for queer people and in permitting sexual minorities and transgender individuals across the country to marry the persons of their choice. These important civil rights gains engendered considerable conservative backlash that threatens the basic equality of LGBTQ people. Over the last few years, big companies have also played a leading part in condemning and resisting that backlash.

CHAPTER 6

Corporate Resistance to
Anti-LGBTQ Rights Backlash

THE YEAR 2012 WAS A CRUCIAL ONE for the LGBTQ rights movement in the United States. During that year, Barack Obama became the first sitting president to embrace equal marriage rights for same-sex couples. At about the same time, polls showed that a majority of Americans, for the first time, supported granting same-sex couples the right to marry. In addition, marriage equality supporters, who had won *only one of more than thirty* ballot-box measures in the previous decade, prevailed in all four such measures placed before voters in 2012—in Maine, Maryland, Minnesota, and Washington State. To put it simply, in 2012 the political dynamics of marriage equality debates shifted, with proponents for the first time holding the upper hand.

The next year saw state legislatures in Delaware, Hawai'i, Illinois, Minnesota, and Rhode Island enact statutes granting same-sex couples the opportunity to marry. These legislative victories took place around the same time the movement gained two crucial judicial victories before the US Supreme Court. In the first case, the Court held that supporters of California's Proposition 8, a state constitutional amendment banning same-sex marriages, did not have standing to defend its validity, a ruling that left in place a lower court's judgment that the measure violated the federal Constitution.

In the second case, the Supreme Court held that the federal Defense of Marriage Act was unconstitutional. Between the Court's two pro-marriage equality rulings in 2013 and the end of 2014, more than twenty federal courts throughout the country struck down same-sex marriage bans. As a result, the number of states allowing same-sex couples to marry more than doubled in 2014, increasing from sixteen to thirty-five. By then, it seemed only a matter of time before the LGBTQ rights movement would achieve its objective of attaining marriage equality in all fifty states.[1]

Social and religious conservatives in the last years of marriage inequality in the United States began shifting their tactics. Although many remained steadfastly committed to trying to stop or reverse the marriage equality gains, neither option seemed realistic after 2013. But what did seem possible, especially in conservative states, was to enact laws allowing employers, landlords, and business owners who opposed same-sex marriage on religious grounds to treat sexual minorities differently from heterosexuals. In other words, once it became increasingly clear that their decades-long campaign aimed at preventing the government from recognizing same-sex marriages was headed for defeat across the country, many social and religious conservatives began to try to limit the legal impact and effect of that recognition. As the number of states that allowed same-sex couples to marry grew, social and religious conservatives became more vehement about the need to enact laws exempting those who opposed same-sex marriage on religious grounds from the application of sexual orientation antidiscrimination laws.[2]

Conservative activists between 2014 and 2016 succeeded in persuading five state legislatures (Arizona, Arkansas, Georgia, Indiana, and Mississippi) to enact so-called religious freedom laws in response to the spread of marriage equality. Dozens of large corporations, including highly prominent ones such as Apple, Google, IBM, and Walmart, forcefully objected to the new measures on the ground that they condoned discrimination against LGBTQ individuals. Several companies, as part of their campaigns against the new measures, announced that they were reconsidering plans to invest and create jobs in states with such laws. The strong and unified opposition by corporate America proved to be too much for conservative elected officials, even in deeply red states. As a result, Republican governors in Arizona and Georgia vetoed the so-called religious freedom laws, while the Arkansas and Indiana legislatures rewrote the provisions in ways that no longer authorized employers and others to use religious belief as a defense against discrimination claims. In the end, only Mississippi retained its anti-LGBTQ rights law.

It bears noting that none of the states that adopted, however briefly, so-called religious freedom laws in response to the spread of marriage equality protected LGBTQ people from discrimination. In other words, private employers, landlords, and businesses were already free under the laws of those states to discriminate against queer people, a fact that rendered largely unnecessary a "religious freedom law" that sought to protect defendants in civil lawsuits from discrimination liability. (In contrast, and not surprising, the more liberal states that did have LGBTQ antidiscrimination laws on the books did not consider adopting religious freedom measures that exempted for-profit businesses from those laws.) Nonetheless, if religious freedom laws are used in the ways that many conservatives want them used in states without sexual orientation antidiscrimination laws, they would negatively impact LGBTQ people in two significant ways: first, they would limit the protections afforded by antidiscrimination measures adopted at the local level by municipalities, counties, and school districts; and second, they would limit the application of future state laws protecting LGBTQ individuals against discrimination.

Marriage equality was not the only policy area that saw conservative backlash to LGBTQ rights gains followed by strong corporate resistance to that backlash. Corporate opposition also proved essential in repealing or defeating legal measures aimed at preventing transgender individuals from using public bathrooms that match their gender identity as opposed to the gender they were assigned at birth. The so-called transgender bathroom issue gained national attention after North Carolina enacted such a law in 2016. Large corporations across the country joined forces with civil rights groups and other liberal advocacy organizations to criticize the North Carolina law on the ground that it targeted transgender individuals for discrimination. Some corporations went so far as to announce that they would rescind preexisting plans to invest in North Carolina or refuse to make new plans for such investments. As had happened with the so-called religious freedom laws, corporate activism on behalf of LGBTQ equality in North Carolina proved instrumental in framing the public debate over a law that sought to render queer people second-class citizens. In the end, corporate activism persuaded the Republican-controlled legislature in North Carolina to partially repeal the transgender bathroom law. Similarly, corporate opposition convinced the GOP-dominated Texas legislature to reject a transgender bathroom bill in 2017.

Marriage Equality and Religious Freedom

The first battle over the enactment of a religious liberty statute in the era of same-sex marriage took place in Arizona in 2014. Raising concerns about the impact that the recognition of same-sex marriages would have on the rights of those who objected to gay unions on religious grounds, conservative legislators in Arizona proposed amendments to the state's religious liberty law. Their principal objective was to prevent same-sex couples from bringing discrimination lawsuits against religious business owners who refused to provide them with wedding-related services and goods.

In 1999, Arizona had enacted a statute, called the Religious Freedom Restoration Act (RFRA), which required the state to show that a compelling government interest justified enforcing a law that substantially burdened a person's exercise of religion. In doing so, Arizona joined the federal government and eighteen other states that enacted RFRAs in the 1990s in response to the Supreme Court ruling in *Employment Division v. Smith*. The Court in that case held that the Constitution does not require that the government exempt religious actors from laws that apply broadly to religious and nonreligious actors alike and that do not target the exercise of religion. At issue in *Smith* was whether Native Americans who smoked peyote as part of religious rituals were entitled, under the First Amendment's Free Exercise Clause, to an exemption from the government's criminalization of the use of that controlled substance. The Supreme Court's conclusion that the Constitution did not mandate the granting of exemptions from generally applicable laws—such as the criminal prohibition against the smoking of peyote—was criticized by many across the political spectrum. Conservatives, as a matter of principle, objected to the ruling's lack of vigorous protection for religious freedom; for their part, liberals worried about the decision's impact on religious minorities who lacked the political power to gain exemptions through the legislative process.[3]

The criticism of *Smith* led to widespread support for RFRAs. For example, the federal version was enacted by Congress over the opposition of only three legislators and was signed by President Bill Clinton in 1993. However, it is important to note that when Congress and some state legislatures were considering RFRAs in the 1990s, no one argued that the new laws limited the ability of the government to enforce *antidiscrimination laws*. Instead, RFRA supporters focused on the burdens imposed on religious believers by other types of measures, such as zoning laws that excluded places of worship from residential neighborhoods, regulations requiring autopsies over the religious objections of survivors, road safety regulations that required the Amish to affix lights and bright warning signs on their buggies in violation of their religious principles, and food preparation regulations that impacted some religious groups like Orthodox Jews.

As marriage equality spread across the country, some business owners (including photographers, bakers, and florists) who opposed same-sex marriage on religious grounds contended that sexual orientation antidiscrimination laws could not constitutionally be applied in ways that required them to provide goods and services for same-sex weddings. State courts generally rejected such claims, concluding that operators of businesses open to the general public had to abide by antidiscrimination laws regardless of whether their reasons for refusing to provide the services or goods were religious or secular. Although one of those disputes reached the Supreme Court in 2018, the majority ruled narrowly in the case: it sided with the religious business owner on the ground that two members of a state agency adjudicating the discrimination claim brought by a same-sex couple had expressed hostility toward religion. In doing so, the Court did not address the bigger question of whether the Constitution limits the ways in which antidiscrimination laws can be applied to business owners who object to providing equal treatment on religious grounds.[4]

In response to state court rulings refusing to mandate exemptions from antidiscrimination laws in cases involving religious business owners who refused to provide LGBTQ customers with goods and services, many conservative politicians and activists demanded new laws that would do just that. As already noted, right-wing legislators in Arizona introduced a bill seeking to amend the state's RFRA. The version of that law adopted in 1999 already prohibited the state from placing a substantial burden on a person's exercise of religion unless it showed the existence of a strict necessity. The 2014 amendment sought to expand the definition of "person" to include for-profit businesses. It also would allow individuals and businesses to use their religious beliefs as a defense in private lawsuits, including ones alleging discrimination.

Although Arizona did not have a state law prohibiting sexual orientation discrimination, such discrimination was prohibited by ordinances in three of the state's municipalities. If the proposed bill became law, it would not be possible for LGBTQ plaintiffs to sue under those ordinances when the employers denied them jobs, landlords denied them housing, and business owners denied them goods and services on the ground that they were required to do so by their religious beliefs. Although the new RFRA bill was written using broad and general language that did not mention LGBTQ issues, it was clear that the advent of marriage equality, and the possibility that religious business owners would be forced to provide goods and services to marrying same-sex couples, was the motivating force behind the planned changes in the law.

Introduced during the highly polarized political environment created by the increasingly successful push for marriage equality across the country, the proposed amendment to Arizona's religious freedom statute met strong resistance. Opponents of the measure expressed grave concerns that the proposal's broad language would allow employers, landlords, and businesses to discriminate not only against LGBTQ people, but against other groups as well. Despite the opposition, the Republican-controlled legislature quickly approved the measure and sent it to Republican governor Jan Brewer for her signature.

At this point, corporations took a leading role in opposing the measure. An Apple executive called the governor to urge her to reject the measure (the company at the time was planning to build a big manufacturing plant in Arizona), while the chairman and CEO of American Airlines wrote her a letter praising Arizona's "economic comeback," but noting that "there is genuine concern throughout the business community that this bill, if signed into law, would jeopardize all that has been accomplished so far." The letter added that "our economy thrives when our doors to commerce are open to all. This bill sends the wrong message." Similarly, Delta Air Lines issued a statement opposing recently proposed religious freedom bills because "if passed into law, these proposals would cause significant harm to many people and will result in job losses. They would also violate Delta's core values of mutual respect and dignity." The Arizona Technology Council sent the governor a letter signed by 107 corporations, including American Express, AT&T, and eBay, opposing the measure. For their part, the leaders of four companies that intended to relocate to Arizona contacted the president of the Greater Phoenix Economic Council to tell him that they would have to reconsider their plans if the bill became law.[5]

In the days that followed, the pressure on the governor to veto the bill mounted as civil rights organizations across the country called for a boycott of Arizona. The leaders of several business groups, including the Arizona Chamber of Commerce and Industry and the Phoenix Chamber of Commerce, wrote the governor a joint letter complaining that "the legislation is . . . already clearly having a negative effect on our tourism industry, one of the largest sectors of the economy. The bill could also harm job creation efforts and our ability to attract and retain talent." The Hispanic Bar Association canceled plans to hold its annual meeting, attended by more than two thousand lawyers, in Phoenix. The NFL, which was planning to hold the Super Bowl in Arizona the following year, announced that it would reconsider its decision if the bill became law. Arizona Republican senator John McCain commented that "the entire business community is galvanized in a way that I have never seen against this legislation."[6]

Several days after the measure landed on her desk, Governor Brewer vetoed the bill. In doing so, she complained that the measure had become a distraction from more important matters such as the need for further economic growth. She also stated that although "religious liberty is a core American and Arizona value, so is no discrimination."[7]

Arizona's bill, like other RFRAs proposed in 2014 and 2015 in response to the spread of marriage equality, sought to grant for-profit corporations the ability to raise religious-based objections to avoid antidiscrimination obligations. At around the same time, the Supreme Court was considering a case called *Burwell v. Hobby Lobby*, which raised a similar issue. That dispute centered on a regulation, issued under the Patient Protection and Affordable Care Act of 2010 (known as Obamacare), requiring most employers of more than fifty employees to provide their workers with health insurance coverage that included free access to FDA-approved contraceptives. The owners of the Hobby Lobby Corporation, a large privately held company that operated five hundred arts-and-crafts stores in thirty-nine states, with a workforce of thirteen thousand employees and estimated annual revenues of $2 billion, objected to the use of some contraceptives on religious grounds because they believed them to induce abortions. The corporation argued that the regulation requiring it to help its employees gain access to the contraceptives forced it to facilitate abortions in violation of its religious liberty rights under the federal RFRA.

The Supreme Court, in a highly controversial opinion, agreed with the company and, in the process, ruled that privately held, for-profit corporations could exercise religion within the meaning of the federal religious freedom law. For many liberal and progressive critics, the Court's ruling in *Hobby Lobby* was reminiscent of its highly contentious opinion of a few years earlier, in *Citizens United v. Federal Elections Commission*, striking down limits on the ability of companies to spend corporate funds to influence the outcome of elections. In these cases, critics argued, the Court had sided with the interests of powerful corporations over the interests of women to have free access to contraceptives (in *Hobby Lobby*) and of entities and individuals with limited financial resources whose voices were likely to be drowned out by corporate electioneering expenditures (in *Citizens United*).[8]

Despite their political defeat in Arizona, right-wing activists, growing increasingly concerned about the number of states required by federal courts to allow same-sex couples to marry and spurred on by the Supreme Court's religious-friendly ruling in *Hobby Lobby*, continued to push hard in other conservative states for laws that would exempt religious dissenters from having to abide by LGBTQ equality measures. In response, Republican legislators introduced more than twenty such bills across the country. In 2015, the Arkansas and Indiana legislatures adopted expansive RFRAs. Not coincidentally, federal courts in both states had recently ruled that same-sex marriage bans were unconstitutional.[9]

Opposition to the Indiana measure began to form several months before its passage. As news about the pending bill spread, the Human Rights Campaign, Lambda Legal, and other liberal groups started working with friendly legislators and businesses to oppose it. After consulting with activists, Cummins, a major engine manufacturer in the state valued at over $19 billion, deployed two in-house lobbyists and an outside lobbying firm to try to defeat the measure. LGBTQ activists also lined up corporate opposition to the bill by encouraging the Indiana Chamber of Commerce, the Indianapolis Chamber of Commerce, Alcoa, Eli Lilly, and Salesforce to publicly criticize the measure. Representatives from Cummins and other large companies testified at legislative hearings in opposition to the bill.[10]

Despite corporate opposition, the Republican-controlled legislature approved the measure along party lines and Governor Mike Pence quickly signed it into law. At that point, criticism of the measure grew stronger and louder. Part of the opposition came from expected quarters, such as Democratic elected officials, civil rights leaders, union representatives, and university presidents. But what really caught Indiana Republican leaders by surprise was corporate America's strong and forceful response to the new law. As Pence put it during a news conference shortly after he signed the measure, "Was I expecting this kind of backlash? Heavens no."[11]

Nine big corporations with a significant presence in the state, including Anthem insurance company and Eli Lilly, wrote to Governor Pence and Republican legislative leaders urging them to "take immediate action" to ensure that the Indiana law would not be used to discriminate "based upon sexual orientation or gender identity." In addition, Salesforce and Angie's List took concrete steps to cut back on their Indiana investments; the former canceled all business events in the state, while the latter—whose CEO, Republican William Oesterle, had managed the political campaign of a former GOP governor—canceled a $40 million project, years in the works, to build its corporate headquarters in Indianapolis and to bring more than one thousand jobs to the area. Jeremy Stoppelman, the founder of Yelp, issued a warning to states like Indiana that "it is unconscionable to imagine that Yelp would create, maintain, or expand a significant business presence in any state that encouraged discrimination." Marriott's CEO said in a speech that the legislation was "pure idiocy from a business perspective. . . . The notion that you can tell businesses somehow that they are free to discriminate against people based on who they are is madness." The Human Rights Campaign released a statement signed by American Airlines, Microsoft, Wells

Fargo, and six other large corporations denouncing efforts across the country to condone discrimination against LGBTQ people in the name of religious freedom. Lobbyists for the manufacturing, health care, and tourism industries in Indiana complained to legislators that the new law was terrible for business. Several months later, Indianapolis reported that the controversy over the state's RFRA had cost the city more than $60 million in convention business.[12]

It is important to note that the negative and forceful corporate response to the Indiana law did not occur by happenstance. Instead, it was the result of months of close work between LGBTQ activists and corporations in opposition to the measure. As *Time* magazine explained, "Without the close alliance between big Indiana businesses and liberal activists, the national outcry . . . over Indiana's new law could have been just a muffled whimper." The vice president of the Human Rights Campaign added, "This was a moment years in the making. The reason we are able to rely on this level of corporate support now is [because] we've cultivated this garden for a long time."[13]

It would be a mistake, therefore, to view corporate political activism on behalf of LGBTQ equality in Indiana and elsewhere as isolated from and independent of the work of LGBTQ groups and other advocacy organizations, at both the national and the grassroots levels. Although the media and the public were paying considerable attention to LGBTQ corporate political activism, it was only one component—an admittedly important one—of the advocacy work done by a broader coalition of organizations that sought to defeat anti-LGBTQ rights measures. It would also be incorrect to claim that corporations at around this time became "leaders" in advancing LGBTQ rights. It is more accurate to say that corporations followed the lead and adopted many positions articulated by LGBTQ groups and other advocacy organizations on issues involving LGBTQ equality in the public sphere. What made corporate advocacy on behalf of LGBTQ equality particularly distinctive was that it was more likely to be discussed and analyzed by the media and the public, while more likely to be noticed, followed, and heeded by elected officials, especially Republican politicians in conservative states.

It was not only large for-profit corporations and liberal groups that criticized the new Indiana law. The NCAA, which has its headquarters in Indianapolis and was about to hold its men's basketball Final Four tournament there, also expressed displeasure with the law and raised the possibility of no longer holding tournaments in the state. NASCAR released a statement expressing that it "was disappointed by the recent legislation passed in Indiana. We will not embrace nor participate in exclusion or intolerance." The *Indianapolis Star* newspaper published a rare front-page editorial with the headline, in large letters, "FIX THIS NOW" that warned the governor that "Indiana is in a state of crisis."[14]

As the pressure mounted, Governor Pence and Republican legislators scrambled to address the political firestorm by holding meetings with business leaders and others to discuss how (not whether) to modify the statute. Less than a week after the law came into effect, the legislature amended it by explicitly stating that it did not authorize businesses to deny employment, housing, goods, and services on the basis of several traits, including race, sex, religion, disability, sexual orientation, and gender identity.

The Arkansas RFRA met a similar fate after it was approved by the state legislature. Republican governor Asa Hutchinson, who initially expressed support for the bill, backtracked following loud corporate opposition. Walmart, the largest private employer in Arkansas (and the country), opposed the bill before it was approved by the legislature, and then, after it passed, urged Hutchinson to veto it. As Walmart's CEO explained on the company's Twitter account, the measure "threatens to undermine the spirit of inclusion present throughout the state of Arkansas and does not reflect the values we proudly uphold." The large data company Acxium, based in Little Rock, also demanded a veto, complaining in a letter to the governor that the measure was "a deliberate vehicle for enabling discrimination" and that "simply stated, this bill inflicts pain on some of our citizens and disgrace upon us all." For his part, Apple's Tim Cook, the first CEO of a Fortune 500 company to publicly identify as gay, wrote an op-ed in the *Washington Post* criticizing the measures approved by the Indiana and Arkansas legislatures: "Our message, to people around the country and around the world, is this: Apple is open. Open to everyone, regardless of where they come from, what they look like, how they worship or who they love. Regardless of what the law might allow in Indiana or Arkansas, we will never tolerate discrimination."[15]

In the face of strong opposition by large corporations and others, Governor Hutchinson asked the legislature to make changes to the bill. The legislators quickly did so, adopting a new version that contained two crucial modifications: first, it did not expressly allow for the religious freedom law to be used as a defense in private litigation; and second, it did not include corporations within the meaning of a "person" protected by the statute.

Georgia legislators in 2016 also enacted a RFRA to protect the ability of businesses operated by religious conservatives to refuse to serve LGBTQ people. A coalition of almost five hundred big and small companies based in Georgia, including Coca-Cola, Delta Air Lines, and Home Depot, criticized the bill for condoning discrimination. The Walt Disney Company and Marvel Studios, both of which routinely filmed movies in the state, threatened to take their business elsewhere "should any legislation allowing discriminatory practices be signed into state law." Viacom urged the governor to "resist and reject the patently discriminatory law being proposed." For its part, the NFL warned that if the measure became law, it would imperil its willingness to choose Atlanta as a site for future Super Bowls. In the face of strong and pervasive corporate opposition, the Republican governor vetoed the bill.[16]

Corporate opposition also proved crucial in making sure that similar bills were not approved by state legislatures to begin with. In Texas, for example, the Texas Association of Business—the state's chamber of commerce—took the lead in opposing that state's RFRA bill. (The same group, as we will soon see, was instrumental in defeating a transgender bathroom bill in 2017.) More than 250

Texas corporations, including American Airlines, Dell, and Texas Instruments, went on the record opposing the bill and pledging to treat their LGBTQ employees equally and fairly.[17]

In the end, the only state that enacted and retained an expansive so-called religious freedom law in response to marriage equality was Mississippi. That state's law, adopted in 2016, is particularly problematic because it—unlike other RFRAs, which aim to protect religious exercise *regardless of the nature of the religious beliefs motivating that exercise*—seeks to protect only three particular religious views, all of which are closely associated with anti-LGBTQ rights positions. The three religious beliefs that are given special protection under the Mississippi law are (1) that marriage should be between a man and a woman; (2) that sexual conduct should only take place within marriage; and (3) that "male (man) or female (woman) refer to an individual's immutable biological sex as objectively determined by anatomy and genetics at time of birth."[18]

From an LGBTQ rights perspective, the Mississippi law is, by far, the broadest religious exemption measure ever adopted by an American jurisdiction. The statute prohibits the government from "discriminating" against businesses that refuse to provide their goods and services for the celebration of marriages that are inconsistent with the three protected religious beliefs. The statute also allows providers to refuse to make services related to gender transition, psychological counseling, or infertility that are inconsistent with the religious views protected by the statute. In addition, the law allows clerks, judges, and justices of the peace to refuse to issue marriage licenses to LGBTQ individuals while continuing to provide them for different-sex couples. Although a federal district court initially struck down the statute as unconstitutional, a court of appeals later overturned that ruling on the ground that the plaintiffs lacked standing to challenge the law.[19]

Corporations and business groups, including Dow Chemical, IBM, Nissan, PepsiCo, Toyota, Tyson Foods, the Mississippi Manufacturers Association, and the Mississippi Economic Council, joined Democrats, civil rights groups, and LGBTQ activists in speaking out against the Mississippi measure. However, big businesses in that largely rural state did not seem to enjoy the same political influence as they had in other conservative states—such as Arizona, Arkansas, Georgia, and Indiana—with greater corporate footprints. While business opposition in other states was effective in dividing Republican elected officials between those who were sensitive to businesses' concerns and those who prioritized socially conservative views, few GOP elected officials in Mississippi seemed to care about corporate objections to the new religious freedom law.

But Mississippi proved to be the exception to the rule. In the other Republican-controlled states, business opposition proved to be crucial in governors vetoing of legislation intended to protect for-profit entities from LGBTQ antidiscrimination obligations, or the watering down of the measures, or the defeating of the bills. As marriage equality was expanding to all fifty states, corporate opposition proved to be crucial in blocking broad legislative proposals intended to significantly limit the scope of laws and regulations, either those already enacted or those that might be enacted in the future, protecting LGBTQ people against discrimination.

There were two main reasons why corporate opposition to RFRAs proved to be so important in defeating or weakening religious freedom bills introduced in the wake of the nationwide expansion of marriage equality. The first was the political influence of large corporations in Republican-controlled states. It bears noting that Republicans held the governorships and enjoyed large majorities in the legislatures of all five states (Arizona, Arkansas, Georgia, Indiana, and Mississippi) that approved the measures in question. It is clear that traditional liberal organizations, such as the minority Democratic Party, civil rights groups, and unions, could not have on their own defeated or weakened the measures in those GOP-dominated states. The positive outcomes for the LGBTQ movement in four out of the five states required the intervention of large corporations and their top executives.

Many of these same firms and individuals were committed supporters and funders of Republican candidates. Indeed, several of the locally based corporations that took the lead in opposing RFRAs were among the most important financial backers of the GOP officials whom they sought to persuade. For example, the employees and political action committees of the Indiana-based Cummins corporation, which lobbied against the bill before it became law and then later pushed Governor Pence to work to repeal it, gave more money (a combined total of $78,000) to Pence's earlier congressional campaigns than any other corporation. For his part, Angie's List CEO William Oesterle, who announced that his company was canceling plans to build its new headquarters in Indianapolis shortly after Pence signed the bill into law, had several years earlier donated $150,000 to Pence's gubernatorial campaign. Furthermore, the employees and political action committees of Eli Lilly, one of the Indiana companies most forcefully opposed to the anti-LGBTQ law, had given Pence a combined total of almost $65,000 for his earlier congressional campaigns. In fact, of the nine Indiana companies that signed a public letter to Pence criticizing him for signing the bill and urging him to work with the legislature to repeal it, six had donated money to his political campaigns. It stands to reason that conservative politicians like Pence, who were already ideologically aligned with business interests, would be especially attuned and sensitive to the perspectives and preferences of their most important corporate supporters.[20]

The second reason why corporate opposition to RFRAs enacted in response to marriage equality proved to be so important in defeating or weakening them was that the companies played a crucial role in framing the policy issues at stake as questions of *discrimination* rather than of religious liberty. The measures in question seemed to pit two sets of values—equality and religious freedom—that most Americans like to believe they are committed to. In the end, the LGBTQ rights movement largely succeeded in defeating or weakening the proposed statutes because a majority of the population following the public debates came to view them as measures that promoted discrimination rather than, as their supporters insisted, laws that protected religious liberty. During the 2014–2016 period, representatives of the country's most influential and widely admired companies issued countless statements and gave scores of interviews and speeches repeatedly emphasizing the same basic point: the proposed laws should be rejected because they condoned discrimination against LGBTQ individuals, and such discrimination was inconsistent with their firms' business interests and corporate values. In the end, that steady corporate drumbeat overwhelmed social and religious conservatives' efforts to persuade the public that the proposed laws were only meant to protect the rights of religious entities and individuals and were not intended to encourage discrimination against anyone.

Of course, it was not just corporations that complained about the discriminatory intent and impact of the proposed laws. Many liberal groups and advocates did the same. But those progressive voices had limited influence in the conservative states that seriously considered RFRAs between 2014 and 2016. It was corporations' participation in the public debates over the meaning and purpose of the proposed measures that, in the end, made the difference and accounted for their defeat or weakening.

Finally, it bears noting that although the LGBTQ rights movement so far has largely succeeded in blocking conservatives' efforts to push for broad religious exemptions benefiting for-profit entities, it has been less successful in preventing the adoption of more limited religious freedom laws. For example, states such as North Carolina and Utah have adopted laws that allow county clerks and magistrates to recuse themselves, due to religious objections, from performing marriages. (Unlike the Mississippi law discussed earlier, however, these provisions do not allow government officials to choose to marry heterosexual couples but not same-sex ones; instead, the excused officials must refrain from performing *all* marriages.) In addition, states such as Michigan and South Dakota have enacted laws that permit private adoption agencies to use religious beliefs to refuse to place children in households headed by LGBTQ individuals. These more limited religious freedom laws do not protect for-profit entities and therefore have not been the subject of corporate scrutiny and criticism. The lack of corporate opposition has made it politically possible for some states to enact these narrower types of laws over the strong objections of LGBTQ groups and their liberal allies.

Corporations and Transgender Rights

Karen Ulane flew combat airplanes for the US Army in Vietnam between 1964 and 1968. A few months after leaving the military, Ulane got a job as a pilot for Eastern Airlines. Ten years later, she took a sick leave from the airline in order to have gender confirmation surgery (also known as sex reassignment surgery). When word about the surgery spread throughout the company, several pilots told their bosses that they would refuse to fly with a transgender pilot. When Ulane attempted to return to her job, the airline fired her because of the unwillingness of others to work with her and the supposed fear that her "condition" would instill in passengers already nervous about flying. Eastern's termination letter also complained that

> to the extent that the operation and the counseling you have undergone have been successful in changing your essential nature from male to female, it has changed you from the person Eastern hired into a different person. You have deliberately and voluntarily undergone this change. No Karen F. Ulane appears on Eastern's seniority list. Eastern would not have hired you had it known you contemplated or might in the future contemplate such an action. By your action, you have severed the employment relationship that existed between Eastern and [you].[21]

Ulane sued the airline, contending that it had violated Title VII's prohibition of employment discrimination on the basis of sex when it fired her. Although a federal trial judge agreed and ordered reinstatement and back pay and other damages exceeding $150,000, a court of appeals reversed that ruling, reasoning that discrimination against transgender individuals had nothing to do with discrimination on the basis of sex. In doing so, the court overlooked the fact that the company, in firing Ulane because she was a woman while being willing to retain her on the job if she had continued to identify as a man, could not have engaged in a clearer form of sex discrimination: what the company in effect told Ulane was "we will retain you if you are a man, but we will fire you if you are a woman." More recent rulings from some federal courts of appeals and the Equal Employment Opportunity Commission have recognized that discrimination against transgender individuals is, in fact, a form of sex discrimination.[22]

In 1985, Boeing fired a transgender female engineer—who was contemplating but had not yet undergone gender surgery—after she insisted in using the company's female bathrooms and wearing feminine clothes to work. Although Boeing claimed it was willing to accommodate the employee after the surgery, it warned her that the company would fire her if she persisted in expressing her femininity at work before the surgery. As for what constituted improperly feminine attire, the company explained that "her attire would be deemed unacceptable when, in the supervisor's opinion, her dress would be likely to cause a complaint were she to use a men's rest room at a Boeing facility." Shortly after that, Boeing fired the engineer when she reported to work wearing a strand of pink pearls that her supervisor believed was "excessively feminine."[23]

The transgender engineer sued Boeing, claiming that the company had violated Washington State's prohibition against discrimination on the basis of disability. The state supreme court eventually rejected that claim, concluding that Boeing fired her not because of her gender dysphoria, but because she violated the employer's rules on acceptable workplace attire. In doing so, the court failed to recognize that the company had treated the plaintiff differently from other female employees given that they were not penalized for wearing feminine clothing. The only thing that distinguished the plaintiff from the other female employees was that she was assigned the male gender at birth and they were not.

The lawsuits brought by transgender plaintiffs against Eastern Airlines and Boeing represented only two of many instances in which companies during the 1970s and 1980s fired employees because of their gender identities. The two cases also reflect how transgender plaintiffs consistently failed to persuade courts that they were protected by statutes that prohibited discrimination on the basis of either sex or disability.[24] In addition, federal law then, as now, does not explicitly prohibit employment discrimination on the basis of gender identity. Minnesota, the first state to prohibit such discrimination, did not do so until 1993. It was not until 2001 that a second state, Rhode Island, did the same. As late as 2010, only a dozen states had laws that explicitly prohibited employment discrimination against transgender individuals.

Despite the lack of clear legal obligations to do so, a growing number of large corporations after the turn of the century began to accommodate and protect the interests of their transgender employees. Most companies that did so had already implemented policies prohibiting discrimination on the basis of sexual orientation and were already offering domestic partnership benefits to their lesbian, gay, and bisexual employees. For these corporations, offering protections to their transgender employees constituted the natural next step in advancing equality and promoting diversity in their workplaces.

The Human Rights Campaign in 2001 identified only twenty private employers in the country, including five Fortune 500 companies (American Airlines, Apple, Lexmark International, Lucent Technologies, and Xerox), that had gender identity nondiscrimination policies. In its 2002 *Corporate Equality Index* rating of 318 companies, including 208 Fortune 500 companies, HRC found that while 92 percent had nondiscrimination policies on the basis of sexual orientation, only 5 percent had a gender identity nondiscrimination policy. The percentages of *Index*-rated companies with such policies increased almost twofold in each of the four years that followed: to 9 percent in 2003; 16 percent in 2004; 28 percent in 2005; and 46 percent in 2006. By 2010, the percentage of rated companies with gender identity antidiscrimination policies had increased to 72 percent and by 2014 the percentage of *Index*-rated companies with such policies reached 86 percent. That number, which included 305 (61 percent) of the Fortune 500 companies, represented the highest level of growth since 2002 in any of the criteria used by HRC to assess private employers' commitment to LGBTQ equality. By 2018, 83 percent of Fortune 500 companies prohibited discrimination on the basis of gender identity.[25]

At first, the only transgender-related criterion that was part of the *Index* ranking process was whether corporations had gender identity antidiscrimination policies. But the *Index* later also studied whether corporations provided at least one transgender-inclusive health-care benefit, such as mental health counseling; medical benefits for hormone treatments; and leaves of absences and medical benefits for surgical procedures. The number of Fortune 500 companies with at least one such benefit increased from 49 (10 percent) in 2009 to 206 (41 percent) in 2012 to 340 (68 percent) in 2014 to 395 (79 percent) in 2018.

Similar to what had happened with issues involving sexual orientation, some of the corporations that had adopted internal transgender-friendly policies also later became advocates for transgender rights in the public sphere. Several large corporations publicly advocated for the enactment of federal and state laws prohibiting employment discrimination on the basis of gender identity. And many of the same large corporations that responded to the backlash against marriage equality gains by publicly campaigning against the adoption of RFRAs intended to counteract that equality also came out forcefully against so-called transgender bathroom laws.

After the turn of the century, as a growing number of states and municipalities started enacting laws prohibiting discrimination on the basis of gender identity, some opponents of LGBTQ rights began to raise spurious concerns that such laws threatened the privacy and safety of bathroom users. It was these concerns that led to the introduction of so-called transgender bathroom bills in about twenty states across the country.

Opponents of transgender antidiscrimination laws claimed, without any basis of fact, that transgender antidiscrimination measures encouraged sexual assaults and harassment in bathrooms. But, of course, laws that criminalized sexual assaults were already on the books. It was also already illegal to enter bathrooms for the purpose of harming or harassing others. Gender identity antidiscrimination laws did not in any way affect or weaken the enforcement of these preexisting laws. Proponents of new bathroom laws could not point to a single incident in which an antidiscrimination law was used as an excuse or justification to engage in illegal conduct in bathrooms. In contrast, there were multiple reports of transgender people being physically assaulted and verbally abused for using bathrooms that matched their gender identity but not their assigned sex at birth.[26]

Although opponents of transgender antidiscrimination laws rallied around the provocative slogan of keeping "men out of women's bathrooms," the reality is that allowing individuals to use bathrooms that match their gender identity does nothing more than allow transgender *women*, for example, to use bathrooms designated to be used by women. What many opponents were really contending was that transgender women were not *real women*, but were instead "men who claim to be women," as the Republican state legislator in Tennessee who introduced a bathroom bill put it. In other words, in pushing for discriminatory, unnecessary, and harmful bathroom laws, opponents were denying or ignoring the very existence of transgender people.[27]

The issue of bathroom use by transgender individuals was the subject of much public attention and debate in Houston in 2015. The year before, the city had become the last major American city to enact an antidiscrimination ordinance; with the support of Houston's openly lesbian mayor, the city council approved a measure prohibiting employers, landlords, and businesses from discriminating on the basis of fifteen protected classes, including race, sex, disability, age, religion, military status, sexual orientation, and gender identity. The following year, conservative activists succeeded in placing before voters a ballot initiative seeking to repeal the civil rights ordinance. The law's opponents, in pushing to repeal a broad civil rights measure that protected, among other things, against racial and religious discrimination, relied exclusively on the purported dangers associated with allowing individuals to use public bathrooms according to their gender identity rather than the sex they were assigned at birth.

In one radio ad sponsored by supporters of the ballot initiative, an unidentified woman claimed she was afraid to raise children in Houston because the new ordinance allowed men to use women's bathrooms, and that their doing so was "filthy," "disgusting," and "unsafe." In a television ad, Lance Berkman, a former baseball star with the Houston Astros, claimed he was worried that his wife and four daughters might be attacked in bathrooms by "troubled men" because of the civil rights ordinance. Another television ad, funded by opponents of the civil rights law, showed a man entering a bathroom and hiding in a stall. After a young girl wearing a school backpack entered the bathroom, the man burst into the girl's stall and closed the door behind him. The narrator then warned viewers that the "bathroom ordinance" (the civil rights law) would allow "any man at any time [to] enter a woman's bathroom simply by claiming to be a woman that day." For his part, a former chairman of the local Republican Party, who was a leading opponent of the civil rights law, claimed that it "clearly allows biological males and even registered sex offenders to enter female showers, bathrooms or locker rooms. We're not willing to compromise the safety of our wives, our mothers and our daughters on the altar of political correctness."[28]

After Houston residents overwhelmingly voted to repeal the civil rights ordinance by a margin of 61 to 39 percent, Dan Patrick, the state's Republican lieutenant governor, told a cheering crowd gathered at a Houston hotel on election night that the campaign had been about "protecting our grandmoms, and our mothers and our wives and our sisters and our daughters and our granddaughters. I'm glad Houston led tonight to end this constant political-correctness attack on what we know in our heart and our gut as Americans is not right."[29]

By the time of the Houston vote in 2015, seventeen states and more than two hundred municipalities had enacted laws prohibiting gender-identity discrimination. In 2016, Charlotte became the first municipality in North Carolina to adopt such a measure, approving an ordinance that prohibited city contractors and places of public accommodation from discriminating on the basis of sexual orientation and gender identity. The Charlotte ordinance was attacked by many religious and social conservatives in the state who, like their brethren in Houston, relied on spurious claims about bathroom privacy and safety. A few weeks later, the Republican-controlled state legislature enacted a law prohibiting municipalities from providing antidiscrimination protection to classes of individuals left unprotected by state law. This meant that since no state statute prohibited discrimination on the basis of either sexual orientation or gender identity, no municipality in the state could provide that protection through its own laws. But the new North Carolina law went even further by including a provision, the first of its kind in the country, which made it illegal for public agencies and schools to allow individuals to use bathrooms and changing facilities that did not correspond to their biological sex as stated on their birth certificates.

The North Carolina measure was approved in a special legislative session that lasted only twelve hours. The bill received unanimous support from Republicans—senate Democrats walked out to protest the irresponsible speed with which the chamber considered the measure—and was signed that same day by Republican governor Pat McCrory. In the days that followed, civil rights groups and corporations issued statements and used social media to criticize the new law. American Airlines (which employed fourteen thousand people in the state) and Bank of America (which is headquartered in Charlotte), along with other companies with operations in the state, including Apple, Biogen, Dow Chemical, and Facebook, strongly objected to the legislation. The CEO of PayPal, which had recently broken ground for a new operations center in Charlotte, announced that it was canceling its planned $3.6 million investment in the center.

PayPal was not the only company to reconsider investing in facilities and jobs in the state. For example, CoStar, a commercial real estate information company, backed out of negotiations to bring 700 jobs to the Charlotte area and instead took the jobs to Virginia; Deutsche Bank scuttled plans to bring 250 jobs to Raleigh; Adidas announced that it was going to build its first shoe factory in the United States near Atlanta rather than in North Carolina because of the new law; and Voxpro, a customer service company, chose to hire one hundred customer service representatives in Georgia and not in North Carolina because, as its founder and CEO put it, "we couldn't set up operations in a state that was discriminating against LGBT people." A study conducted by the Associated Press in 2017 estimated that the bathroom law would cost North Carolina $3.7 billion in lost business over the next twelve years.[30]

In the month following the adoption of the controversial law, organizers canceled more than twenty conventions in North Carolina, costing the state about $2.5 million in revenue. For its part, the national retailer Target, in response to the furor created by the North Carolina measure, announced that it would allow transgender employees and customers to choose bathrooms and fitting rooms that matched their gender identity. A group of fifty-three large investors, including Morgan Stanley Investments and RBC Wealth Management, with more than $2 trillion in combined assets, issued a public letter denouncing the North Carolina law and calling it "bad for business."[31]

Big companies were not the only entities that strongly objected to the law. The NAACP called for a national economic boycott of the state. And, in a particularly painful blow to a college basketball–loving state, the NCAA relocated championship tournament games scheduled to be played in North Carolina during the 2016–2017 academic year, including those that would have been part of the Division I men's basketball tournament. The NCAA also warned the state that if it did not rescind its controversial new law, North Carolina could lose the opportunity to host the association's sporting events through 2022. The Atlantic Coast Conference—which includes North Carolina State University, the University of North Carolina, and Duke University—followed the NCAA's lead by moving all its athletic championship tournaments out of the state because of the anti-LGBTQ law. For its part, the NBA moved its All-Star game from Charlotte to New Orleans. Bruce Springsteen, Pearl Jam, Ringo Starr, and Cirque du Soleil, among other performers, canceled shows in the state. More than twenty cities and five states (including New York and Washington) prohibited their employees from traveling to North Carolina on government business.

Governor McCrory tried to quell the furor over the transgender bathroom law by signing an executive order affording state employees protection from discrimination on the basis of sexual orientation and gender identity. But this step did not satisfy opponents of the bathroom law; for them, nothing short of repeal of the blatantly discriminatory law would do. LGBTQ plaintiffs and the Obama administration separately sued North Carolina, arguing that the law violated the Constitution and federal statutes. Roy Cooper, the Democratic state attorney general who was running for governor, agreed with these claims and refused to defend the bathroom law in the courts. A few months later, Cooper defeated McCrory in a razor-thin gubernatorial election, a victory widely understood to reflect voters' discontent with the national backlash against the state engendered by the transgender bathroom bill.

A few weeks after the 2016 election, Charlotte repealed its anti-discrimination ordinance in a failed attempt to reach a compromise with Republican state legislators. But in 2017, those legislators and Cooper reached a compromise whereby the legislature repealed the controversial bathroom law while at the same time (1) placing a moratorium on new local antidiscrimination ordinances until 2020 and (2) requiring that future regulation of bathroom use be done by the state legislature rather than by local officials. Most LGBTQ groups and activists appropriately criticized the compromise because it left queer people throughout the state without antidiscrimination protections and without the ability to gain them for several years. But at least the infamous transgender bathroom measure was no longer the law. As had happened with other anti-LGBTQ measures enacted in conservative states in recent years, most commentators agreed that business opposition to the North Carolina law proved crucial to its eventual demise.

It should be pointed out that, as had happened in other states, many corporate critics of the North Carolina law had helped fund the political campaigns of the Republican legislators who voted for the bill and of the Republican governor who signed it into law. The corporations did so by contributing to so-called super PACs, such as the Republican State Leadership Committee and the Republican Governors Association. One report concluded that thirty-six companies that came out against the law (including Bank of America, Citigroup, Google, and Pfizer) had given a combined $10.8 million to those two super PACs in recent election cycles. The PACs then spent some of that money to "help elect five of the bill's sponsors, 13 other legislators who voted for it, and governor McCrory."[32]

From an LGBTQ rights perspective, it is obviously problematic for corporations to help fund the campaigns of politicians who support anti-LGBTQ laws. That funding reflects the ways in which campaigns for public office in this country have become beholden to the financial interests of corporations, especially after the Supreme Court in *Citizens United* struck down a federal campaign law aimed at limiting corporate electioneering spending in the weeks leading up to elections. It is nothing less than shameful and hypocritical for large American businesses and their top executives, many of whom repeatedly insist they are committed to LGBTQ equality, to continue to be the most important funders of Republican politicians who support anti-LGBTQ laws, presumably because those individuals also support antiregulatory and other corporate-friendly policies.

The continued corporate funding of anti-LGBTQ politicians exposes some of the important limits of corporate support for queer equality. It is essential, going forward, that LGBTQ activists pressure companies not only to oppose anti-LGBTQ bills after they are proposed, but also to cease giving money to politicians who sponsor and endorse those measures. It is not enough, as happened in North

Carolina, for large corporations to wait until *after* anti-LGBTQ laws are adopted to complain to the officials they helped elect about the discriminatory impact of the measures enacted by those very same officials. It is crucial that progressives pay greater attention to the political funding decisions of leading American companies in order to publicize and condemn their continued financial support for elected officials who support anti-LGBTQ measures. In the end, corporations that fund the campaigns of anti-LGBTQ politicians, such as those who supported the North Carolina bathroom law, are subsidizing bigotry and prejudice.

Corporate opposition to a proposed transgender bathroom measure was also crucial to its defeat in Texas. In 2016, Lieutenant Governor Patrick called for the enactment of a bathroom law that would prohibit cities and counties from telling private businesses which bathroom policies to adopt. The measure also sought to prohibit individuals from using their gender identity, as opposed to their biologically assigned sex, in choosing which restrooms, showers, and locker rooms to use in government buildings and public schools. As Patrick put it, when speaking in support of what he dubbed the "Women's Privacy Act," if municipalities, counties, or school districts in the state enacted regulations protecting transgender people from discrimination, it would "allow men to go into a bathroom because of the way they feel [and] we will not be able to stop sexual predators from taking advantage of that law, like sexual predators take advantage of the internet."[33] At around the same time, Patrick led a group of officials from thirteen conservative states in legally challenging an Obama administration's policy guideline warning public schools that they would violate Title IX if they barred transgender students from using bathrooms that matched their gender identity. The Trump administration later rescinded that guideline.

In response to calls by Patrick and other state Republican leaders for a transgender bathroom law, a group of five hundred small businesses in Texas wrote an open letter to state legislators urging them to reject such a measure. As the letter explained, "We oppose any Texas legislation—broad or narrow—that would legalize discrimination against any group. That kind of legislation doesn't just go against our values to be welcoming to everyone, it [also] jeopardizes the businesses we've worked so hard to create, and it threatens the jobs and livelihoods of everyday Texans." For their part, the board of directors of the Texas Association of Business (TAB)—the state's most powerful business group, representing companies with a combined two million employees and $8 billion in assets—approved legislative priorities that called for opposing both RFRAs that permitted discrimination and transgender bathroom laws. The TAB also commissioned researchers at the Austin-based St. Edwards University to study the economic impact on the state if the legislature enacted either type of law.[34]

The study concluded that the Texas economy could lose up to $8.5 billion and 185,000 jobs due to corporate cutbacks in investments if the legislature adopted anti-LGBTQ rights measures. In announcing the release of the study at a press conference, the TAB president stated, "We now face overwhelming data about the risk of damage to the economy and reputation of our great state resulting from legislation that would allow for discrimination. Businesses from across Texas have come together to urge the Texas Legislature to reject discrimination and embrace public policy that keeps Texas open for business."[35]

Not surprisingly, TAB's study was not well received by LGBTQ rights opponents. As one recently elected Republican state legislator put it, "The TAB is known for shamelessly pushing crony capitalism, but they generally stay away from the hot buttons. Well now the phony pro-business group in Texas has finally showed its true colors and wants to open business owners up to fines and lawsuits if they don't give troubled men unfettered access to women's bathrooms."[36]

After the regular 2017 legislative session ended without the bathroom bill being adopted into law, Republican governor Greg Abbott called a special legislative session to consider that measure (along with others). But, as the *New York Times* reported, "a barrage of corporate advertising and activism has the potential to sink legislation restricting transgender bathroom use that has been a flash point in the state's culture wars." The newspaper noted that although liberal religious groups and transgender advocates were part of the coalition that opposed the bill, it was "big business [that] has been a dominant force throughout the debate." In addition to the TAB, fifty Fortune 500 companies, including many with a significant presence in Texas—such as American Airlines, Apple, Capital One, IBM, Intel, Southwest Airlines, and United Airlines—came out against the proposed legislation.[37]

The corporate strategy in opposition to the Texas bill "included a seven-figure radio ad buy, strategically targeted letters signed by prominent chief executives, lobbying blitzes throughout the Capitol and rallies on the Capitol grounds." IBM alone took out two full-page ads in Texas newspapers the day before the special legislative session started opposing the bill; the company also brought in some of its top executives to meet with Republican legislative leaders and the governor to express their displeasure with the proposed law. The Republican chair of the House of Representatives committee to which the bill was sent put it this way: "Corporate America is stepping forward, speaking loudly about the fact that this will have a chilling effect on business opportunity in this state. I'm hearing from many major corporations about this bill and the effect it will have."[38]

A representative of the conservative Texas Pastor Council expressed great frustration at the powerful and effective corporate activism against the bathroom bill: "I don't think anybody has seen corporations engage on an issue like this outside the framework of taxes and regulations in our memory. I think it's a combination of a rising moral bankruptcy in corporate America, in which the only thing they support is their image and their bottom line." For its part, the Family Research Council put out a video campaign titled Big Business Hypocrisy criticizing large companies for demanding that "Texas expose women and children to policies that could endanger them in the most private of places" while refusing to "enact the same unsafe policies in their own facilities."[39]

The strong and negative reaction by many on the right to corporate political activism on behalf of LGBTQ equality reflected the growing tension between two traditional supporters of the Republican Party: business executives and social conservatives, a tension that left GOP elected officials awkwardly in the middle. As the journalist James Surowiecki explained in the *New Yorker*, "To many conservative business leaders, today's social-conservative agenda looks anachronistic and is harmful to the bottom line; it makes it hard to hire and keep talented employees who won't tolerate discrimination. Social conservatives, meanwhile, think that Republican leaders are sacrificing Christian principles in order to keep big business happy."[40]

In the end, opponents prevailed in defeating the Texas bill, which was never even scheduled for a vote in the House of Representatives. Corporate political activism overwhelmed the influence of social and religious groups and activists even in a deeply red state such as Texas, where traditional conservatives have dominated politics for decades. There is little doubt that *but for* corporate opposition to the bathroom bill, it would have become the law in Texas. Without corporations, the coalition of liberal groups in the state that objected to the bathroom law would not have had the political clout to defeat the measure on its own.

The legislative defeats of anti-LGBTQ rights measures in states like Arizona, Indiana, Georgia, North Carolina, and Texas seemed to take the political momentum away from socially conservative activists in red states, activists who had spent years working to amass large Republican majorities in state legislatures. As the *New York Times* put it in 2018, "With elections looming and major corporations watching, the social issues that have provoked bitter fights in recent years across the conservative South—including restroom access for transgender people and so-called religious freedom measures—are gaining little legislative momentum in statehouses this year. . . . A combination of fear, fatigue and legislative mathematics appear to be behind the shift. Many people believe that states have grown wary of provoking a pronounced corporate backlash like the one North Carolina experienced in 2016."[41]

There were examples of this new political dynamic involving

transgender rights in several conservative states. In South Carolina, a transgender bathroom law, opposed by Republican governor Nikki Haley, languished in a legislative committee for more than a year. In South Dakota, the Republican governor—who admitted he had never knowingly met a transgender person—vetoed a bill that would have required public school students to use bathrooms that matched their assigned sex at birth. In doing so, he emphasized the strong opposition to the bill by Citigroup and Wells Fargo, two important employers in the state. And in Tennessee, a lawmaker who introduced a similar measure withdrew the proposal after only one week.

Two years earlier, the CEO of Scripps Networks Interactive, a major employer in Tennessee, had told employees that his company would "consider re-evaluating future investment" in the state if the legislature approved a then pending bill that would require transgender students at public schools and universities to use bathrooms that corresponded to their assigned gender at birth. The proposed bill, the CEO explained, "runs entirely contrary to the core values on which this company was founded." In addition, sixty companies, including Airbnb, Alcoa, Dow Chemical, Hewlett Packard, and Williams-Sonoma, working with the Human Rights Campaign, had sent a letter to the Republican Speaker of the House and the Senate president expressing their opposition to the bill.[42]

In short, the strong corporate objections to the North Carolina bathroom law and the similar Texas bathroom bill, which followed on the heels of forceful corporate criticisms of RFRAs proposed in response to marriage equality, sent a powerful message to elected officials in conservative states. As the *New York Times* explained, "Though the bills have often been popular with conservative voters, they go down very poorly with another important constituency: big business. Officials in states hoping to attract major investments from out-of-state corporations—like Amazon's second headquarters—say they drew a lesson from the boycotts and cancellations that North Carolina suffered over its bathroom bill." In Georgia, the Republican Speaker of the House told a radio station that any proposed legislation that "creates headwinds" for economic growth was unappealing. For his part, the governor's chief of staff urged Georgia Republican candidates "to remember [that] when [you] speak, those headlines go as quick and as far as the CEO's desk."[43] The bottom line was that conservative politicians in red states seemed to have learned important and, for supporters of the anti-LGBTQ measures, unpleasant lessons about the power and influence of large corporations in American politics and society.

It should be noted that, despite the setbacks in promoting anti-LGBTQ rights measures, conservative state legislatures have continued to enact highly restrictive abortion laws. For example, at around the time that the LGBTQ movement was defeating RFRAs and transgender bathroom bills, the Oklahoma legislature enacted a provision (vetoed by the governor) banning all abortions; South Dakota and South Carolina joined fifteen other states in banning abortions after twenty weeks of pregnancy; and Alabama, Mississippi, and West Virginia banned the most common second-trimester abortion procedure. Several state legislatures enacted laws in 2019 essentially banning almost all abortions.[44]

One thing that distinguishes the culture war issue of abortion from that of LGBTQ equality is that while large corporations remain scrupulously neutral on the former, they have become heavily invested in the latter. Without the type of political support and activism that corporations provided to LGBTQ rights groups, free choice activists in conservative states have been politically unable to prevent the enactment of highly restrictive abortion measures. This has meant that proponents of free choice in those states have had to rely entirely on the courts to protect women's reproductive rights. In contrast, the political boost given by corporate political activism to the LGBTQ rights movement in conservative states has allowed that movement, since the Supreme Court's same-sex marriage decisions, to defeat anti-LGBTQ rights measures not through lawsuits, but in state legislatures and in the court of public opinion.

It is undoubtedly the case that, as with their growing public advocacy of sexual orientation equality measures, corporate opposition to transgender bathroom laws was motivated in part by business considerations. Laws such as the one enacted in North Carolina and considered in several other jurisdictions made it more difficult for companies in those states to attract the best and most qualified employees. But, as had happened with issues related to sexual orientation, the companies also objected to the measures because they were fundamentally inconsistent with their expressed values of diversity, inclusion, and equality. From the perspective of some of the nation's largest and most important corporations, anti-LGBTQ laws are not only bad for business, but they are also, as a matter of principle, unacceptable because they seek to render sexual minorities and transgender individuals second-class citizens.

Looking Beyond *Citizens United*

T HIS BOOK BEGAN with accounts of rampant corporate discrimination against queer people in the 1970s. It ends with accounts of forceful and effective political activism by corporations on behalf of LGBTQ rights in the 2010s. Early LGBTQ rights activists who are no longer with us would likely not recognize a society in which large and influential corporations are important supporters of LGBTQ equality. As this book has sought to show, significant changes in corporate policies and practices as they relate to LGBTQ issues, implemented during a span of only a few decades, have had profound consequences for both the firms themselves and for the greater society.

The transformation in corporate thinking about queer equality, resulting in substantial and influential corporate political activism on behalf of that equality, raises important and broader questions about the role of corporations in our democracy. As seen by the starkly different responses to *Citizens United v. Federal Elections Commission*, the ruling in which a closely divided Supreme Court struck down limits on the ability of companies to spend corporate funds to influence elections in the weeks before voters head to the polls, many in our society have conflicting views on the desirability and appropriateness of corporate political activity.[1]

Supporters of *Citizens United* take the position that for-profit corporations, like other associations of individuals, are entitled to advocate on behalf of government policies and political candidates that they believe advance their interests. From this perspective, corporate participation in policy debates and elections strengthens rather than threatens democracy. If the objective behind protecting free speech rights is to promote a robust marketplace of ideas, then the government should not limit the ability of certain entities, simply because of their for-profit corporate forms, to contribute to that marketplace by advocating for their policy choices and preferred candidates for elected office.

In sharp contrast, critics of *Citizens United* complain that the ruling reinforces a troubling feature of our democracy: the ways in which wealthy institutions and individuals exert undue influence on who gets elected and, after elections, on the setting of government policies. From this perspective, for-profit corporations, with the enormous amounts of money the law allows them to amass, should not be permitted to use that money in ways that distort our democracy by drowning out the voices—and discouraging the participation in elections—of those with significantly fewer financial resources. These critics argue that placing limits on the ability of wealthy corporations to use their successes in the economic sphere to dominate the political sphere promotes rather than threatens a truly robust and ideologically diverse marketplace of ideas.

One interesting consequence of corporate political activism on behalf of LGBTQ equality is that it complicates both of these narratives. During the debates over so-called religious freedom laws and transgender bathroom measures, many on the right decried the outsize corporate influence on the setting of public policy on LGBTQ issues. In doing so, they avoided making the point that they so often make in other contexts: that corporations, too, have rights to free speech. At the same time, many on the left welcomed and celebrated corporate political advocacy on behalf of LGBTQ rights positions. In doing so, they avoided making the point that they so often make in other contexts: that corporations routinely exert an undue and distorting influence on our democratic system. Debates over LGBTQ rights have turned many conservatives into critics (at least temporarily) of corporate political activism and participation in the setting of government policy, while converting many liberals into supporters (at least temporarily) of that activism and participation.

There are lessons for both sides arising from this apparent mutual incongruity. In the context of LGBTQ rights, social and religious conservatives have experienced firsthand what it means politically to be on the wrong side of corporate priorities, power, and influence. As traditional conservatives have learned from political disputes over issues such as the intersection of marriage equality and religious freedom, it is not easy—indeed, it is frequently *impossible*—for activists (regardless of their ideologies, beliefs, or objectives) to prevail in important public policy debates in the face of committed corporate opposition. This might suggest to some conservative supporters of *Citizens United* that placing reasonable limits on the ability of for-profit corporations to spend money to influence the outcome of elections may promote rather than undermine democracy.

At the same time, several of this century's LGBTQ rights debates have shown those on the left that corporate priorities, power, and influence can sometimes be deployed in ways that advance social change and reforms by, for example, helping expand opportunities and promote equality. Depending on the issue and circumstances, corporations can sometimes be allies of those who are fighting for a more fair, just, safe, and equal society. This might suggest to some on the left that it may be inappropriate to limit the ability of corporations to participate in public policy debates.

All this takes us right back to *Citizens United*. Few other US Supreme Court rulings in the last twenty years have impacted the workings of our democracy to a greater extent than *Citizens United*. But as important as that decision has turned out to be, it "only" addressed the question of whether corporations (and unions) can use their general funds to seek to influence the outcome of elections through advertisements and other means of communication in the weeks leading up to elections. I put the word *only* in quotation marks above because, although the issue addressed by *Citizens United* is profoundly important to how political campaigns are financed, and therefore immensely important to the workings of our democracy, the Court's decision did not, as some believe, address the broader question of whether corporations that are not members of the press have free speech rights to begin with.

That broader question was largely settled by the Supreme Court in 1978 when it held, in *First National Bank of Boston v. Bellotti*, that the government cannot limit the ability of for-profit corporations to participate in public policy debates, including by using corporate funds to support or oppose particular legislative proposals or ballot measures. The Massachusetts law at issue in *Bellotti* prohibited companies from spending corporate funds to influence ballot measures involving issues that did not affect their "property, business, or assets." The Court held that the statute was unconstitutional because the First Amendment protects "the liberty to discuss publicly and truthfully all matters of public concern."[2]

In considering the implications of *Bellotti*, we should keep in mind that many social and religious conservatives have complained during recent LGBTQ-rights debates that corporations have been improperly speaking on matters that go beyond their internal corporate affairs. If the Supreme Court had upheld the Massachusetts statute at issue in *Bellotti*, it might have been constitutional for the North Carolina legislature, for example, to have responded to the forceful and effective corporate criticism of its transgender bathroom law by enacting a statute limiting corporate speech to issues that affect companies directly. Specifically, conservative North Carolina legislators could have contended that who uses which bathrooms in government-owned buildings does not involve the "property, business, or assets" of corporations. After *Bellotti*, it is clear that such a law would be unconstitutional. It is also clear that had corporations not been allowed to participate vigorously in public debates over the appropriateness of the rash of anti-LGBTQ rights bills introduced in conservative states around the time the Supreme Court recognized the constitutional right of queer people to marry the individuals of their choice, many more of those provisions would be on the books today.

At the same time, it is important to recognize that the Court's holding in *Bellotti* that for-profit corporations have rights to free speech does not mean it decided *Citizens United* correctly forty years later. The principal problem with the Court's reasoning in *Citizens United* is that it failed to appreciate the extent to which wealthy and powerful corporations, through unlimited *electioneering* expenditures in support of or opposition to particular candidates, can commandeer and distort the process through which the people select their representatives. Given that real danger, the Free Speech Clause should not be understood to preclude the enforcement of reasonable regulations limiting corporate electioneering expenses, with the objective of preventing wealthy corporate interests from displacing and overwhelming less well-funded voices and perspectives on whom voters should choose to represent them. There is also a clear democratic interest in making sure that candidates for political office are not beholden to the preferences of the highest bidders. The people's trust in our democratic system depends on the belief that their representatives are looking out for their best interests rather than only protecting those of the powerful and the wealthy.

It is also important to note that the campaign financing reform law struck down in *Citizens United* did not seek to restrict the *hundreds of millions of dollars* that large corporations spend every year in lobbying efforts aimed at influencing legislation and government policy. Between 1998 and 2018, for example, the US Chamber of Commerce spent $1.4 billion in lobbying activities. During that same twenty-year period, General Electric spent $355 million on lobbying efforts, while Boeing and Exxon Mobil, to name just two additional companies, spent $266 million and $246 million, respectively.[3]

Corporations also pay millions of dollars to gain access to government officials by, for example, funding most of the weeklong festivities in Washington, DC, that accompany presidential inaugurations. As the *New York Times* explained in 2017, the group that organized President Donald Trump's inauguration that year "raised more than $100 million, . . . nearly double the record for an inauguration, with much of it coming in six- and seven-figure checks from America's corporate suites." For instance, Boeing donated $1 million and Chevron pledged $500,000 to pay for inauguration parties and gatherings. As the *Times* noted, in exchange for the money, "Mr. Trump's most prolific donors . . . gain access to what amounts to a parallel inauguration week, carefully planned and largely out of public sight, during which they can mingle with members of the incoming administration over intimate meals and witness Mr. Trump's ascension from the front rows."[4]

The campaign reform law struck down in *Citizens United* also did not attempt to interfere with the ability of corporate-run political action committees (PACs) to pay for election ads and to contribute money to the campaigns of particular candidates. Corporate PACs raise money through voluntary donations from employees, shareholders, and their families. In 2010, the year in which *Citizens United* was decided, PACs raised $1.2 billion and contributed $433 million of those funds directly to candidates for political office. The vast majority of that money was raised and spent by corporate PACs. As a result, Justice John Paul Stevens was absolutely correct when he ended his dissent in *Citizens United* by noting that even if the "American democracy is imperfect, few outside the majority of this Court would have thought its flaws included a dearth of corporate money in politics."[5]

Citizens United is a threat to our democracy because it burst open the floodgates of corporate electioneering expenditures—a campaign financing system that was already awash with corporate cash and influence became even more so for three principal reasons. First, the ruling allows the direct expenditure of unrestricted amounts of corporate treasury money for electioneering purposes as long as the expenditures are not coordinated with candidates for elected office. Second, corporations now have the right to support candidates indirectly by donating money to so-called super PACs that, unlike ordinary PACs, are able to accept unlimited contributions as long as they spend the funds without coordinating with candidates. In 2012 alone, corporations gave $70 million to super PACs. Finally, corporations are now free to give unlimited amounts of money to groups, such as trade associations and other private organizations, which can use the funds for electioneering purposes. Unlike money donated to PACs and super PACs, donations to these groups do not have to be reported to the Federal Elections Commission.[6]

In short, the Supreme Court committed a grave error when it held that the First Amendment does not permit campaign finance reforms that seek to limit the spending of corporate money to influence the outcomes of elections. However, it is a different matter altogether to contend that the First Amendment allows the government to limit the ability of corporations to speak on public policy issues—ranging from the desirability of government regulations that affect the private sector to the advisability of free trade policies to the appropriateness of anti-LGBTQ rights laws—in ways that do not call for the election or defeat of particular candidates for political offices. Even if the Court in *Citizens United* had upheld the government's authority to limit the electioneering expenditures of corporations in the weeks leading up to an election, such a ruling would not have permitted public officials to prevent corporations from speaking more broadly on economic, social, and political issues.

Some on the right have claimed that corporate support for LGBTQ equality creates, as a commentator for the conservative *National Review* magazine put it, a "cognitive dissonance" for "leftists who blame businesses for corrupting the democratic process."[7] But there is, in fact, no such dissonance if we distinguish between the expending of corporate funds to influence the outcome of elections (the type of corporate political campaign funding at issue in *Citizens United*) and corporate speech that is part of wider debates over government policies. The use of unlimited amounts of corporate funds to influence the outcomes of elections constitutes a greater threat to our democracy than corporate participation in public policy debates that are disconnected to whether one candidate or another should serve as the people's representative. It is therefore not inconsistent to be critical of *Citizens United* while recognizing that corporations have a constitutional right to participate in debates over government policy.

There are some who seem to believe that because corporations are not people, they do not have free speech rights. But the Free Speech Clause does not limit its protections to "people." Instead, it simply reads "Congress shall make no law . . . abridging the freedom of speech." Once we recognize that a huge panoply of associations of people—including nonprofit corporations ranging from the ACLU to the Scouts BSA to the NAACP to the Democratic Party—have rights to free speech, then it is not at all clear why associations formed primarily to pursue profits should not have at least some rights to free speech as well.

It bears noting that the Supreme Court in *Citizens United* did not hold, as some critics have suggested, that corporations are people. As law professor Adam Winkler explains, "Corporate personhood—the idea that a corporation is an entity with rights and obligations separate and distinct from the rights and obligations of its members—is entirely missing from the court's opinion."[8] Instead, the Court emphasized the political nature of the speech that was subject to regulation and the threat to democratic principles when the government decides who gets to participate (and who does not) in election-related advocacy. Rather than viewing corporations as independent entities with a personhood of their own, the Court in *Citizens United* looked behind the corporate veil and focused on the interests of corporations' members.*

———

* In his book *We the Corporations: How American Businesses Won Their Civil Rights* (2018), Winkler provides a comprehensive historical study of the constitutional rights of corporations in the United States. In doing so, he argues persuasively that when the Supreme Court has recognized corporations as "people" (that is, as entities whose interests are distinct from those of their members), it has almost always denied their constitutional claims. In contrast, when the Court has refused to entertain the notion of corporate personhood and instead focused on the interests of their members, it has generally expanded the scope of the constitutional rights of corporations. This means, paradoxically, that those who oppose corporate constitutional rights may want to emphasize rather than criticize the notion of corporations as people.

Some have argued that for-profit corporations should not have free speech rights because they are nothing more than law-created entities. These critics point out that the government charters and regulates for-profit corporations while immunizing their owners from liability arising from corporate actions. Since for-profit corporations are artificial entities created through legal mechanisms, it is argued, the Constitution does not grant them rights to free expression. The problem with this contention is that nonprofit corporations are also chartered and regulated by the government. In addition, the law immunizes members of nonprofit corporations from liability arising from the actions of the organizations to which they belong. Again, as long as it is widely accepted that nonprofit corporations have some rights to free speech protected by the First Amendment, it is not clear why for-profit corporations that are not members of the press should be denied all constitutional rights to free expression.

What *does* distinguish for-profit corporations from nonprofit ones is that only the former are legally able to amass huge amounts of money. It can be argued that big companies can use their large amounts of corporate wealth to dominate public policy debates and, in the process, overwhelm the voices of less well-funded speakers in the same way that, after *Citizens United*, corporations can use their wealth to affect the outcomes of elections by drowning out the voices of others.

In a democratic system, the government has a compelling interest in making sure that the people trust that elections reflect the actual choices and interests of a majority of voters rather than the preferences of wealthy corporations. It is also reasonable to conclude that because persons vote and corporations do not, the latter should be subject to greater restrictions in their ability to influence the outcome of elections through cash expenditures and contributions than the former.

But granting the government the authority to prevent for-profit corporations from contributing altogether to the marketplace of ideas in matters related to government policy and legislation is inconsistent with the basic purposes of the Free Speech Clause in ways that placing reasonable limits on the ability of corporations to influence the outcomes of elections does not. It is inconsistent with democratic objectives to allow the government to decide which associations and individuals get to participate (and which do not) in public policy debates. The future of our democracy depends on the government's willingness to abide by constitutional principles of neutrality in regulating and fostering the marketplace of ideas.

It is true that for-profit corporations routinely exercise their free speech rights to oppose progressive laws and regulations aimed at protecting and promoting the public's health, safety, and general welfare. It is also true that if it were not for corporate opposition, more of those measures would be in place today. On the other hand, if corporations did not have free speech rights, conservative activists in red states would have succeeded in persuading elected officials in recent years to enact a significantly greater number of anti-LGBTQ laws. But, either way, the purpose of the Free Speech Clause, like most constitutional provisions, is not to make it more likely that one political camp or another will attain its objectives in particular public policy disputes. Instead, the basic purpose of the clause is to restrict the government's ability to determine who is able to express which ideas.

Of course, to argue that for-profit corporations have some rights to free speech does not mean that those rights trump government interests in all instances. Under well-established constitutional principles, for example, the government can prohibit companies from advertising their goods and services in false or misleading ways. In addition, the free speech rights of corporations should not be understood to preclude the government's long-recognized constitutional power to adopt reasonable regulations to protect the health and safety of individuals, even when doing so limits corporate discretion. Furthermore, the free speech rights of for-profit corporations should not immunize them from the application of antidiscrimination laws. The government has a compelling interest in guaranteeing equal treatment for all and, as a result, the First Amendment should never be understood to grant a constitutional right to discriminate to for-profit entities that make their goods and services available to the general public. Finally, as already noted, I believe the Supreme Court in *Citizens United* committed a grave error in concluding that corporations cannot constitutionally be prevented from spending unlimited amounts of corporate funds to influence who gets elected to public office.

In short, the appropriate question is not *whether* for-profit corporations should have constitutionally protected rights of expression, but is instead *which* free speech rights the Constitution accords them. It is reasonable to conclude that, given their nature and functions, corporations should have fewer free speech rights than human beings. For example, the right to vote and to choose who governs us as a people, a right that has crucial free speech implications, is appropriately limited to human beings. And as law professor Kent Greenfield explains, while it violates the Free Speech Clause to require human beings to speak in ways that they do not want to speak, it does not violate the Constitution to require corporations, over their objections, to disclose information about, for example, their finances or the safety of their products and workplaces.[9] But it goes too far to contend that corporations should have *no* constitutionally protected rights to free expression.

It is also important to distinguish between the constitutionally protected right of corporations to participate in public policy debates and the substantive positions that companies take on particular issues. Other participants in those debates should and must subject corporate policy positions to rigorous scrutiny. In particular, it seems to me that the appropriate response to corporate participation in public policy debates is not to try to prohibit them from contributing to the marketplace of ideas. Instead, the proper response is to vigorously criticize corporations when their positions and proposals, as they frequently do, impede the promotion of social welfare goals and the attainment of social justice objectives, while praising companies when they contribute, as they sometimes do, to the reaching of those ends.

Some commentators on the left have warned that despite corporate support for LGBTQ equality, progressive activists should not engage in political coalition work with corporations because they are unreliable allies in the pursuit of progressive goals and reforms, given that they are ultimately conservative institutions exclusively concerned with profits and wealth maximization. As one commentator puts it, "For corporations, progressivism is always adopted out of expediency. They're no partners to left movements. The solution, as always, is to mobilize and build power from below."[10]

But it seems to me that progressives should not put themselves in the position of always having to choose between harnessing corporate political activism, on the one hand, and engaging in grassroots activism in the pursuit of progressive objectives, on the other. As this book has explained, the two forms of activism have worked effectively *together* to defeat or weaken anti-LGBTQ measures in conservative states where liberal advocacy groups enjoy limited political influence.

It is probably true that those on the left who believe that a just society requires a fundamental restructuring or replacement of basic capitalist principles are unlikely to help their cause by working in coalition with large and powerful corporations on any issue. But progressives who do not want to replace capitalism as such, but who instead want to reform it in ways that make it more humane and less likely to promote entrenched and damaging forms of economic and social inequalities—perhaps along the lines of what some social democracies in Western Europe have been able to achieve—should consider working with corporations on those issues, such as LGBTQ equality, climate change, and immigration reform, where the priorities and values of at least some large corporations overlap with those of the progressive movement. At the same time, it is crucial for progressives to remain critical of corporate objectives and principles—manifested, for example, in corporate support for anti-union, anti-regulation, and antitax policies—that undermine rather than promote social welfare and justice reforms.

It is also important to acknowledge that some critics on the left have argued that the LGBTQ rights movement made a moral and strategic mistake in allying itself with corporate interests in pursuit of a narrow agenda of LGBTQ rights rather than seeking more broadly to tackle issues of wealth redistribution and widespread social and economic inequalities engendered by modern day capitalism.[11] Although it is difficult to know with any certainty, it is possible that if leading LGBTQ rights organizations had refused to work closely with large corporations in promoting LGBTQ equality and had instead taken a more oppositional stance toward big business with the aim of reducing corporate power in order to promote greater wealth redistribution, our society today would be less unequal across the board. At the same time, it is also possible that had leading LGBTQ rights organizations pursued an explicit anticorporate and economically redistributive political agenda that went beyond LGBTQ equality issues, they would have had little impact in changing corporate objectives, reducing corporate power in American society, or persuading the government to redistribute wealth aggressively. But either way, there can be little doubt of the following: a refusal by the LGBTQ movement to work with corporations on issues of mutual interest would have made it more difficult for the movement both to attain the important LGBTQ rights gains of recent years and to effectively oppose the forces of conservative backlash aimed at reversing or limiting those gains. For that reason, this book has focused on the road taken rather than the roads forsaken by the LGBTQ rights movement as it sought, in the decades following Stonewall, to challenge corporate America and, more recently, to ally itself with big businesses in the pursuit of queer equality.

The recent strong corporate support for LGBTQ equality has partially disrupted the traditional political alliance between big business and Republican elected officials in conservative states. In addition, the queering of corporate America has to some extent disrupted the ideological cooperation between big businesses, on the one hand, and social and religious conservatives, on the other, which has centered on promoting small government and free markets. It seems to me that progressive causes in the United States would benefit from encouraging similar political and ideological fissures that might further weaken or disrupt the powerful coalition of corporations, economic libertarians, and social and religious conservatives that has, since the early days of the Reagan administration, been so effective in opposing liberal public policies.

At the same time, it is important to recognize the limits of corporate support for LGBTQ equality. Large American corporations have done close to nothing in challenging or criticizing harmful government policies affecting sexual minorities and transgender individuals in some of the foreign countries where they conduct business. It is also troubling that large American businesses (and their political action committees), most of which repeatedly insist they are committed to LGBTQ equality, continue to be among the most important funders of Republican politicians who support anti-LGBTQ laws. It seems that many large companies, in making campaign funding decisions, are willing to look the other way on issues related to LGBTQ equality and focus instead on whether the politicians in question support antiregulatory and other corporate-friendly policies. It is hypocritical for companies and their executives to strongly oppose anti-LGBTQ measures while simultaneously giving thousands of dollars to the political campaigns of the most important and vociferous proponents of those laws. By funding the campaigns of anti-LGBTQ politicians, such as those who supported the North Carolina bathroom law, corporations are doing nothing less than subsidizing bigotry and prejudice.

LGBTQ activists, going forward, should expose and condemn corporations that continue (1) to do business in countries with oppressive anti-LGBTQ laws without criticizing or opposing those laws and (2) to fund candidates for political office in the United States with anti-LGBTQ rights agendas. It would be helpful, in this regard, if the Human Rights Campaign added these corporate omissions and actions to its annual *Corporate Equality Index*. The HRC should deny perfect scores to corporations that insist in silently doing business in countries with oppressive anti-LGBTQ laws and in subsidizing the political campaigns of American politicians who sponsor or endorse anti-LGBTQ laws. In addition, the HRC and other LGBTQ organizations should expand the criteria they use to praise good (and criticize bad) corporate citizenship beyond issues related to queer equality. LGBTQ rights groups should join coalitions of other progressive organizations in pressuring corporations to implement policies that, for example, protect the environment, support workers' rights, and reduce the huge and growing disparities between what top executives and low-level employees earn.

Left critics are correct when they note that corporate America routinely prioritizes profits over the well-being of some segments of society. But, in my estimation, that is not reason enough for progressives to categorically reject working with big businesses on those issues in which there is common ground. For LGBTQ rights activists, creating political alliances with corporations on issues of mutual interest may be particularly important going forward, given that the Supreme Court may be in the firm control of conservative justices for years to come. This means that it may not be possible for LGBTQ rights proponents in the foreseeable future to rely on judicial intervention as a way of addressing the harms and injuries caused by discriminatory laws and policies as they have in the recent past. In this possibly changed judicial environment, the ability to defeat anti-LGBTQ measures in legislatures and in the court of public opinion becomes even more crucial than it has been in years past. And the chances of successes in legislative and political arenas, especially in conservative states, are greatly enhanced if LGBTQ activists and large corporations continue to work together in advocating on behalf of LGBTQ equality.

The bottom line is that there is no easy response to the question of whether corporate participation in public policy debates benefits or harms society. Instead, the answer, like the nature of politics itself, is messy and complicated, and, by necessity, depends on the particular issues and circumstances in question.

There is little doubt that corporate engagement with issues related to LGBTQ equality in recent years has worked to the benefit of many sexual minorities and transgender individuals. The positive consequences for the LGBTQ movement and, I would argue, for the broader society resulting from the corporate promotion of LGBTQ equality were partly due to decades of LGBTQ rights activism that targeted and engaged with the practices and values of large corporations in the United States. It turns out that LGBTQ activism aimed at the private sector has been as important as activism directed at the government in transforming the ways in which the American society understands, treats, and regulates sexual minorities and transgender individuals.

Acknowledgments

I WOULD LIKE TO THANK Sarah Dadush, Donna Dennis, Carlos Gonzalez, Doug NeJaime, Ed Stein, Scott Skinner-Thompson, Cynthia Williams, Adam Winkler, and Timothy Zick for taking the time to read earlier sections of this manuscript and for providing me with many helpful and thoughtful suggestions for improvement. I presented portions of this book at a faculty colloquium at the Yeshiva University Cardozo School of Law. I thank participants for their comments and questions regarding some of the book's findings and claims. I am also very appreciative of having been able to use, in researching and writing this book, primary sources available at the New York Public Library and at the Lesbian Herstory Archives in Brooklyn, New York.

It is sometimes the case that publishing houses feel like homes for authors. That is true for me—publishing this book with Beacon Press has been a coming home of sorts. I would like to thank everyone at Beacon for their unfailing encouragement and support through the years, especially Joanna Green and Gayatri Patnaik.

This book is dedicated to my son, Sebastian, and my daughter, Ema. I wrote the book while Ema was in the process of socially transitioning genders. During that time, I gained a great deal of strength from, and marveled at, both Ema's unyielding courage and

Sebastian's unyielding love for his sister. It is fair to say that my daughter's journey has deepened my understanding of some of the transgender issues that I address in this book.

Finally, little of what I have been able to accomplish professionally or personally would be possible without the love and support of my husband, Richard. I am profoundly grateful to him for the countless ways in which he makes me feel like the luckiest person on earth.

Notes

Note from Series Editor

1. "A Message from CEO, Erin Uritus, on Trans Military Ban," Out & Equal: Workplace Advocates, 2019, https://outandequal.org/a-message-from-ceo-erin -uritus-on-trans-military-ban.

Introduction

1. "Ma Bell Gives In to SIR, But Gays Want It to Be Legal," *Advocate*, September 1, 1971, 6, describing the 1968 refusal to publish the ad; "Ma Bell Will Ignore San Francisco's Ordinance," *Advocate*, July 19, 1972, 4; Philip Hager, "Pacific Bell Will Pay $3 Million to End Gay Bias Case," *Los Angeles Times*, December 5, 1986.

2. Jena McGregor, "Wal-Mart CEO Speaks Out Against 'Religious Freedom Bill' in Arkansas," *Washington Post*, April 1, 2015; Monica Davey et al., "Indiana and Arkansas Revise Rights Bill, Seeking to Remove Divisive Parts," *New York Times*, April 2, 2015. For Walmart's gradual embrace of LGBTQ rights positions, see Jeremy Lybarger, "Why Walmart Became LGBT Friendly," *Advocate*, August 31, 2016; Hiroko Tabachi and Michael Barbaro, "Walmart Emerges as Unlikely Social Force," *New York Times*, April 1, 2015.

3. See, for example, S. E. James, *The Report of the 2015 U.S. Transgender Survey* (Washington, DC: National Center for Transgender Equality, 2016); *The Cost of the Closet and the Rewards of Inclusion* (Washington, DC: Human Rights Campaign, 2014); Brad Sears and Christy Mallory, *Documented Evidence of Employment Discrimination and Its Effects* (Los Angeles: Williams Institute, 2011). On the phenomenon of LGBTQ people and other minorities covering in the workplace, see Kenji Yoshino, *Covering: The Hidden Assault on Our Civil Rights* (New York: Random House, 2006).

4. Although chapter 6 explores efforts by some states to grant legal immunity to business owners who object to LGBTQ equality on religious grounds, a full exploration of that topic goes beyond the scope of this book. For a fuller exploration, see Carlos A. Ball, *The First Amendment and LGBT Equality: A Contentious History* (Cambridge, MA: Harvard University Press, 2017).

5. See, for example, Parija Kavilanz, "America's Biggest Businesses Are Standing by Their Dreamer Employees," *CNN Business*, January 18, 2018; Zach Wichter, "C.E.O.s See a 'Sad Day' After Trump's DACA Decision," *New York Times*, September 5, 2017; Nick Wingfield and Daisuke Wakabayashi, "Tech Companies Fight Trump Immigration Order in Court," *New York Times*, January 30, 2017.

6. See, for example, Daniel Victor, "'Climate Change Is Real': Many U.S. Companies Lament Paris Exit," *New York Times*, June 1, 2017; Brad Plummer, "A Year after Trump's Paris Pullout, U.S. Companies Are Driving a Renewables Boom," *New York Times*, June 1, 2018. See also Adam Winkler, "Corporate Political Conscience: Why Big Business Is Suddenly into Liberal Politics," *New Republic*, April 30, 2018.

7. Citizens United v. Federal Elections Commission, 558 U.S. 310 (2010). I explore the interplay of *Citizens United* and the queering of corporate America in this book's conclusion.

CHAPTER 1 A (Very) Brief History of Corporations in America

1. William G. Roy, *Socializing Capital: The Rise of the Large Industrial Corporation in America* (Princeton, NJ: Princeton University Press, 1997), chap. 3.

2. Oscar Handlin and Mary F. Handlin, "Origins of the American Business Corporation," in *Enterprise and Secular Change: Readings in Economic History*, ed. Frederic Lane and Jelle Riemersma (Homewood, IL: Richard Irwin, 1953), 103, 123. See also John Micklethwait and Adrian Woolridge, *The Company: A Short History of a Revolutionary Idea* (New York: Random House, 2003); Naomi R. Lamoreaux and William J. Novak, eds., *Corporations and American Democracy* (Cambridge, MA: Harvard University Press, 2018).

3. Adam Winkler, *We the Corporations: How American Businesses Won Their Civil Rights* (New York: W.W. Norton, 2018), 39.

4. Winkler, *We the Corporations*, 43.

5. 17 U.S. 518 (1819); Morrell Heald, *The Social Responsibilities of Business: Company and Community, 1900–1960* (New York: Oxford University Press, 1970); Roy, *Socializing Capital*.

6. Naomi Lamoreaux, *The Great Merger Movement in American Business, 1895–1904* (New York: Cambridge University Press, 1988); Lawrence Mitchel, *The Speculation Economy: How Finance Triumphed over Industry* (San Francisco: Berrett-Koehler, 2007).

7. Micklethwait and Woolridge, *The Company*.

8. See, for example, Nikki Mandell, *The Corporation as Family: The Gen-*

dering of Corporate Welfare, 1890–1930 (Chapel Hill: University of North Carolina Press, 2002); Andrea Tone, *The Business of Benevolence: Industrial Paternalism in Progressive America* (Ithaca, NY: Cornell University Press, 1997).

9. Kent Greenfield, *Corporations Are People Too (And They Should Act Like It)* (New Haven, CT: Yale University Press, 2018), 35.

10. Dodge v. Ford Motor Company, 204 Mich. 459, 468 (1919).

11. *Dodge v. Ford Motor Company.*

12. Milton Friedman, *Capitalism and Freedom* (Chicago: University of Chicago Press, 1962), 133; Committee for Economic Development, *Social Responsibility of Business Corporations* (New York: CED, 1971), quoted in Archie B. Carroll, "A History of Corporate Social Responsibility: Concepts and Practices," in *The Oxford Handbook of Corporate Social Responsibility*, ed. Andrew Crane et al. (New York: Oxford University Press, 2008), 19, 29.

13. See, for example, Neil Jacoby, *Corporate Power and Social Responsibility: A Blueprint for the Future* (New York: Simon & Schuster, 1973); Andrew Crane et al., eds., *The Oxford Handbook of Corporate Social Responsibility* (New York: Oxford University Press, 2008); Archie B. Carroll et al., eds., *Corporate Responsibility: The American Experience* (New York: Cambridge University Press, 2012).

14. Executive Order 8802 (1941); Nancy MacLean, *Freedom Is Not Enough: The Opening of the American Workplace* (Cambridge, MA: Harvard University Press, 2006), 22.

15. Jennifer Delton, *Racial Integration in Corporate America, 1940–1990* (New York: Cambridge University Press, 2009), 21, 54.

16. MacLean, *Freedom Is Not Enough*, 38.

17. MacLean, *Freedom Is Not Enough*, 42, 58.

18. James Peck, "Minority Stockholders vs. Jim Crow—Continued," *Crisis* (June–July 1952), 367; Derek Charles Catsam, *Freedom's Main Line: The Journey of Reconciliation and the Freedom Rides* (Lexington: University Press of Kentucky, 2009), 56–58; R. D. G. Wahdwani, "Kodak, FIGHT, and the Definition of Civil Rights in Rochester, New York, 1966–1967," *Historian* 60, no. 1 (1997): 59–75.

19. Delton, *Racial Integration in Corporate America*, 168–73. See also William J. Collins, "The Labor Market Impact of State-Level Antidiscrimination Laws, 1940–1960," *Industrial and Labor Relations Review* 56, no. 2 (2003): 244–72.

20. MacLean, *Freedom Is Not Enough*, 43–44; Delton, *Racial Integration in Corporate America*, 23, 41.

21. Frank Dobbin, *Inventing Equal Opportunity* (Princeton, NJ: Princeton University Press, 2009), 27.

22. MacLean, *Freedom Is Not Enough*, 18–19.

23. Delton, *Racial Integration in Corporate America*, 55, 67, 173.

24. Delton, *Racial Integration in Corporate America*, 5.

25. Executive Order 10925 (1961).

26. Delton, *Racial Integration in Corporate America*, 188–91. See also Dobbin, *Inventing Equal Opportunity*, chap. 3.

27. Equal Employment Opportunities: Hearings on H.R. 405 Before the Subcommittee on Labor of the House Committee on Education and Labor, 88th Cong., 1st Sess. 497 (1963) (Letter from Theron J. Rice, US Chamber of Commerce, June 27, 1963); MacLean, *Freedom Is Not Enough*, 67–68, quoting "Forced Hiring of Negroes—How It Would Work," *U.S. News & World Report*, July 29, 1963, 83. For a detailed exploration of NAM's position regarding the Civil Rights Act of 1964 and other antidiscrimination laws, see Delton, *Racial Integration in Corporate America*, chap. 7.

28. MacLean, *Freedom Is Not Enough*, chap. 3; Timothy J. Minchin, "Black Activism, the Civil Rights Act of 1964, and the Racial Integration of the Southern Textile Industry," *Journal of Southern History* 65, no. 4 (1999): 809–44.

29. Delton, *Racial Integration in Corporate America*, 225.

30. Jules Cohn, "Is Business Meeting the Challenge of Urban Affairs?," *Harvard Business Review* (March–April 1970): 68–82; Herbert H. Haines, "Black Radicalization and the Funding of Civil Rights: 1957–1970," *Social Problems* 32, no. 1 (1984): 31–43; Delton, *Racial Integration in Corporate America*, 225–26; Griggs v. Duke Power Company, 401 U.S. 424 (1971).

31. Delton, *Racial Integration in Corporate America*, 230.

32. Dobbin, *Inventing Equal Opportunity*.

33. Delton, *Racial Integration in Corporate America*, 138; MacLean, *Freedom Is Not Enough* 310–11.

34. MacLean, *Freedom Is Not Enough*, 316.

35. Dobbin, *Inventing Equal Opportunity*, 140.

36. Delton, *Racial Integration in Corporate America*, 281.

CHAPTER 2 LGBTQ Corporate Activism in the 1970s

1. "L.A. Bank's Form Asks That Question," *Advocate*, March, 1970, 5; "Ma Bell Will Ignore San Francisco's Ordinance," *Advocate*, July 19, 1972, 4; Dan Baum, *Citizen Coors: An American Dynasty* (New York: HarperCollins, 2000), 66; Larry Gross, *Up from Invisibility: Lesbians, Gay Men, and the Media in America* (New York: Columbia University Press, 2001).

2. For an exploration of this workplace phenomenon, primarily across racial lines, see Cynthia Estlund, *Working Together: How Workplace Bonds Strengthen a Diverse Democracy* (New York: Oxford University Press, 2003).

3. Ken Bronson, *A Quest for Full Equality* (2004), https://www.qlibrary .org/wordpress/wp-content/uploads/2018/11/JACKBAKERQuest.pdf.

4. "Survey Starts Drive on Job Discrimination," *Advocate*, July 22, 1970, 2; "Three Big Companies Say They Hire Gays," *Advocate*, September 30, 1970, 5.

5. "Honeywell Faces Bias Charge at Minnesota University," *Advocate*, April 25, 1973, 8; Lars Bjorson, "A Quiet Win: Honeywell Yields," *Advocate*, April 10, 1974, 13.

6. I explore the connection between LGBTQ proponents' exercise of free speech rights and the movement's attainment of basic civil and fundamental rights for sexual minorities in Carlos A. Ball, *The First Amendment and LGBT Equality: A Contentious History* (Cambridge, MA: Harvard University Press, 2017).

7. Bill Beardemphl, editorial, *Vector*, no. 3 (February 1965): 6; and Bill Beardemphl, "S.I.R.'s Statement of Policy," *Vector*, no. 1 (December 1964): 1, quoted in Nan Amilla Boyd, *Wide-Open Town: A History of Queer San Francisco to 1965* (Berkeley: University of California Press, 2003), 213, 228.

8. John D'Emilio, "Gay Politics and Community in San Francisco Since World War II," in *Hidden from History: Reclaiming the Gay and Lesbian Past*, ed. Martin Bauml Duberman, Martha Vicinus, and George Chauncey Jr. (New York: New American Library, 1989), 464.

9. "Ma Bell Gives into SIR, but Gays Want It to Be Legal," *Advocate*, September 1, 1971, 6; "Ma Bell Will Ignore San Francisco's Ordinance," *Advocate*, July 19, 1972, 4.

10. "Ma Bell Will Ignore San Francisco's Ordinance," 4.

11. "Ma Bell Zapped in San Francisco," *Advocate*, May 23, 1973, 5.

12. "San Francisco Commission Takes on Ma Bell," *Advocate*, July 30, 1975, 4; Philip Hager, "Pacific Bell Will Pay $3 Million to End Gay Bias Case," *Los Angeles Times*, December 5, 1986.

13. "Ma Bell Zapped," 5; "Ma Bell Must End Bias," *Advocate*, June 30, 1976, 10.

14. "Battle of Ma Bell Spreads to Minnesota," *Advocate*, August 29, 1973, 14.

15. "ACLU Lawsuit Will Challenge Northwestern Bell Ban," *Advocate*, October 10, 1973, 12.

16. "Rights Bill Passed in Minneapolis," *Advocate*, April 24, 1974, 6; "Northwestern Bell Settles Past Bias," *Advocate*, August 28, 1974, 1.

17. Lois Kathryn Herr, *Women, Power, and AT&T: Winning Rights in the Workplace* (Boston: Northeastern University Press, 2003); Marjorie Stockford, *The Bell Women: The Story of the Landmark AT&T Sex Discrimination Case* (New Brunswick, NJ: Rutgers University Press, 2004).

18. For all quotations in the text, see "Ma Bell Decrees: No More!," *Advocate*, August 28, 1974, 1.

19. AT&T did not actually amend its employee nondiscrimination policy by adding sexual orientation until the following year (1975). By then, IBM had become the first American corporation to amend its policy in that way.

20. " 'No Discrimination Here,' Seven More Say," *Advocate*, May 7, 1975, 5.

21. Gay Law Students Association v. Pacific Telephone and Telegraph Company, 595 P.2d 592 (Ca. 1979). A federal court that same year sided with the phone company by holding that the prohibition against sex discrimination in Title VII of the Civil Rights Act of 1964 did not bar discrimination on the basis of sexual orientation. DeSantis v. Pacific Telephone and Telegraph, 608 F.2d 327 (9th Cir. 1979).

22. David L. Kirp, "Uncommon Decency: Pacific Bell Responds to AIDS," *Harvard Business Review* (May–June 1989): 140–51, 146.

23. Sam B. Puckett and Alan R. Emery, *Managing AIDS in the Workplace* (New York: Basic Books, 1988).

24. Kirp, "Uncommon Decency," 148–49; Daniel B. Baker, Sean O'Brien Strub, and Bill Henning, *Cracking the Corporate Closet: The 200 Best (and Worst) Companies to Work For, Buy From, and Invest In If You're Gay or Lesbian—and Even If You Aren't* (New York: Harper Business, 1995), 176–77. On the 1986 AIDS ballot initiative, see David L. Kirp, "LaRouche Turns to AIDS Politics," *New York Times*, September 11, 1986; Jay Matthews, "LaRouche's Call to Quarantine AIDS Victims Trails in California," *Washington Post*, October 26, 1986.

25. "The Homosexual," *CBS Reports*, March 7, 1967.

26. Joseph Epstein, "Homo/Hetero: The Struggle for Sexual Identity," *Harper's*, September, 1970, quoted in Gross, *Up from Invisibility*, 43.

27. Gross, *Up from Invisibility*, 45.

28. Gross, *Up from Invisibility*, 47.

29. Gross, *Up from Invisibility*, 45–46.

30. Gross, *Up from Invisibility*, 47–48. See also Kathryn C. Montgomery, *Target: Prime Time, Advocacy Groups and the Struggle over Entertainment Television* (New York: Oxford University Press, 1989), 79–85.

31. "Smash! Bleep! Clean Up! Gays Zap Network Center," *Advocate*, April 10, 1974, 1; Gross, *Up from Invisibility*, 49.

32. Montgomery, *Target: Prime Time*, 90; "Outraged Lesbians Zap NBC," *Advocate*, December 18, 1974, 1; "Top-Level NBC Meeting," *Advocate*, December 18, 1974, 7; "FCC, Networks Hear Gay Case," *Advocate*, December 29, 1974, 7.

33. *Up from Invisibility*, 48–49; Montgomery, *Target: Prime Time*, 90–95.

34. "'No Discrimination Here,' Seven More Say," *Advocate*, May 7, 1975, 5; "CBS Television Network Issues Revised Personnel Application Forms," *Advocate*, March 10, 1976, 10.

35. "Mattachine Raps CBS on Job Discrimination," *Advocate*, July 22, 1970, 4.

36. Ron Becker, *Gay TV and Straight America* (New Brunswick, NJ: Rutgers University Press, 2006); Stephen Topiano, *The Prime Time Closet: A History of Gays and Lesbians on TV* (New York: Applause Theater & Cinema Books, 2002).

37. Erin Cole and Allyson Brantley, "The Coors Boycott: When a Beer Can Signaled Your Politics," Colorado Public Radio, October 2, 2014, https://www.cpr.org/news/story/coors-boycott-when-beer-can-signaled-your-politics; Allyson Powers Brantley, "'We're Givin' Up Our Beer for Sweeter Wine': Boycotting Coors Beer, Coalition-Building, and the Politics of Non-Consumption, 1957–1987," PhD diss., Yale University, 2016.

38. Brantley, "We're Givin' Up Our Beer for Sweeter Wine," 65–66.

39. Randy Shilts, *The Mayor of Castro Street: The Life and Times of Harvey Milk* (New York: St. Martin's Press, 1982), 83–84.

40. Baum, *Citizen Coors*, 66.

41. Brantley, "We're Givin' Up Our Beer for Sweeter Wine," 135, 146.

42. Baum, *Citizen Coors*, 121.

43. Brantley, "We're Givin' Up Our Beer for Sweeter Wine," 209.

44. Alan Belasen, *The Theory and Practice of Corporate Communication* (Los Angeles: Sage Publication, 2008), 69; "Over a Barrel: Men at Coors Find the Old Ways Don't Work Anymore," *Wall Street Journal*, January 19, 1979, quoted in Brantley, "We're Givin' Up Our Beer for Sweeter Wine," 267.

45. Brantley, "We're Givin' Up Our Beer for Sweeter Wine," 233–34; "Coors Changes Policies," *Advocate*, March 22, 1978, 22; "I've Heard Coors' Side and I'm Satisfied," Coors advertisement, *Advocate*, April 5, 1979, 14; "Rocky Mountain Hype? The Coors Controversy," *Advocate*, November 16, 1977, 11.

46. "Rocky Mountain Hype?," 12.

47. Baker et al., *Cracking the Corporate Closet*, 103; Brantley, "We're Givin' Up Our Beer for Sweeter Wine," 371–72.

48. Baum, *Citizen Coors*, 345–46.

49. Brantley, "We're Givin' Up Our Beer for Sweeter Wine," 375.

50. Bruce Mirken, "Coors Controversy Boils Statewide," Corporations.org (1997), https://www.corporations.org/coors/lgb2.html.

CHAPTER 3 AIDS Corporate Activism in the 1980s

1. Lawrence K. Altman, "Rare Cancer Seen in 41 Homosexuals," *New York Times*, July 3, 1981.

2. John-Manuel Andriote, *Victory Deferred: How AIDS Changed Gay Life in America* (Chicago: University of Chicago Press, 1999), 68; "Senator Helms and the Guilty Victims," editorial, *New York Times*, June 17, 1987.

3. See, for example, Leckelt v. Board of Commissioners of Hospital District 1, 909 F.2d 820 (5th Cir. 1990); City of New York v. New Saint Mark's Bath, 497 N.Y.S.2d 979 (Sup. Ct. 1986).

4. *Epidemic of Fear: A Survey of AIDS Discrimination in the 1980s and Policy Recommendations for the 1990s* (New York: American Civil Liberties Union, 1990), 1, 22.

5. *Epidemic of Fear*, 23.

6. Baker et al., *Cracking the Corporate Closet*, 38; Puckett and Emery, *Managing AIDS in the Workplace*, 56; Phil Tiemeyer, *Plane Queer: Labor, Sexuality, and AIDS in the History of Male Flight Attendants* (Berkeley: University of California Press, 2013), 151–54.

7. Puckett and Emery, *Managing AIDS in the Workplace*, 48–62; Baker et al., *Cracking the Corporate Closet*, 163–64; Marilyn Chase, "Corporations

Urge Peers to Adopt Humane Policies for AIDS Victims," *Wall Street Journal*, January 20, 1988. In 1991, a federal appellate court ruled that a self-insured employer did not violate the Employee Retirement Security Act (ERISA) when it singled out HIV-positive employees by placing a $5,000 lifetime limit on AIDS-related health claims without doing the same for any other diseases. McGann v. H&H Music Co., 946 F.2d 401 (5th Cir. 1991).

8. Kirp, "Uncommon Decency," 140, 142.

9. Kirp, "Uncommon Decency," 143.

10. Kirp, "Uncommon Decency," 144–48.

11. Puckett and Emery, *Managing AIDS in the Workplace*, 74.

12. Puckett and Emery, *Managing AIDS in the Workplace*, 75.

13. Puckett and Emery, *Managing AIDS in the Workplace*, 77.

14. Puckett and Emery, *Managing AIDS in the Workplace*, 77–78; Baker et al., *Cracking the Corporate Closet*, 38–39; Chase, "Corporations Urge Peers."

15. A survey of one thousand companies in 1987 resulted in only thirty of them acknowledging that they had written AIDS policies. Jesus Sanchez, "Written Job Guarantees for AIDS Victims Rare," *Los Angeles Times*, May 22, 1987.

16. Forrest Briscoe, M. K. Chin, and Donald C. Hambrick, "CEO Ideology as an Element of the Corporate Opportunity Structure for Social Activists," *Academy of Management Journal* 57, no. 6 (2014): 1786–1809.

17. Puckett and Emery, *Managing AIDS in the Workplace*, 139.

18. Tiemeyer, *Plane Queer*, 185.

19. Puckett and Emery, *Managing AIDS in the Workplace*, 80, 85–86.

20. Susan M. Chambré, *Fighting for Our Lives: New York's AIDS Community and the Politics of Disease* (New Brunswick, NJ: Rutgers University Press, 2006), 118.

21. Chambré, *Fighting for Our Lives*, 140.

22. Chambré, *Fighting for Our Lives*, 140–41.

23. Peter Arno and Karyn L. Feiden, *Against the Odds: The Story of AIDS Drug Development, Politics, and Profits* (New York: HarperCollins, 1992), 40–41.

24. Chambré, *Fighting for Our Lives*, 122–23; Douglas Crimp and Adam Rolston, *AIDS Demographics* (Seattle: Bay Press, 1990), 28.

25. Chambré, *Fighting for Our Lives*, 138; Arno and Feiden, *Against the Odds*, chap. 6.

26. Andriote, *Victory Deferred*, 177; Raymond A. Smith and Donald P. Haider-Markel, *Gay and Lesbian Americans and Political Participation: A Reference Handbook* (Santa Barbara, CA: ABC/CLIO, 2002), 302; Arno and Feiden, *Against the Odds*, 55; Bruce Nussbaum, *Good Intentions: How Big Business and the Medical Establishment Are Corrupting the Fight Against AIDS* (New York: Atlantic Monthly Press, 1990), 179–80.

27. Arno and Feiden, *Against the Odds*, 55; Brian O'Reilly, "The Inside Story of the AIDS Drug," *Fortune*, November 5, 1990; Simon Garfield, "The Rise and Fall of AZT," *Independent*, May 1, 1993.

28. Nussbaum, *Good Intentions*, 177–78; Arno and Feiden, *Against the Odds*, 137–41; James Krellenstein, Aaron Lord, and Peter Staley, "Greed Allows an Epidemic to Persist," *New York Times*, July 17, 2018; "A Million Americans Need This Drug. Trump's Deal Won't Help Enough of Them," editorial, *New York Times*, May 13, 2019.

29. Andriote, *Victory Deferred*, 219–20.

30. Arno and Feiden, *Against the Odds*, 128–30; Crimp and Rolston, *AIDS Demographics*, 115–16.

31. Arno and Feiden, *Against the Odds*, 59, 132.

32. "AZT's Inhuman Cost," editorial, *New York Times*, August 28, 1989; Arno and Feiden, *Against the Odds*, 134–35.

33. Arno and Feiden, *Against the Odds*, 135–37; Crimp and Rolston, *AIDS Demographics*, 117.

34. Arno and Feiden, *Against the Odds*, 137; Chambré, *Fighting for Our Lives*, 154; Baker et al., *Cracking the Corporate Closet*, 139.

35. Arno and Feiden, *Against the Odds*, 178–79, 223; Baker et al., *Cracking the Corporate Closet*, 139.

36. Baker et al., *Cracking the Corporate Closet*, 140–41.

37. Baker et al., *Cracking the Corporate Closet*, 142–43.

38. Andriote, *Victory Deferred*, 204–5; Chambré, *Fighting for Our Lives*, 155–58.

39. Maureen Taylor, Gabriel M. Vasquez, and John Doorley, "Merck and AIDS Activists: Engagement as a Framework for Extending Issues Management," *Public Relations Review* 29 (2003): 257–70, 264–65.

40. Lawrence K. Altman, "New Study Questions Use of AZT in Early Treatment of AIDS Virus," *New York Times*, April 1, 1993.

41. Lewis A. Grossman, "AIDS Activists, FDA Regulation, and the Amendment of America's Drug Constitution," *American Journal of Law and Medicine* 42 (2016): 687–742, 687. See also Chambré, *Fighting for Our Lives*, 146–52; Michael Specter, "Pressure from AIDS Activists Has Transformed Drug Testing," *Washington Post*, July 2, 1989.

42. Erik Ose, "Jesse Helms' Shameful Legacy Cannot Be Whitewashed," *Huffington Post*, July 21, 2008; Edward I. Koch, "Senator Helms's Callousness Toward AIDS Victims," *New York Times*, November 7, 1987.

43. Irvin Molotsky, "Program to Fight AIDS Cleared by Senate, 87–4," *New York Times*, April 29, 1988; Ose, "Jesse Helms' Shameful Legacy Cannot Be Whitewashed."

44. Peter Staley, "In Memory of Jesse Helms, and the Condom on His House," *Poz*, July 8, 2008.

45. N. Offen, E. A. Smith, and R. E. Malone, "From Adversary to Target Market: The ACT-UP Boycott of Philip Morris," *Tobacco Control* 12 (2003): 203–7, 204; Baker et al., *Cracking the Corporate Closet*, 98.

46. Offen et al., "From Adversary to Target Market."

47. Offen et al., "From Adversary to Target Market."

48. Baker et al., *Cracking the Corporate Closet*, 98–99.

49. Offen et al., "From Adversary to Target Market"; Baker et al., *Cracking the Corporate Closet*, 99, 157.

50. Tiemeyer, *Plane Queer*, 186–87; John Gallagher, "Ugly American," *Advocate*, September 6, 1994, 29.

51. John Gallagher, "Flight Risk," *Advocate*, December 29, 1993, 31.

52. Tiemeyer, *Plane Queer*, 189–91; Gallagher, "Ugly American," 30.

53. Erica Ciszek, "A Corporate Coming Out: Crisis Communication and Engagement with LGBTQ Publics," *Case Studies in Strategic Communications* 5 (2016): 72–98.

54. Andriote, *Victory Deferred*, 2.

55. George Chauncey, *Why Marriage? The History Shaping Today's Debate* (New York: Basic Books, 2004), 95–104.

CHAPTER 4 Corporate Domestic Partnership Benefits in the 1990s

1. Craig A. Bowman and Blake M. Cornish, "A More Perfect Union: A Legal and Social Analysis of Domestic Partnership Ordinances," *Columbia Law Review* 92 (1992): 1164–211.

2. William J. Wiatrowski, "Family-Related Benefits in the Workplace," *Monthly Labor Review* (March 1990): 28–33.

3. Baker v. Nelson, 191 N.W.2d 185 (Minn. 1971); Singer v. Hara, 522 P.2d 1187 (Wa.Ct.App. 1974); Jones v. Hallahan, 501 S.W.2d 588 (Ky.Ct.Ap. 1973).

4. Tamar Lewin, "Suit over Death Benefits Asks, What Is a Family?," *New York Times*, September 21, 1990.

5. Rovira v. AT&T, 817 F. Supp. 1062 (S.D.N.Y. 1993). The court also concluded that an employer did not violate the Employee Retirement Security Act (ERISA) when it refused to provide DPBs.

6. Nicole C. Raeburn, *Changing Corporate America from Inside Out: Lesbian and Gay Workplace Rights* (Minneapolis: University of Minnesota Press, 2004), 42.

7. "HIV and AIDS—United States, 1981–2000," *Morbidity and Mortality Weekly Report* (Atlanta: Centers for Disease Control and Prevention, June 1, 2001), 430.

8. Sally Kohn, *The Domestic Partnership Organizing Manual for Employee Benefits* (Washington, DC: Policy Institute of the National Gay and Lesbian Task Force, 1999), 1.

9. The issue of corporate support for affirmative action programs in the 1980s and 1990s is discussed in chapter 1. That corporate support continued into the new century. For example, when conservative activists challenged the constitutionality of affirmative action in the educational context during the Obama years, forty-five major corporations—including Apple, Johnson & Johnson, and Shell—filed a brief with the US Supreme Court asking it to allow affirmative action programs in educational institutions to remain in place. Brief

of Fortune-100 and Other Leading American Businesses as *Amici Curiae* in Support of Respondents, Fisher v. University of Texas, 136 S.Ct. 2198 (2016).

10. Raeburn, *Changing Corporate America from Inside Out*, 259.

11. Carlos A. Ball, *From the Closet to the Courtroom: Five LGBT Lawsuits That Have Changed Our Nation* (Boston: Beacon Press, 2010), chap. 3. The US Supreme Court struck down the Colorado constitutional amendment in Romer v. Evans, 517 U.S. 620 (1995), before it went into effect.

12. Schaefer v. City & County of Denver, 973 P.2d 717 (Colo.Ct.App. 1998); Crawford v. City of Chicago, 710 N.E.2d 91 (Ill.App. 1999); City of Atlanta v. Morgan, 492 S.E.2d 193 (Ga. 1997); Connors v. City of Boston, 714 N.E.2d (Mass. 1999); Lilly v. City of Minneapolis, 527 N.W.2d 107 (Minn. Ct.App. 1995); Arlington County v. White, 528 S.E.2d 706 (Va. 2000).

13. For example, in the early 2000s, conservative members of Congress proposed a constitutional amendment that would have prohibited the recognition of same-sex marriages, as well as civil unions and domestic partnership benefits instituted as a result of judicial rulings. In stark contrast, the proposed amendment would not have interfered with the ability of private employers to offer DPBs to their employees. See S.J. Res. 40, 108th Congress, 2nd Session (2004).

14. Mireya Navarro, "Disney's Gay Policy for Gay Employees Angers Religious Right in Florida," *New York Times*, November 29, 1995; Gustav Niebuhr, "Baptists Censure Disney for Gay-Spouse Benefits," *New York Times*, June 13, 1996; Allen R. Myerson, "Southern Baptist Convention Calls for Boycott of Disney," *New York Times*, June 19, 1997.

15. Laura Evenson, "Apple Draws Fire over Gay Benefits," *San Francisco Chronicle*, November 4, 1993.

16. David Tuller, "Gay Issue Blocks Apple Plant in Texas," *San Francisco Chronicle*, December 1, 1993; Sam Howe Verhovek, "Texas County Retreats over Apple's Gay Policy," *New York Times*, December 8, 1993.

17. Barbara Pressly Noble, "At Work: Benefits for Domestic Partners," *New York Times*, June 28, 1992.

18. Catherine Iannuzzo and Alexandra Pink, "Benefits for the Domestic Partners of Gay and Lesbian Employees at Lotus Development Corporation" (thesis, Simmons College Graduate School of Management, November, 1991).

19. Kohn, *Domestic Partnership Organizing Manual for Employee Benefits*, 11; Barbara Whitaker, "Partner Benefits Have a Surprising Lack of Takers," *New York Times*, April 27, 1997.

20. Tom Gara, "The Corporate Approach to Gay Rights, Circa 1991," blog, *Wall Street Journal*, March 19, 2014.

21. "Lotus Offers Benefits for Homosexual Pairs," *New York Times*, September 7, 1991.

22. Foray v. Bell Atlantic, 56 F. Supp. 2d 327 (S.D. N.Y. 1999); Baehr v. Lewin 852 P.2d 44 (Haw. 1993). See also Irizarry v. Board of Education of Chicago, 251 F.3d 604 (7th Cir. 2001) (rejecting claim that the school district

violated the Equal Protection Clause when it made DPBs available to same-sex domestic partners but not to cohabiting heterosexual couples).

23. Kohn, *Domestic Partnership Organizing Manual for Employee Benefits*, 4.

24. William M. Bulkeley, "Lotus Flap over Extending Benefits to Partners of Gay Employees," *Wall Street Journal*, October 25, 1991.

25. In re Guardianship of Kowalski, 478 N.W.2d 790 (Minn.Ct.App. 1991) (guardianship); Braschi v. Stahl Associates, 543 N.E.2d 49 (N.Y. 1989) (succession to rent-controlled apartment). For the background and impact of the *Braschi* case, see Ball, *From the Closet to the Courtroom*, chap. 1.

26. Iannuzzo and Pink, "Benefits for the Domestic Partners of Gay and Lesbian Employees at Lotus Development Corporation"; Bulkeley, "Lotus Flap over Extending Benefits to Partners of Gay Employees."

27. Thomas A. Stewart, "Gay in Corporate America," *Fortune*, December 16, 1991.

28. Raeburn, *Changing Corporate America from Inside Out*, 5; Pat Baillie and Julie Gedro, "Perspective on Out & Equal Workplace Advocates Building Bridges Model," *New Horizons in Adult Education and Human Resource Development* 23, no. 2 (2009): 39–46. By 2005, employees at 115 Fortune 500 companies had formed LGBTQ groups. Briscoe et al., "CEO Ideology as an Element of the Corporate Opportunity Structure for Social Activists," 1794. Interestingly, this study found that "the CEOs of companies with LGBT employee group foundings were significantly more liberal, as gauged by their publicly observable political donation patterns, than were the CEOs of companies in which LGBT employee groups did not form," 1801.

29. Raeburn, *Changing Corporate America from Inside Out*, 3, 252.

30. Raeburn, *Changing Corporate America from Inside Out*, 1.

31. Baker et al., *Cracking the Corporate Closet*, 5.

32. Briscoe et al., "CEO Ideology as an Element of the Corporate Opportunity Structure for Social Activists," 1790.

33. W. E. Douglas Creed and Maureen A. Scully, "Song of Ourselves: Employees' Deployment of Social Identity in Workplace Encounters," *Journal of Management Inquiry* 9, no. 4 (2000): 391–412, 399–400, 404.

34. Karen Thompson and Julie Andrzejewski, *Why Can't Sharon Kowalski Come Home?* (San Francisco: Spinsters, 1989).

35. Creed and Scully, "Song of Ourselves," 402.

36. Forrest Briscoe and Sean Safford, "The Nixon-in-China Effect: Activism Imitation, and the Institutionalization of Contentious Practices," *Administrative Science Quarterly* 53, (2008): 460–91, 472.

37. Raeburn, *Changing Corporate America from Inside Out*, 137–38.

38. Kohn, *The Domestic Partnership Organizing Manual for Employee Benefits*, 49.

39. Kohn, *The Domestic Partnership Organizing Manual for Employee Benefits*, i.

40. Corporate Equality Index 2002, Human Rights Campaign; Raeburn, *Changing Corporate America from Inside Out*, 248.

41. Corporate Equality Index 2002, Human Rights Campaign, 143.

42. Corporate Equality Index 2003, Human Rights Campaign, 1; Corporate Equality Index 2009, Human Rights Campaign, 2, 14.

43. Timothy Werner, *Public Forces and Private Politics in American Big Business* (New York: Cambridge University Press, 2012), 89–90.

44. Mary Leonard, "Corporate Competition Is Leading the Way in Providing Domestic Partners with Dependable Benefits," *Boston Globe*, April 5, 1998.

45. See, for example, Hinman v. Dep't of Pers. Admin., 213 Cal. Rptr. 410 (Ct. App. 1985); Ross v. Denver Dep't of Health & Hosps., 883 P.2d 516 (Colo. Ct. App. 1994); Rutgers Council of AAUP Chapters v. Rutgers, 689 A.2d 828 (N.J. App. Div. 1997). Although the Alaska Supreme Court held that the failure to provide domestic partnership benefits had violated an earlier version of a state law that prohibited discrimination on the basis of marital status, the legislature mooted the issue when it amended the statute so that it did not apply to employment benefits. University of Alaska v. Tumeo, 933 P.2d 1147 (Alaska 1997).

46. "The Equal Benefits Ordinance: A Six Month Report," San Francisco Human Rights Commission, January 6, 1998. Eventually more than a dozen municipalities and one state (California) adopted similar laws. Christian Mallory and Brad Sears, "An Evaluation of Local Laws Requiring Government Contractors to Offer Equal Benefits to Domestic Partners," Williams Institute, February 2012.

47. The trade association failed in its lawsuit. See Air Transport Association v. City and County of San Francisco, 266 F.3d 1064 (9th Cir. 2001). For another failed legal challenge to the ordinance, see S.D. Myers Inc. v. City and County of San Francisco, 253 F.3d 461 (9th Cir. 2001). For an exploration of United Airlines' initial support of the lawsuit followed by its change of heart and its adoption of DPBs, see Tiemeyer, *Plane Queer*, 201–9. For an exploration of DPBs activism aimed at United Airlines, including by its own employees, see Ryan Patrick Murphy, "United Airlines Is for Lovers? Flight Attendant Activism and the Family Values Economy in the 1990s," *Radical History Review* (Winter 2012): 100–12.

48. For an exploration of the crucial role that the United Auto Workers played in persuading the three large automobile companies to adopt DPBs, see Monica Bielski Boris, "Fighting for Equal Treatment: How the UAW Won Domestic Partnership Benefits and Discrimination Protection for Lesbian, Gay, and Bisexual Members," *Labor Studies Journal* 35, no. 2 (2010): 157–80. For an exploration of LGBTQ activism within and by unions, see Miriam Frank, *Out in the Union: A Labor History of Queer America* (Philadelphia: Temple University Press, 2014).

49. Elizabeth Davison and Joy Rouse, "Exploring Domestic Partnership

Benefits Policies in Corporate America," *Journal of Homosexuality* 48, no. 2 (2004): 21–44, 23.

50. Antonia Juhasz, "What's Wrong with Exxon?," *Advocate*, September 3, 2013.

51. John Howard, "The Cracker Barrel Restaurants," in *Understanding and Managing Diversity: Readings, Cases, and Exercises*, ed. Carol Harvey and M. June Allard (New York: Prentice Hall, 2011), 187; Peter T. Kilborn, "Gay Rights Groups Take Aim at Restaurant Chain That's Hot on Wall Street," *New York Times*, April 9, 1992.

52. On shareholder activism and LGBTQ rights, see Neal Rane, "Twenty Years of Shareholder Proposals After *Cracker Barrel*: An Effective Tool for Implementing LGBT Employment Protections," *University of Pennsylvania Law Review* 162 (2014): 929–77; Josephine Roy, "Non-Traditional Activism: Using Shareholder Proposals to Urge LGBT Non-Discrimination," *Brooklyn Law Review* 74 (2008): 1513–38.

CHAPTER 5 Corporate LGBTQ Advocacy in the Public Sphere

1. Laura Patrice, "In Gay Marriage Fight, Some Companies Take a Stand," *USA Today*, July 29, 2012; Schuyler Velasco, "Chick-fil-A Supporters Send Message: Eat Chicken," *Christian Science Monitor*, August 1, 2012.

2. See, for example, Katherine Sender, *Business Not Politics: The Making of the Gay Market* (New York: Columbia University Press, 2004); Susan McPherson and Laura Clise, "Big Business Increasingly Supports Gay Rights," *Harvard Business Review*, September 28, 2012; "Big Business at End of Rainbow," *Tampa Bay Times*, June 28, 2014.

3. A 2006 study suggests that the adoption by large corporations of LGBTQ-friendly policies has "an effect on public policy adoption of state-level gay rights policies. [The evidence] suggests that the higher the percentage of Fortune 500 companies with nondiscrimination policies in a state, the more likely the state will be to adopt a gay rights policy." Roddrick A. Colvin, "Innovation of State-Level Gay Rights Laws: The Role of Fortune 500 Corporations," *Business and Society Review* 111 (2006): 363–86, 380.

4. Carlos A. Ball, *The Morality of Gay Rights: An Exploration in Political Philosophy* (New York: Routledge, 2003).

5. Bowers v. Hardwick, 478 U.S. 186 (1986).

6. Martha Groves, "Frequent Job Bias Leaves Little Recourse, Gays Say," *Los Angeles Times*, October 5, 1991; Martha Groves, "Shell Must Pay $5.3 Million in Gay Bias Case," *Los Angeles Times*, June 18, 1991.

7. "Governor Vetoes Gay Job Bias Bill," *Los Angeles Times*, October 4, 1991.

8. Elaine Herscher and Dan Levy, "Gay Rights Protest Turns Violent," *San Francisco Chronicle*, October 1, 1991; Victor Merin, "March by 1000 Gay Activists Halts Business," *Los Angeles Times*, October 6, 1991; David Ferrell, "Wilson's Veto Energizes Gay Rights Movement," *Los Angeles Times*, November 17, 1991.

9. George Skelton, "Wilson Signs Bill on Gay Job Rights," *Los Angeles Times*, September 26, 1992.

10. Todd Bishop and Dan Richman, "Corporations Weigh Social Issues Against Bottom Line," *Seattle Post-Intelligencer*, April 28, 2005.

11. Janet Tu, "Controversy Sparked on Microsoft's Stance [on] Gay-Rights Bill," *Seattle Times*, April 22, 2005.

12. Kim Peterson, "Gay Group Wants Award Back from Microsoft," *Seattle Times*, April 23, 2005; Brier Dudley, "Microsoft Gay Workers Call for Action," *Seattle Times*, April 30, 2005.

13. Andrew Garber and Brier Dudley, "Microsoft Decides to Back Gay Rights Bill," *Seattle Times*, May 7, 2005; Steve Ballmer, email to Microsoft employees, May 6, 2005.

14. Andrew Gerber, "Major Companies Back Gay Rights Legislation," *Seattle Times*, January 12, 2006.

15. Chris McGann, "A Long-Awaited Win for Gay Rights," *Seattle Post-Intelligencer*, January 28, 2006.

16. Jean Latz Griffin, "Gay, Lesbian Rights Gain Support: 3 Companies Endorse Equality in Housing, Jobs, Accommodations," *Chicago Tribune*, April 17, 1995; Jennifer Jacobs and Jason Clayworth, "Firms Support Bill Shielding Gays from Discrimination," *Des Moines Register*, April 3, 2007; Marc Gunther, "Queer, Inc.: How Corporate America Fell in Love with Gays and Lesbians," *Fortune*, November 30, 2006.

17. Gunther, "Queer Inc."

18. Letter from Jerre Stead, CEO of AT&T, to Senator Edward Kennedy, Hearing of the Committee on Labor and Human Resources on S.2238, 103rd Congress, Second Session, July 28, 1994, 47.

19. Gallup Poll, March 15–17, 1996; Gallup Poll, April 22–24, 1993; Gallup Poll, June 4–8, 1992.

20. Testimony of Charles Gifford, President and CEO, FleetBoston Financial Corporation, Hearing of the Committee on Health, Education, Labor, and Pensions on S.1284, 107th Congress, Second Session, February 27, 2002, 9.

21. Testimony of Robert Berman, Director of Human Resources and Vice President, Hearing of the Committee on Health, Education, Labor, and Pensions on S.1284, 107th Congress, Second Session, February 27, 2002, 11. An Eastman Kodak representative had also testified in 1996 in support of ENDA before a subcommittee of the House of Representatives. Testimony of Michael Morley, Senior Vice President, Eastman Kodak, Hearing before the Subcommittee on Government Programs of the Committee on Small Business, House of Representatives, 104th Congress, Second Session, July 17, 1996, 14–15.

22. Testimony of Kelly Baker, Vice President for Diversity, General Mills, Inc., Hearing before the Subcommittee on Health, Employment, Labor, and Pensions, Committee on Education and Labor, U.S. House of Representatives, 110th Congress, First Session, Serial No. 110–60, September 5, 2007, 32–34; Testimony of Virginia Nguyen, Diversity and Inclusion Team Member, Nike

Corporation, Hearing of the Committee on Health, Education, Labor, and Pensions on S.1584, 111th Congress, First Session, November 5, 2009, 33–34.

23. Kevin Bogardus, "Gay Rights Activists Turn to Fortune 500," *The Hill*, November 6, 2013.

24. Bogardus, "Gay Rights Activists Turn to Fortune 500."

25. Gunther, "Queer Inc."

26. J. Simons, "Gay Marriage: Corporate America Blazed the Trail," *Fortune*, June 14, 2004; Goodridge v. Department of Public Health, 798 N.E.2d 941 (Mass. 2003).

27. Simons, "Gay Marriage."

28. Kerrigan v. Commissioner of Public Health, 957 A.2d 407 (Ct. 2008); In re Marriage Cases, 183 P.3d 384 (Cal. 2008); Varnum v. Brien, 763 N.W.2d 862 (Iowa 2009); Gunther, "Queer Inc."

29. Frank Phillips, "Leaders Oppose Bid to Ban Gay Marriage," *Boston Globe*, July 6, 2008; "Pacific Gas and Electric Donates $250,000 to Oppose Ballot Measure," *Sacramento Bee*, July 30, 2008.

30. Michelle Quinn, "Anti-Prop 8 Campaign Gets a Boost from Apple," *Los Angeles Times*, October 25, 2008.

31. "Microsoft, Boeing, and Other Big Companies Support Gay Rights," *Seattle-Post Intelligencer*, September 14, 2009; "Seattle Chamber of Commerce Supports Same-Sex Partnerships," *Seattle-Post Intelligencer*, September 15, 2009; Andrew Garber, "Microsoft, Others Endorse Same-Sex Marriage Legislation," *Seattle Times*, January 20, 2012.

32. Melissa Maynard, "Business Playing Key Role in Gay Marriage Push," *Stateline*, March 21, 2012; "Ballmer, Gates Open Wallets to Defend Gay Marriage Law," *Seattle Times*, July 3, 2012; Rachel La Corte, "Amazon.com Founder Backs Gay Marriage," *Trenton Times*, July 28, 2012.

33. Mike Hughlett, "General Mills Against Gay Marriage Ban," *Minneapolis Star-Tribune*, June 15, 2012; Baird Hegelson, "Businesses Drawn into Fight Over Marriage Amendment," *Minneapolis Star-Tribune*, August 11, 2012.

34. "Coalition Opposes Ban on Gay Marriage," *Louisville Courier-Journal*, August 22, 2013; Mark Niquette and Tom Jones, "Eli Lilly, Cummins Fight Against Indiana Gay-Marriage Ban," *Bloomberg*, January 15, 2014; Jena McGregor, "Corporate America's Gay Rights Evolution," *Washington Post*, March 3, 2014.

35. "Chamber Opposes Gay Marriage Bill," *Indianapolis Star*, October 23, 2013.

36. Tony Cook, "Big State Legislative Wins for Business Interests, Not Social Conservatives," *Indianapolis Star*, March 16, 2014.

37. Susanne Craig, "Blankfein to Speak Out for Same-Sex Marriage," *New York Times*, February 5, 2012; Andrew Ross, "Gay Marriage Has Friends in Business," *San Francisco Chronicle*, March 1, 2013.

38. Brief of 278 Employers and Organizations Representing Employers as Amici Curiae in Support of Respondent, United States v. Windsor, U.S. Supreme Court (2013), 33.

39. Brief of 379 Employers and Organizations Representing Employers as Amici Curiae in Support of Petitioners, Obergefell v. Hodges, U.S. Supreme Court (2015), 36–37, citing Katie Kopansky and Jerry Cacciotti, *The Cost of Inconsistency: Quantifying the Economic Burden to American Business from the Patchwork Quilt of Marriage Laws* (New York: Marsh & McLennan, 2014).

40. Brief of 379 Employers and Organizations Representing Employers as Amici Curiae in Support of Petitioners, Obergefell v. Hodges, U.S. Supreme Court (2015), 22, citing Feng Li and Venky Nagar, "Diversity and Performance," *Management Science* 59 (2013): 529.

41. Brief of 379 Employers and Organizations Representing Employers as Amici Curiae in Support of Petitioners, Obergefell v. Hodges, 26–27.

42. "Same-Sex Marriage: What Is at Stake for Corporate America," *Knowledge@Wharton*, March 27, 2013.

43. McGregor, "Corporate America's Gay Rights Evolution."

44. "Our Position on California's No on 8 Campaign," blog, Google, September 26, 2008, https://googleblog.blogspot.ch/2008/09/our-position-on -californias-no-on-8.html, quoted in Florian Wettstein and Dorothea Baur, " 'Why Should We Care About Marriage Equality?' Political Advocacy as a Part of Corporate Responsibility," *Journal of Business Ethics* 138 (2016): 199–213, 203.

45. Brief of 278 Employers and Organizations Representing Employers as Amici Curiae in Support of Respondent, United States v. Windsor, 35–36; Brief of 379 Employers and Organizations Representing Employers as Amici Curiae in Support of Petitioners, Obergefell v. Hodges, 41–42. In 2019, more than two hundred businesses, with a total of more than seven million employees, filed a brief with the Supreme Court asking it to rule that Title VII of the Civil Rights Act of 1964 prohibits employment discrimination against sexual minorities and transgender individuals. To conclude otherwise, the brief argued, would "undermine the nation's business interests." Brief of 206 Businesses as Amici Curiae in Support of Employees, Bostock v. Clayton County et al., U.S. Supreme Court (2019), 8.

46. Wettstein and Baur, "Why Should We Care About Marriage Equality?," 206.

CHAPTER 6   Corporate Resistance to Anti-LGBTQ Rights Backlash

1. Hollingsworth v. Perry, 570 U.S. 693 (2013); United States v. Windsor, 570 U.S. 744 (2013).

2. See Carlos A. Ball, *The First Amendment and LGBT Equality: A Contentious History* (Cambridge, MA: Harvard University Press, 2017), chap. 7; Douglas NeJaime and Reva B. Siegel, "Conscience Wars: Complicity-Based Conscience Claims in Religion and Politics," *Yale Law Journal* 124, no. 7 (May 2015): 2516–91.

3. Employment Division v. Smith, 494 U.S. 872 (1990).

4. For examples of the state court rulings, see Elane Photography, LLC v. Willock, 309 P.3d 53 (N.M. 2013); Craig v. Masterpiece Cakeshop, Inc.,

370 P.3d 272 (Col.Ct.App. 2015); Klein v. Oregon Bureau of Labor and Industries, 410 P.3d 1051 (Or.Ct.App. 2017); State v. Arlene's Flowers, Inc., 389 P.3d 543 (Wash. 2017); Gifford v. McCarthy, 137 A.D.3d 30 (N.Y. App. Div. 2016). For the US Supreme Court ruling, see Masterpiece Cakeshop v. Colorado Civil Rights Commission, 138 S.Ct. 719 (2018). On that ruling, see Carlos A. Ball, "The Baker and the Boxer," *Beacon Broadside*, June 14, 2018, http://www.beaconbroadside.com/broadside/2018/06/the-baker-and-the -boxer.html.

5. Fernanda Santos, "Governor of Arizona Is Pressed to Veto Bill," *New York Times*, February 24, 2014; "Business Leaders Laud Brewer's Veto of Bill," *Arizona Republic*, February 27, 2014; McGregor, "Corporate America's Gay Rights Evolution."

6. "Religious-Rights Bill Hurting State, Business Leaders Say," *Arizona Republic*, February 25, 2014; Fernanda Santos, "Arizona Governor Vetoes Bill on Refusal of Service to Gays," *New York Times*, February 26, 2014; Gail Collins, "The State of Arizona," *New York Times*, February 26, 2014.

7. Santos, "Arizona Governor Vetoes Bill on Refusal of Service to Gays."

8. Burwell v. Hobby Lobby Stores, Inc., 573 U.S. 682 (2014); Citizens United v. Federal Elections Commission, 558 U.S. 310 (2010).

9. Baskin v. Bogan, 766 F.3d 648 (7th Cir. 2014); Jernigan v. Crane, 64 F. Supp.3d 1260 (E.D. Ark. 2014).

10. Sam Frizell, "How Gay Rights Won in Indiana," *Time*, April 2, 2015; Jeff Swiatek and Tim Evans, "9 CEOs Call for Changes to 'Religious Freedom Law,'" *Indianapolis Star*, March 30, 2015.

11. Harry Bruinius, "Religious Freedom Act: Are Businesses Becoming More Socially Conscious?," *Christian Science Monitor*, March 31, 2015.

12. Michael Hiltzik, "Legalized Bias: A Great Way to Hinder Growth," *Los Angeles Times*, April 1, 2015; Bruinius, "Religious Freedom Act"; Frizell, "How Gay Rights Won in Indiana"; Michael Barbaro and Erik Eckholm, "Indiana Law Denounced as Invitation to Discriminate Against Gays," *New York Times*, March 27, 2015; Mark McKinnon, "We Republicans Lost on Gay Rights," *Politico*, June 1, 2015; Andrew Bender, "Indiana's Religious Freedom Act Cost Indianapolis $60 Million in Lost Revenue," *Forbes*, January 31, 2016.

13. Frizell, "How Gay Rights Won in Indiana."

14. "Governor Pence, Fix Religious 'Freedom Law' Now," editorial, *Indianapolis Star*, March 30, 2015.

15. Dean Starkman and Andrea Chang, "Social Issues Are Now Their Business," *Los Angeles Times*, April 2, 2015; Tim Cook, "Pro-Discrimination 'Religious Freedom' Laws Are Dangerous," *Washington Post*, March 29, 2015; Bruinius, "Religious Freedom Act."

16. Alan Blinder, "Business to Play Key Role as Georgia Weighs Bill on Religion and Gay Rights," *New York Times*, March 22, 2016; Ted Johnson, "Disney, Marvel to Boycott Georgia if Religious Liberty Bill Is Passed," *Variety*, March 23, 2016.

17. Jena McGregor, "CEOs Oppose Georgia Push to Let Faith-Based Groups Refuse Certain Services," *Washington Post*, March 18, 2016; McKinnon, "We Republicans Lost on Gay Rights."

18. Mississippi Statute, House Bill 1523 (2016).

19. Barber v. Bryant, 193 F. Supp.3d 677 (S.D. Miss. 2016), reversed by 860 F.3d 345 (5th Cir. 2017).

20. Cole Stangler, "Indiana 'Anti-Gay Law': Firms Criticizing Pence Funded Him as He Fought LGBT Rights," *International Business Times*, April 2, 2015.

21. Ulane v. Eastern Airlines, Federal District Court for Northern Illinois, 1984, Plaintiff's Exhibit #1, https://catalog.archives.gov/id/12008912.

22. Ulane v. Eastern Airlines, 581 F. Supp 821 (N.D. Ill. 1984), reversed by 742 F.2d 1081 (7th Cir. 1984). For more recent cases, see, for example, EEOC v. R.G. & G.R. Harris Funeral Homes, Inc., 884 F.3d 560 (2018); Glenn v. Brumby, 663 F.3d 1312 (11th Cir. 2011); Macy v. Holder, EEOC Appeal No. 0120120821 (2012). In 2019, the US Supreme Court agreed to decide whether discrimination against transgender individuals violates Title VII.

23. Doe v. Boeing, 846 P.2d 531, 533–34 (Wash. 1993).

24. For other failed lawsuits, see, for example, Kirkpatrick v. Seligman & Latz, Inc., 636 F.2d 1047 (5th Cir. 1981); Sommers v. Budget Marketing Inc., 667 F.2d 748 (8th Cir. 1982); Holloway v. Arthur Andersen, 566 F.2d 659 (9th Cir. 1977).

25. Corporate Equality Index, Human Rights Campaign, 2002, 2003, 2004, 2005, 2006, 2010, 2014, 2018.

26. Carlos A. Ball, "A New Stage for the LGBT Movement: Protecting Gender and Sexual Multiplicities," in *After Marriage Equality: The Future of LGBT Rights*, ed. Carlos A. Ball (New York: New York University Press, 2016), 157, 172–74.

27. Megan Boenke, "Scripps Networks, Other Companies Urge Lawmakers to Nix Transgender Bill," *Knoxville Sun-Sentinel*, April 14, 2016.

28. Mimi Swartz, "The Equal Rights Fight over Houston's Bathrooms," *New York Times*, October 27, 2015; Lisa Falkenberg, "Anti-Ordinance Campaign's Scare Tactics Need to Be Flushed," *Houston Chronicle*, August 26, 2015; Katherine Driessen, "Claims about Bathroom Access Dominate HERO Debate," *Houston Chronicle*, October 15, 2015; Manny Fernandes, "Tactics and Antagonists Draw Attention to Houston Rights Vote," *New York Times*, October 31, 2015.

29. Manny Fernandes and Mitch Smith, "Houston Voters Reject Broad Anti-Discrimination Ordinance," *New York Times*, November 4, 2015.

30. Emery P. Dalesio and Jonathan Drew, "Price Tag of North Carolina LGBT Law: $3.76B," Associated Press, March 27, 2017.

31. Jonathan M. Katz and Erik Eckholm, "Anti-Gay Laws Bring Backlash in Mississippi and North Carolina," *New York Times*, April 6, 2016; Shivani Vora, "North Carolina and Mississippi See Tourist Backlash After LGBT Laws," *New York Times*, April 22, 2016; Rachel Abrams, "Target Steps Out in

Front of Bathroom Choice Debate," *New York Times*, April 27, 2016; "Dozens of Investors Say North Carolina Bathroom Law 'Bad for Business,' " *New York Times*, September 26, 2016.

32. Alex Kotch, "Businesses Opposing N.C.'s HB2 Helped Elect Legislators Behind It," *Facing South*, April 5, 2016, https://www.facingsouth.org/2016/04/businesses-opposing-ncs-hb2-helped-elect-legislato. See also Alex Kotch, "Companies Opposing N.C. 'Bathroom Bill' Funding Pro-McCrory Political Group," *Facing South*, August 10, 2016, https://www.facingsouth.org/2016/08/companies-opposing-nc-bathroom-bill-funding-pro-mccrory-political-group.

33. Chuck Lindell, "No Transgender Bathroom Law, Texas Businesses Urge GOP," *Austin-American Statesman*, October 25, 2016.

34. Lindell, "No Transgender Bathroom Law, Texas Businesses Urge GOP."

35. *Keep Texas Open for Business: The Economic Impact of Discriminatory Legislation on the State of Texas* (Austin: Texas Association of Business, 2016); Lauren McGaughy, "Texas Could Lose $8.5B If Anti-Gay or Transgender Bathroom Laws Are Passed, Study Claims," *Dallas News*, December 6, 2016.

36. Lana Shadwick, "Biz Group Claims Bathroom Ban Bad for Texas," *Breitbart*, December 9, 2016, https://www.breitbart.com/border/2016/12/09/biz-group-claims-trans-bathroom-bans-bad-texas/.

37. David Montgomery, "Texas Transgender Bathroom Bill Falters Amid Mounting Opposition," *New York Times*, August 8, 2017.

38. Montgomery, "Texas Transgender Bathroom Bill Falters Amid Mounting Opposition."

39. Montgomery, "Texas Transgender Bathroom Bill Falters Amid Mounting Opposition."

40. James Surowiecki, "Unlikely Alliances," *New Yorker*, April 25, 2016.

41. Alan Blinder, "Wary, Weary or Both, Southern Lawmakers Tone Down Culture Wars," *New York Times*, January 22, 2018.

42. Boenke, "Scripps Networks, Other Companies Urge Lawmakers to Nix Transgender Bill."

43. Blinder, "Wary, Weary or Both, Southern Lawmakers Tone Down Culture Wars."

44. Amber Phillips, "14 States Have Passed Laws This Year Making It Harder to Get an Abortion," *Washington Post*, June 1, 2016; Sabrina Tavernise, "How Banning Abortion in the Early Weeks of Pregnancy Suddenly Became Mainstream," *New York Times*, April 18, 2019.

CONCLUSION Looking Beyond *Citizens United*

1. Citizens United v. Federal Elections Commission, 558 U.S. 310 (2010).

2. First National Bank of Boston v. Bellotti, 435 U.S. 765 (1978). For an illuminating exploration of the circumstances leading up to the *Bellotti* litigation, see Adam Winkler, *We the Corporations: How American Businesses Won Their Civil Rights* (New York: W. W. Norton, 2018), 310–23.

3. "Lobbying: Top Spenders, 1998–2018," *Open Secrets*, Center for Responsive Politics, https://www.opensecrets.org/lobby/top.php?showYear=a&index Type=s.

4. Nicholas Fandos, "Corporations Open the Cash Spigot for Trump's Inauguration," *New York Times*, January 15, 2017.

5. Citizens United v. Federal Elections Commission, 558 U.S. 310, 479 (2010) (Stevens, J., dissenting).

6. Winkler, *We the Corporations*, 372. Following *Citizens United*, a federal court of appeals held that limits to contributions to super PACs are unconstitutional. Speechnow.org v. Federal Elections Committee, 599 F.3d 686 (D.C. Cir. 2010) (en banc).

7. Celina Durgin, "Corporations and the People: Who Influences Whom?," *National Review*, March 30, 2016.

8. Winkler, *We the Corporations*, 364. Kent Greenfield argues that the concept of corporations as "people," that is, entities that are separate and independent from their owners and managers, allows the law to hold them accountable for their actions and, to the extent that corporations enjoy constitutional rights, serves to limit what could be abusive governmental authority. Greenfield advises progressives to encourage rather than fight corporate personhood because if corporations were more like people, they would seek objectives that go beyond wealth maximization. Kent Greenfield, *Corporations Are People Too (And They Should Act Like It)* (New Haven, CT: Yale University Press, 2018).

9. Greenfield, *Corporations Are People Too*, 145–53.

10. Paul Blest, "The Myth of the Progressive Capitalist," *Jacobin Magazine*, April 2016.

11. See, for example, Blest, "The Myth of the Progressive Capitalist"; Nico Lang, "Money Talks: The Hidden Downsides to Corporate America's Fight for LGBT Equality," *Quartz Media*, March 31, 2016; Jason Kirby, "The Limits of Corporate Do-Goodery," *McLean's Magazine*, August 3, 2015. For a scholarly critique of the LGBTQ movement's embrace of identity politics and equality rights at the expense of more progressive goals based on wealth redistribution and legal protection for the most vulnerable members of the LGBTQ community (such as the young, the poor, and people of color), see Libby Adler, *Gay Priori* (Durham, NC: Duke University Press, 2018). See also Lisa Duggan, *The Twilight of Equality? Neoliberalism, Cultural Politics, and the Attack on Democracy* (Boston: Beacon Press, 2003); Alexandra Chasin, *Selling Out: The Gay and Lesbian Movement Goes to Market* (New York: St. Martin's Press, 2000).

Index

Abbott, Greg, 187
Abbott Laboratories, 81, 84
ABC, 46–47, 48
abortion, 120, 191
ACLU, 39, 61–62, 145
ACT UP, 73–82, 87, 88
Adidas, 183
Aetna, 147
affirmative action, 26–28, 102, 220n9
AFL-CIO, 52, 53, 55
African Americans, 17–25, 28, 56, 112. *See also* racial discrimination
AIDS: and American Airlines, 89–91; and Bank of America, 65–67, 69; and Coors Brewing Company, 55; corporate response to, 58, 62–72, 116–17; and disability discrimination, 69; and domestic partnership benefits, 100–101, 107–8, 114; and early days of epidemic, 59–62, 72–73; and employment discrimination, 61–62; and HIV testing, 44; and Pacific Bell, 44, 64–65, 67, 69, 71; and pharmaceutical companies,

3, 74–85, 151; and Philip Morris boycott, 86–89
AIDS Coalition to Unleash Power. *See* ACT UP
Airbnb, 140, 190
Alabama, 191
Alcoa, 25, 147, 168, 190
Amazon, 140, 147
American Airlines: and AIDS, 89–91; and domestic partnership benefits, 122; and gender identity discrimination, 178; and opposition to religious freedom laws, 165, 168, 172; and opposition to transgender bathroom laws, 182, 188; and sexual orientation discrimination, 40
American Express, 148, 165
American Family Association of Indiana, 145
American Foundation for AIDS Research (amfAR), 79, 87
American GI Forum, 51
American Psychological Association, 47
Americans for Democratic Action, 39

California Manufacturing Association, 131, 132
California Public Utilities Commission, 36
campaign finance reform. See *Citizens United v. Federal Elections Commission*; political action committees (PACs)
Capital One, 188
Cargill, 144
CBS, 45–46, 47, 48, 49
Centers for Disease Control and Prevention (CDC), 59, 61, 66, 67, 86
Chamber of Commerce, 24, 197. *See also* Arizona Chamber of Commerce; Boston Chamber of Commerce; California Chamber of Commerce; Indiana Chamber of Commerce; Indianapolis Chamber of Commerce; Phoenix Chamber of Commerce; San Francisco Chamber of Commerce; Seattle Chamber of Commerce; Texas Association of Business (TAB)
Charlotte (North Carolina), 182, 184
Chavez, Cesar, 51
Chevron, 67, 122, 139, 198
Chick-fil-A, 127
Chrysler, 122
Cincinnati, 135–36
Citibank. *See* Citigroup
Citigroup, 67, 96, 147, 185, 190
Citizens to Restore Fairness (Cincinnati), 136
Citizens United v. Federal Elections Commission, 7–8, 167, 185, 93–96, 197–200, 201, 203. *See also* First Amendment
Civil Rights Act of 1964, 23–24, 25, 26, 35, 41, 157, 227n45
clarithromycin, 81

Clinton, Bill, 163
Coca-Cola, 25, 139, 171
Colorado, 51, 55, 103, 132
Committee for Economic Development, 15
Congress of Industrial Organizations (CIO), 18. *See also* AFL-CIO
Congress for Racial Equality, 19
Cook, Tim, 170–71
Cooper, Roy, 184
Coors Brewing Company, 3, 31, 34, 50–57, 87, 133. *See also* MillerCoors
Corporate Equality Index, 119, 124, 178–79. *See also* Human Rights Campaign (HRC)
corporate social responsibility, 14, 15–16, 25
corporations: and their brands, 32; and conservatives, 140, 188–89, 196, 205–6; and diversity, 6, 16, 27–29, 44, 102, 116, 123, 137, 148; and donations to AIDS and LGBTQ groups, 80, 87, 119, 129, 136, 143, 144, 145; and environmental regulations, 7, 16, 204; and funding of Republican candidates, 5, 85–86, 87, 151, 173–74, 185–86, 198, 206; and immigration restrictions, 7, 204; and LGBTQ nondiscrimination policies, 3, 17, 49, 54, 85, 90, 98–100, 125, 178–79; and the LGBTQ policies of foreign countries, 156, 206; and marriage equality, 141–49; and opposition to the Defense of Marriage Act, 147; and opposition to religious freedom laws, 4–5, 160, 165–66, 167–75, 179, 187; and opposition to transgender bathroom laws, 4–5, 161–62, 179, 182–85, 186–90; as people, 200, 231n8;